Praise for 7

"*Timely Death* tackles the last taboo with a reasoned and compelling thoughtfulness, enabling readers to attain a useful level of informed awareness." FAMILY PRACTICE MAGAZINE

"Anne Mullens has provided a unique overview of the complex issues surrounding physician-assisted death in Canada, the U.S. and the Netherlands. Combining patient narratives, interviews with activists on both sides of the debate, and a review of published materials, she explores the tensions between the individual and society, and between policy and practice. *Timely Death* is an important read for those looking for a balanced understanding of this emotionally laden subject."

TIMOTHY E. QUILL, M.D., PROFESSOR OF MEDICINE AND
PSYCHIATRY, UNIVERSITY OF ROCHESTER

"The Senate Special Standing Committee on Euthanasia and Assisted Suicide learned that Canadians were more afraid of dying than they were of death. Anne Mullens' book is an important contribution to the ongoing debate. Sooner or later politicians — like all of us — will be required to enter that debate. *Timely Death* should be their primer."

SENATOR SHARON CARSTAIRS

"Anne Mullens has written a sensitive, comprehensive and compassionate overview of the complex issues of euthanasia and assisted suicide. The moving stories of individuals and families are powerful witness to the need to offer terminally or incurably ill competent adults a choice other than continued suffering, indignity and pain or pharmaceutical oblivion. I hope this book will be widely read."

SVEND ROBINSON, MP

TIMELY

ANNE MULLENS

DEATH

WHAT WE CAN EXPECT AND
WHAT WE NEED TO KNOW

Vintage Canada
A Division of Random House of Canada

FIRST VINTAGE CANADA EDITION, APRIL 1997

Canadian Cataloguing in Publication Data

Mullens, Anne
Timely death:
what we can expect and what we need to know

ISBN 0-679-97038-9
1. Right to die.   I. Title.
R726.M855 1997   197'.7   C96-932147-3

Printed and bound in the United States of America

This book is dedicated to the memory of
the following people:

Bill Davies
Gayle Stelter
Jan Smit
Jeanne Verheijen
Douglas Alan Miller
Gordon Howard
Cynthia Verbonac-Sigurdson
Brian Burkell
and
Rodney Mitchell

Author's Note

THE NAMES in this book, save for two exceptions, are real; there are otherwise no composites and no pseudonyms. The people whose stories appear in these pages were willing to allow their names and their personal details to appear in the hope that their experiences might somehow make a difference to the lives of others. To all of them, I am greatly indebted.

Acknowledgements

THIS BOOK could not have been written without the help and support of numerous people. The board members of the Atkinson Foundation in Public Policy at *The Toronto Star* selected my proposal to examine euthanasia and assisted suicide, recognizing it was a social policy issue that demanded deeper study. If not for them, this book would never have happened. The foundation's generous support gave me the time and the financial resources to carry out the necessary research. In those early stages, my research assistants, Deborah Tucker and Patrick Martin, as well as Adele Jushka at the foundation, Abe Rotstein at the University of Toronto, and John Ferri at *The Toronto Star*, all contributed to the successful completion of the research project that appeared as an extensive newspaper series in *The Toronto Star*. It might have stopped there, had not my agent, Denise Bukowski, and Louise Dennys at Alfred A. Knopf Canada agreed with me that the research material and the subject itself deserved further expansion in a book. My editor, Diane Martin, at Knopf, was a joy and a pleasure to work with for her enthusiasm, her direction, and her considerable editorial skills.

More than one hundred people gave of their time, knowledge and experiences as interview subjects, and while some of them may not agree with my conclusions, I am nevertheless indebted to all of them for their participation. Some deserve special mention. Russel Ogden was instrumental in helping track down the story of Kolitalik. Timothy Quill, Gerrit Kimsma, Michael Downing, Debra Braithwaite, Tyleen Katz, Coby Tschanz, Rae Westcott and Gabor Maté all gave of their time and allowed me the journalist's greatest privilege, that of simply observing them in action. Part of the task of collecting information from around the world was made easier by the services of Deathnet, established by John Hofsess, which provides complete unedited electronic transcripts, documents and news stories concerning the right-to-die through the Internet. John's e-mail messages about breaking news were appreciated in the times I'd become too busy to log-on. Thanks, too, to Derk Van Dassen, of Markham, for his skill in Dutch translation.

Greatest thanks goes to the individuals and families who shared their pain, grief and knowledge to add a personal touch to the issues and to keep this frequently esoteric and academic topic grounded in the experiences of real people. To Alice Davies, Ray Stelter, Carol Ogilvie, Hélène Smit, Jan Verheijen, Tom Sigurdson, Mary Howard, Pat Burkell, Donna Wilson, Lillian Bayne and Mike Hayes, a heartfelt thank you for giving me the honour of telling your stories. Special mention goes to Louise Normandin-Miller, Ron Pal, and Rodney Mitchell who started off as interview subjects and became good friends, enriching both the pages and my life in the process. Thanks, too, to the many individuals who shared their personal stories and views and yet do not appear in the book. Nevertheless, they played important roles in my approach to the issues.

Annabel Lapp and Dina Correale provided me with an ideal office environment, complete with friendship, good conversation and pots of afternoon tea, all conducive to writing. Journalist and friend Deborah Wilson read the early chapters and her critique and encouragement were greatly appreciated. My father,

Dr. Ted Mullens, and my mother, Elizabeth Mullens, read and commented on the entire manuscript and as sceptical observers of the debate still needing to be convinced, served as perhaps my most discerning audience.

The research and writing of this book often took me away from my precious, wonderful girls, Kate and Madeline, and the only way I could live with that was to know they were in the safe and loving hands of one of the following: my mother, my mother-in-law Pat Baldrey, Linda Pabalate, or my husband Keith Baldrey. Keith, as always, provided love, encouragement, understanding and humour, shouldering much of the burden on the home front while I worked on this seemingly endless project.

Finally, a thanks and warm remembrance to Sue Rodriguez, who spurred me, and all the country, to think about the issues.

Contents

Preface

STARING
AT THE SUN

"DEATH, like the sun," said the seventeenth-century French writer, La Rochefoucauld, "should not be stared at."

I think, three years ago, I would have agreed with him. I had no desire, then, to take a hard look at death. I was a young mother, with another baby on the way. I was revelling in the wonders and miracles of new life. I feared death and its ability to snatch away all that mattered to me, to take not only my life, but even more frighteningly, the lives of those I love. And as my list of loved ones was growing ever-longer with the addition of a husband, in-laws, nieces, nephews, friends, and my own children, I felt my vulnerability to the pain and finality of death grow ever greater.

Like many, I had an unspoken, almost unacknowledged, superstition that if I looked too hard at death, if I recognized its menacing and constant presence on the periphery of our lives, if I talked openly about it, and — good heavens — if I went so far as to accept it and even plan for its eventuality, it would be to invite it into my sphere. Become comfortable with Death, the niggling superstition seemed to say, and it might think it was welcome. Better to ignore it.

There was another factor, too, that made me reluctant to

embark on a deep exploration of death: it would be a downer. To stare at death would be depressing, morbid, and unnatural, I thought. It would be too intense and heavy. It would invite neurosis and obsession. At that time I thought someone at the end of life has reason to ponder death; someone who is still on the young side of middle age, like me, must be slightly weird or ill to do so. I confess that whenever I would meet a relatively young person who was devoting her time and energy to the issue of the right-to-die, the tiny question would creep into the back of my mind: "What's wrong with her? Does she have a terminal illness? Did someone close to her die horribly?"

Now I believe we'd all be wiser if we stared at death a little more. I might never have started on my own three-year exploration of death, however, if I hadn't received a fax one afternoon in late August of 1992. I had no idea as I watched the fax slide out of my machine that it would change my life and send me down a path investigating the needs and rights of dying individuals.

At the time I was the Vancouver Island reporter for *The Vancouver Sun,* a paper for which I had worked for more than ten years, covering mostly medicine and science. About eighteen months earlier I had left the medical beat and moved to Victoria to join my husband a few weeks before the birth of our first child. After my maternity leave, I set up the Vancouver Island bureau in the front bedroom of our home.

I had been at the new job eight months and I missed writing about medicine. I longed for a meaty story that combined the complex mix of medical and scientific details, perhaps hinging on a bit of controversy and societal dilemma, wrapped up in a compelling story of a human being. That fax contained it all. From John Hofsess, director of the Victoria-based Right To Die Society, it stated he was representing a forty-two-year-old Sidney woman, dying of amyotrophic lateral sclerosis (ALS), who wanted to challenge the law that prevented her from getting help to die. Her name was Sue Rodriguez and he was offering me the first print interview with her. Did I want it? Of course I did. I knew from reading the few paragraphs of the fax that it was a great story with mythological proportions, a David trying to battle society's Goliaths. Here was a dying woman, whose disease was robbing her of strength and movement and conventional power, taking on the most powerful institutions and structures of our land: the medical profession, the government, religion, and the law. Not only that, but she was staring face to face with death, and attempting to dictate her own terms.

In early September of 1992 I drove out to the rural backroads of the Saanich Peninsula to meet Sue. We sat for two hours or more in the dappled shade around the white patio table in her backyard and talked about her life and her approaching death. Although she could only eat soft foods, she was in relatively good health then, from outward appearances. Her gait was unsteady, but she was still walking on her own. Her speech was still completely clear.

I was familiar, however, with the path that lay ahead of her. An aunt of mine died of ALS in the early 1980s, and as a medical reporter I had written about the incurable disease's baffling, relentless and destructive progress. I knew that often it tended to hit athletic people like baseball's Lou Gehrig, the Iron Horse, who gave the disease its better known name. Leaving the brain intact, but inch by inch destroying the muscles and nerve paths of the body, the disease brings on death in three to five years, its course often described as being buried alive.

I was amazed at this beautiful young woman's composure, her clear-headed, matter-of-factness in the face of her terminal illness. I was charmed by her humour and intelligence. When her eight-year-old son, Cole, ran into the backyard from school to kiss her on the cheek and tell her about his day before he went into the house, I was overwhelmed by the tragedy of it all. As a young mother myself, I could not help but ask: "What would I do in her situation? Would I have such composure, such humour? Would I want the same thing?" I wasn't sure what my choice would be, but I knew, from the moment I met Sue Rodriguez, that I too would at least want the freedom to make a choice.

Over the next six months, however, as I covered her court challenge for *The Vancouver Sun* and then for *The Toronto Star*, as I grew to know Sue better, I began to realize that such a choice is much more complex than I had at first imagined. Like the Ukrainian Matryoshka dolls — which upon opening, reveal another doll, and another, and yet another, each one worthy of individual examination, yet still fitting together as a whole — law, medicine, ethics, religion, philosophy, sociology, human psychology, history and public policy all played a role in whether an individual should be allowed to ask someone else to help them die.

The more I wrote about Sue and the reaction others had to her fight — the ardent supporters, the passionate opposition — the more certain I became that the issue would become *the* social policy issue of the next few decades. I knew that even after Sue was gone, as long as it was illegal to ask another to help you die, other individuals would continue to come forward into the public arena to tell their story. This is the classic dilemma that pits the desires of the individual against the perceived needs of the state. I became convinced that as a society we will be struggling for some time to find the correct balance between the two. For each one of us this topic begins to take on individual meaning, particularly among the aging baby boom generation, as death increasingly touches the sphere of our experience. Now, many of us find ourselves worried about our elderly parents, or even our own health while still rearing our children. As this trend continues we will all feel a need to have a deeper understanding of the issues and of what might be at stake if we take death into our own hands.

I discovered that, rather than being depressing and morbid, the issue of choices in death is fascinating and edifying, even uplifting. It is rich with moving stories of individuals at the same time as it is rife with inconsistencies and snags. It is a compelling conundrum. Yet I was frustrated with my inability as a newspaper journalist to detail the many nuances of this complex, difficult topic in fifteen inches of news copy. I felt unable to present cohesive, in-depth reporting on such a huge and varied issue. The subject was too big to fit with the rigours of daily journalism. Writing about issues concerning the slow and steady change in perception about death and dying was like covering the changes to the landscape caused by a glacier rather than an avalanche. In the pages of our newspapers it is easier to cover the effects wrought by sudden slides and floods than by slow-moving events like a glacier, even though, in the scheme of things, the glacier actually changes the landscape more permanently and dramatically.

Accordingly, thanks to an Atkinson Fellowship in Public Policy, I embarked on a year of research about euthanasia and assisted suicide. I spent six weeks in the Netherlands, interviewed experts in England, Scotland, Germany, the United States and Canada. In those countries I talked to doctors, ethicists, advocacy groups, lawyers and lawmakers. I read innumerable documents, articles and books on the topic and heard countless stories of dying individuals and their families. I spent time with palliative care teams, and I held the hands of the dying and listened to their distressed relatives. In all I interviewed more than one hundred individuals in five countries.

The research grew into something much larger than looking at the pros and cons of whether we should afford individuals the choice, and the help, to die. It grew to encompass all decisions at the end of life and who makes them — the individual, the medical profession, or society. It spread to cover the needs of the dying, such as the provision of comprehensive palliative

care. Its roots reached down into history, culture, religion, philosophy and long-held taboos. The resulting newspaper series,
called "Dying for Leadership" appeared in *The Toronto Star* in
October of 1994. Yet, despite the series' length, I found there
were more stories of individuals to tell, more texture and detail
and complexity to impart, and more questions to ask so that
the reader could assimilate a deep and balanced understanding
of our current rights and the rights that perhaps we should have
at the end of life. This book is a consideration of those rights.
Individuals need to know what they can do, now, without
breaking laws or resorting to violent methods of suicide, to
bring about a more peaceful end. Therefore we must look
honestly at the strengths and weaknesses of palliative care; the
benefits of advance directives and living wills, and their shortcomings; the legal options of terminating treatments, withholding medication or withdrawing life support treatment, and
what happens when they go wrong.

Perhaps the most troubling and thorny area of these last
rights is what society should allow for those who are incompetent to make decisions for themselves. It is one thing for a
rational, undepressed individual like Sue Rodriguez to make
a conscious decision that the burden of living has grown too
great. But what do we do about the individual with Alzheimer's
disease who has never talked with his family about what
he wants, or the handicapped child, like Tracy Latimer, who
appears to be in pain, but is unable to tell others what her
choice would be and what makes life meaningful for her? This,
without question, is the most problematic territory in staking
out our last rights.

Writing this book, for me, has been as much a personal journey as an intellectual one. By staring at death, I have come to
appreciate life all the more. I have lost my fear of death, but not
my respect for it. I have found truth in the existentialist belief
that the awareness of the ever-present possibility of death is

what makes real life possible. That awareness and acceptance shows itself in both big and little ways. I've written a living will. I've talked to my parents, my husband and my sisters about death and our attitudes long before, we hope, any of us will have need to use that information. I am cognizant of not leaving things unsaid, of mending my bridges, of keeping my psychological space clean. I say "I love you" frequently to the important people in my life. I try, as much as possible, to live in the moment. Staring at death, in fact, has enabled me to get more out of life.

1

BILL'S
CHOICE

BILL DAVIES was a powerfully built man. Even in his sixties there was a robust vitality to him, a fluidness that spoke of a life of physical activity and of natural agility once taken almost for granted. Perhaps that was why it was so hard for him when his cancer hit. He had always had a mind of his own, a pride in his self-reliance, and that, coupled with the relentlessness of the disease, made his increasing infirmity too much to bear.

When Alice first laid eyes on him in London's Victoria and Albert Museum he was fresh from working his way across the Atlantic on a tramp steamer. It was 1951 and he was twenty-five. She was an eighteen-year-old Swiss au pair, working for a family in London to improve her English. Their eyes met across a spinet near the museum entrance. It was a charged glance and Alice didn't really mind that, after that *coup de foudre*, he seemed to be following her through the museum. When she was leaving he was at the exit. He asked her to join him in the museum coffee shop and she accepted.

Over their more than forty years together, Alice and Bill often marvelled at the seeming fatedness of their meeting, how they had been so drawn to each other. Alice, with her dark, swept-back hair and noble carriage, looked like a queen to Bill. Alice was intrigued by Bill's mix of bookishness and physical power — she'd never met a man who looked even faintly like him in Switzerland.

During the thirty minutes they sat in the coffee shop, they laughed over the chicory-flavoured water that was sold as coffee and the inedible lard-and-flour concoction called Bavarian pastry in rations-time London. Of course, they weren't too interested in the food anyway, as it was, after all, just the pretext. From that conversation she learned that Bill was from New Westminster, British Columbia, and he had been an officer in the Canadian Army, but just as his contingent was about to be shipped overseas, World War II ended. He'd been determined to get to England anyway, so after graduating with a degree in English and History and earning his teacher's certificate, he joined the crew of the tramp steamer the HMS *Argofax*.

It was years before Alice, by then his wife, learned the full story of his Atlantic crossing, how in the middle of the ocean a mutiny had broken out among the *Argofax*'s disgruntled crew and Bill had stopped a shipmate from taking the captain's life. When the *Argofax* landed in Cardiff, Bill was hailed as a hero. To hold back such a crucial part of the story was just like Bill, says Alice fondly. He was never boastful nor one to parade his accomplishments. In the same way, he had never told his mother when he was named top cadet in Canada as a teen in the Seaforth Highlanders.

At the end of their coffee, since neither Bill nor Alice could find a pen or a piece of paper, Bill had run through the London Underground chanting "Byron-0421" until he found a man with a pen and a scrap piece of newsprint onto which he could jot Alice's phone number. Eight months later they were married in a church in New Westminster. Alice knew she was entwining her life with that of a fine and decent man. Forty-two years later, after Bill's tragic, violent death, she still thought that was true.

Except for a heart attack in his early fifties, Bill always seemed healthy. They had often remarked on the almost magical good fortune of their life together — like the amazing week in 1952 when three momentous events happened all at once: their first son, Ken, was born; Bill got a job teaching highschool English and History; and they found the idyllic twenty-acre piece of property on the edge of a mountain with a stunning view over the Fraser Valley. On the property was a tiny, one-room shack that became their home while Bill built their new house by hand. It was three concentric circles, with Stone Henge-like columns supporting the roof, walls and large glass windows that took advantage of the view. The design was strong, singular and intelligent, just like Bill. Each evening, Bill would make the concrete blocks for the columns and walls by hand, pouring twenty pounds of cement into each form. He could make fifteen blocks a night. At that rate, it took ten years to build the house, during which time the family grew by two more children in the tiny shack. Alice not only raised the children, but also chickens, goats and a flourishing vegetable garden on their fertile piece of land.

Their years together were full and varied. For two years in the 1960s they lived in Africa where Bill taught at a teacher's college; in the 1970s, Alice earned a diploma in adult education and taught inmates in a minimum security prison in Agassiz. As the children grew older, the Davies expanded their ranks with an adopted child and two Native Indian foster children who each became integral and important individuals in their family. Bill fed his passion for history, reading up to a book a day. He collected music from around the world. One of his favourite activities was splitting wood for their wood-burning stoves. He built a little wood shed and tool shop on a grassy ledge below the house and made a wooden platform as his wood-chopping site. As his eye took in the magnificent view, he'd swing the axe handle, savouring the fluid motion of his body and the satisfaction of the resounding crack as the axe cleft the wood. He and Alice aged gracefully together.

Then one day when Bill was retired and sixty-four, he began to bleed heavily after doctors gave him a drug to dissolve a blood clot that was threatening to trigger another heart attack. The unexpected bleeding told doctors something else was happening in his body. What they found was bowel cancer and another spot of cancer on his liver. "There was never any talk of cure," says Alice, "just controlling the pain and the rate of growth of the cancer." Bill wrote in a diary after the diagnosis:

> The doctor said I probably had the cancer growing for 20 years — that is certainly a thought provoker. Meanwhile from India is news of an earthquake in which more than 30,000 people were snuffed out in their sleep. So where does anyone see anything beyond random chance shaping destiny? I have had a delightful, healthy life, which suddenly, with cancer, signals the end. They, in India, never saw the end coming.

Bill had surgery to remove the cancerous section of bowel and later on, radiation and chemotherapy to slow the growth and improve Bill's pain control, but the cancer was never cured. Fortunately, there were four good years with little pain or disability. By 1993, however, when Bill was sixty-eight, his condition began to worsen. He was in almost constant pain, as if someone were stabbing a dagger in his chest. It took a few months to find that the cancer had spread through his liver to the bones of his sternum. Over the spring and summer of 1993, cancer infiltrated his rib cage and his lungs. There was nothing doctors could do except try to keep Bill comfortable, but even that, as time went on, proved impossible. His legs swelled to more than twice their normal size so that he could no longer bend his knees and the skin on them ulcerated. He was taking more than sixty milligrams of oral morphine syrup four times a day as well as morphine pills, but still his pain would break through. Bill was miserable. In late September, 1993, he wrote in his diary:

> Aching, desperate feeling . . . I wish to leave life — to die and have it all over with . . . I am trapped between pain, or being doped so that I fumble and doze always. Even my dreams are shaped by this trap so there isn't the night hours of healing the mind one normally gets. I wake at two or three and feel frustration and despair due to my dreadful alternatives — pain, or doped beyond the ability to enjoy the small things which constitute life's joys.

He lost his appetite for food. Even though Alice lovingly tried to cook his favourite dishes or tempt him with new flavours, all he could manage was just a few bites. He existed, instead, on liquid meals of Boost, but he soon lacked the strength to even open the pull-tab on the can. Alice had to open it for him and he could hardly finish a full glass. He abhorred the relentless constipation brought on by the morphine which even constant laxatives or enemas did little to relieve. His diary became full of descriptions of the indignity he felt at having to have a catheter empty his bladder or to have Alice give him enemas to cleanse his bowels. "I can neither urinate nor crap without artificial aid."

The morphine made him too dozy to drive a car, nor could he comfortably ride as a passenger, as his legs would not bend to get into the seat and motion made him nauseated.

In his diary he wrote about his concern for what his ever diminishing abilities were doing to Alice:

> One's relationship to one's mate changes in some ways for the worse. How much and for how long can they be expected to

give at their own personal cost? Does one's mate give up the little outings or even big holidays entirely as I now must?

For the first time in forty-two years of marriage, he moved into another bed, sleeping on the cot in his study so that his night-time restlessness, pain and agitation would not disturb Alice's sleep. There was no palliative care program at the local hospital, but even if there had been, Bill would have been reluctant to be admitted into hospital; he wanted die at home, surrounded by all he loved and worked for. There were regular visits from home care nurses who would change the dressing on his oozing leg and attempt to keep him comfortable, but Bill disliked the frequent change of staff, each new face going over the same medical history often in an artificially chipper way. "They mean so well, the nurses," he wrote, "but oh, how insulting and patronizing some of them are without meaning to be."

All that year, he had watched as another British Columbian, forty-two-year-old Sue Rodriguez, dying of amyotrophic lateral sclerosis (ALS), blazed upon the Canadian scene. He knew that if she was successful in her fight to have a doctor help her end her life in the time and manner of her choosing, that he, too, might seek the same end. His vision of the perfect death was to lie in Alice's arms in their double bed, surrounded by flowers, and give himself a lethal injection or be injected by someone else. Then he would drift off to sleep to a selection of Bach or Mozart.

On September 29, 1993, the Supreme Court of Canada brought down its decision on the Rodriguez petition. The esteemed judges were split five to four, illustrating how divisive the question of assisted death had become in Canadian society. What went unnoticed by Bill Davies and by most commentators, was that the majority judges agreed that Sue Rodriguez's rights to liberty and security of the person, as set out under section 7 of the Canadian Charter of Rights and Freedoms, were indeed being stepped on by laws that denied her an assisted suicide. The five judges ruled, however, the infringement was reasonable and necessary in a democratic society because to change the laws would put other vulnerable people at risk and would devalue the sanctity of life. Sue Rodriguez was told that she must accept the loss of her individual freedom for the welfare of others.

The four dissenting judges, however, all declared that the infringement wasn't reasonable or necessary; laws could be written or guidelines made that would allow Sue Rodriguez the liberty to control the timing of her death while other members of society were still protected. As dissenting Justice Beverly McLachlin noted, "Sue Rodriguez is being asked to bear the burden of the chance that other people in other situations may act criminally to kill others or improperly sway them to suicide. She is asked to serve as a scapegoat." The fear is that unless assisted suicide is prohibited, it would be used as a cloak, not for suicide, but for murder, yet McLachlin noted a "person who causes the death of an ill or handicapped person without that person's consent can be prosecuted under the provisions for culpable homicide," in the Criminal Code. The law against assisted suicide was therefore arbitrary and unjustified.

Chief Justice Antonio Lamer also disagreed with the majority, but on the grounds that the law prohibiting assisted suicide was discriminatory and therefore against section 15 of the Canadian Charter of Rights and Freedoms. While able-bodied Canadians could commit suicide, Sue Rodriguez, who was physically incapable of taking her own life, was denied assistance. Justice Lamer noted that the reasons behind the law prohibiting assisted suicide were indeed worthy — the protection of vulnerable people from being manipulated or coerced by others to end their lives — but the law was too broad. "I remain unpersuaded," he wrote, "that it is not possible to design legislation that is somewhere between complete decriminalization and absolute prohibition."

To Bill Davies, the esoteric legal arguments didn't really matter; what did matter was that, by the narrowest of margins, his hoped-for death was not to be. His thoughts turned to suicide. On the day the judgment was rendered, Bill's diary reads:

> Suicide seems like an act of violence against the family, but although that may be true, the more important feeling is that of the sufferer who has the right to do with his life what he wishes, once the obligations to the family have been done. Well, I have done mine. I've been a devoted husband for 42 years. The children have received all I can or could give as a father. I hope that they can realize and accept that I want my freedom from life.

Since his cancer diagnosis, he had talked at length with Alice about life and death — they had seen their relationship grow even deeper by these frank and open talks about mortality. He was not depressed, rather he was resigned. "My life has been happier and longer than most humans who have ever lived," he wrote in early October. But resorting to suicide concerned him, particularly the impact on his family and how he would do it. A morphine overdose was out of the question because he had been on large doses for a number of months and his body had become accustomed to the drug. A large dose would be unlikely to kill him. Besides, he was beyond the stage of swallowing comfortably. What other options were there? Bill's diary reveals his deliberations:

> Oct. 1, 5 a.m. — I am dopey & hurting & sleepy but I can't sleep for pain. I can't stop the pain even though I am using a lot of morphine syrup, but I must try. *Alice* — at last you must face what we both knew would happen some day.

The price of deep love is probably deep sorrow for the survivors. . . . Am I scared? I am ambivalent whenever I think of it. The actual moment of killing oneself — how do I do it? Obviously, I don't want pain and I don't want any chance of failure. . . . Suicide presents a responsibility to the actor. Where do I leave my body? In what "condition" do I hope it to be when the unfortunate finders find it? For instance, I wish to die here on our property, perhaps in "Alice's copse" but that would then haunt the place for her. I don't want to die inside the house for that same reason. How do I inform my people? I can't just disappear and hope that a search party is lucky and finds me soon. Someone should know. Who should that be? A friend? The police? An immediate relative? How does one cushion them, or hint . . .

A few days after that entry, Bill told Alice he wanted to commit suicide and he asked her for permission to take his life, to break the covenant of their marriage vows so that he was responsible only for himself.

"I could have been selfish and put on a show to stop him from taking his life. But I'd been his sole caregiver for four years and I knew how it was for him. I could not be selfish. My last act of love was to give him my permission." Alice even tried to help him. Books (such as *Final Exit*) and right-to-die organizations adamantly reject violent methods of suicide such as jumping from bridges or shooting oneself with a gun. Instead they recommend that people seek out a sympathetic doctor who will write out a prescription for a fatal dose of barbiturates. In the last week of October Alice visited her doctor and Bill's doctor to see if either could furnish the self-deliverance Bill craved. But she was too worried about the law to ask outright for a fatal prescription. "I didn't want to put them at risk of prosecution. I just kept saying, 'Bill wants out, he really needs to go,'" Alice said.

Neither doctor picked up on her veiled request. One told her that if his own wife were dying, he would see to it that she wouldn't suffer, but his hand didn't move on the prescription pad for Alice. The other doctor told her he had seen horribly botched suicides where people had aimed a gun at their heart. To make a quick and final end, he said, it was best to aim between the eyebrows. Alice didn't know whether that information was meant specifically for Bill or whether the doctor was just telling her what he knew about suicide, but instead of a prescription, Alice returned home with that advice.

On October 23, 1993, Bill wrote the last paragraph in his diary: "I am inwardly revelling in the knowledge that my freedom is soon. The chains that imprison me, everyday a little more and a little more unpleasantly, are about where I find the balance has moved from worth living to the reverse." A week later, after writing notes to Alice, his six children, friends and police, Bill walked with his wife and eldest son down the narrow stone stairs to the grassy ledge below the house. By the shed where he would chop wood was a chair and an old .22 rifle, a gun that he'd inherited from his father but rarely used because he abhorred hunting. Alice stood by him as he took five sleeping pills out of his pocket and swallowed them — a precaution in case he was unsuccessful in killing himself so that it might be more difficult to revive him. Then she and her son hugged and kissed him good bye. Ken went out to stand in the meadow to give his father his privacy. Alice stayed by her husband's side until Bill sent her away.

Bill turned the chair so that his back was to the magnificent view and aimed the rifle at the triangle between his eyes. Alice, not knowing what to do, vacuumed so she wouldn't hear the shot. Later, after Ken had come to get her, Alice descended the stone stairs and turned the corner with fear and trepidation about what she might find. Bill's body was slumped in the chair, two tiny trickles of bright red blood oozing from a clean, round hole between his eyes and another at the back of his head. "I gathered him in my arms and hugged him and kissed him and cried, my sweetie, my sweetie."

Alice called her doctor because Bill's doctor was out of town, but she didn't tell him that Bill had shot himself. When she took the doctor to Bill's body, he was obviously shaken and upset, Alice recounts. "He needed a few minutes to compose himself." The doctor then called the police and the coroner, who questioned Alice and Ken separately. "Everyone was very gentle with me, but I learned later that one of the RCMP officers grilled Ken very hard." Alice and Ken told them everything they knew and gave them all of Bill's writing. What his notes contained was explanation enough.

To his six children he said not to grieve too much, because there was no sadness in his death, he was happy to be going. To the police, he stated that he accepted full responsibility, that no one persuaded him to kill himself, and he forbade any attempt to save him. To Alice, he expressed his love and thanked her for giving him the greatest freedom to release himself from the burden of living. He told her: "I hope you can soon enter upon your individual life with our wonderful marriage as the solid foundation upon which to build whatever future you choose." And to his friends and acquaintances he wrote:

An Open Letter To Anyone Who Is Puzzled By My Death:
In my opinion, every person has the right to leave life when he feels the time has come and when he has prepared his immediate family for the event as well as he can. This I have done. I have chosen to balance the steadily decreasing pleasures against the steadily increasing problems as my body fails me in one function after another . . . So each one of us is faced sometime with the choice — does one stop the misery at the point one chooses or does one let a heartless nature destroy the person at its own rate? I made my choice.

For Alice, although she knew that Bill had done what he wanted, her sorrow was tinged with bitterness at laws that prevented her husband from having a more peaceful death. "No one should have to die alone, in such a violent way," she says.

The question facing Canadians — indeed facing all Western nations — as the twenty-first century dawns is whether as a democratic society we can risk giving Bill Davies or Sue Rodriguez a choice. Can a doctor (or another person for that matter) be permitted to give them a lethal injection at their request, or write a fatal prescription which they then take themselves, without harming the fabric of our society or putting our most vulnerable citizens at risk? That is the crux of the euthanasia and assisted suicide debate.

It is a debate that asks the following questions:

- In the scheme of the universe, should human beings have the right to control the circumstances of their deaths or must that be left to God or nature?
- If the acceptance or rejection of euthanasia comes down to one's personal moral or religious beliefs, what is the role of government in either limiting or accommodating moral choice?
- Where should the line be drawn between the rights of the individual and the needs of society?
- Would the availability of euthanasia or assisted suicide diminish the reverence for life or decrease public tolerance for those with illness, disability or infirmity who choose not to end their lives?
- If euthanasia or assisted suicide is allowed, should only doctors be allowed to administer it? Would giving doctors the power to end our lives erode the ethos of the medical profession or shift the nature of the doctor-patient relationship? Does the medical profession even want the responsibility of helping patients die?

- Would the options of euthanasia or assisted suicide, because they are cheaper to the health care system, undermine the provision of palliative care and other services for the dying?
- Will society begin to condone the termination of the lives of suffering, disabled or dying individuals who haven't asked for euthanasia because others feel it is "for their own good"?
- Will establishing the right to die create a feeling of an obligation to die by individuals who fear their illness or disability may be a burden to their families or to society?
- If we allow euthanasia as a compassionate form of killing, will nefarious individuals be able to disguise acts of murder and go unpunished?
- Can the practice of euthanasia and assisted suicide be contained by legal limits? How do we enforce and regulate an act that can take place in private between a patient and a doctor, and after the patient's death, may only come to light if the doctor chooses to reveal it by self-incrimination?

Variations of those questions are being wrestled within many nations — Canada, the U.S., England, Australia, Japan, France. Nine judges at the Supreme Court of Canada, faced with Sue Rodriguez's petition, decided these questions should be asked by Parliament rather than by the courts. A select committee of the House of Lords in England pondered the same in 1993. And they were the questions investigated by the Special Senate Committee on Euthanasia and Assisted Suicide, which reported in the spring of 1995, and like the Supreme Court justices were split as to whether the laws prohibiting assisted suicide should be re-written to allow a competent individual to ask a doctor for a fatal prescription. In Canada, as in most Western nations, our current Criminal Code prohibits both assisted suicide and euthanasia, even for the most compassionate motives. No one may counsel, aid or abet a suicide; to do so is a crime punishable by up to fourteen years in jail. No one may deliberately take the life of another, even in mercy and at the person's explicit request. To do so is murder and punishable with a minimum life term. As Barney Sneiderman, a professor of law and medical ethics at the University of Manitoba, notes, "It doesn't seem fair, does it? Prompted by mercy and compassion, you kill a person at his earnest request and that is murder. Prompted by rage and anger, you kill a non-consenting victim and that is manslaughter."

The definition of voluntary euthanasia is the giving of a lethal injection to an individual at his request; assisted suicide is that of providing a fatal prescription which the person takes themselves. Is there a moral difference between the two? Most ethicists believe not, since both require the complicit assistance of another person to bring the death about. In fact, to allow assisted suicide but not euthanasia, many argue, would discriminate against individuals who are unable to perform the act themselves, either because they are physically disabled or are too sick to swallow medication. Many people, however, particularly in the medical profession, are more comfortable with only allowing assisted suicide and not euthanasia, as the patient retains the final control of the death and can at the last minute change his or her mind. As well, it removes the onus on the physician to actually end the patient's life. Indeed, in the Netherlands recently, where euthanasia has been about six times more frequent than assisted suicide, the Royal Dutch Medical Association issued new guidelines saying, where possible, the patient should be the one to perform the act to make it easier, emotionally, on physicians.

In the last decade of the twentieth century it has become clear that an increasing number of people are dissatisfied with the legal proscription against aid-in-dying and want either legislative change or are willing to defy the law to obtain the death they want. *Final Exit*, a suicide how-to book written by right-to-die advocate Derek Humphry rocketed to the top of the best-seller lists in 1991 and sold more than 500,000 copies, showing that people were eager for information about how to control their deaths. Around the same time, Dr. Jack Kevorkian was helping his first patients die in the back of his Volkswagen van, making him a hero in some peoples' eyes and the devil in disguise to others. Canadian social worker and researcher Russel Ogden documented thirty-four cases of assisted suicide among people with AIDS, the first empirical research that showed these deaths are indeed occurring in great secrecy despite the law. Although Ogden's research only looked at assisted deaths in the AIDS population, after his report, dozens more people approached him with stories of death among people with cancer, ALS and other terminal illnesses. What was of most concern about Ogden's research was that half of the AIDS deaths did not go smoothly — friends or family had to intervene, smothering patients with plastic bags or pillows after a drug overdose didn't work, or subsequently injecting heroin, using razor blades to slit the wrist, or in one case using a gun. "What we have now is the equivalent of back-alley abortions," Ogden concluded.

In Canada since 1991, five legislative attempts have been made to change the law to allow assisted suicide through private members' bills, two of which were put forward by New Democratic Party member Svend Robinson, who publicly acknowledged his presence at Sue Rodriguez's death. All died on the order paper. In the United States since 1991 more than fifteen states have considered, or are still considering, legislation to allow assisted suicide, which either have or most likely will be defeated by narrow margins. Washington, California and Oregon, have put euthanasia or assisted suicide bills to public referendum. Oregon's bill was passed by voters, just 51 per cent in favour to 49 per cent against, but the bill has yet to come into force because it has been held up in legal challenges. Although euthanasia and assisted suicide have been carried out for almost twenty years in the Netherlands, the acts are still technically illegal in that country. As such, in 1995, the Northern Territory of Australia became the first jurisdiction in the world to pass a bill allowing assisted suicide under strict guidelines.

Increasingly, too, cases in which individuals have defied the law have come before courts in Canada and the United States. Five times since 1991 Canadians who helped another person to die were found guilty of lesser offences, such as administering a noxious substance, and given suspended sentences. Similar cases have come before U.S. courts, only for the defendants to be given a suspended sentence or acquitted, too. By 1995, even the Internet had become an active medium for both sides of the debate. John Hofsess, of the Right To Die Society of Canada, teamed up with Derek Humphry to create DeathNet, an information service on the World Wide Web that provides complete transcripts of the Senate hearings, court transcripts, news stories and documents from around the world. Then pro-life organizations set up Life Net to provide their own interpretation of the issues. In Ontario, Austin Bastable, a Windsor man with multiple sclerosis, set up his own home page to detail his attempts to obtain an assisted suicide.

At the centre of the debate in favour of assisted suicide or euthanasia is a belief in personal autonomy and self-determination; individuals have the right to determine what happens to their own bodies. Like Bill Davies or Sue Rodriguez, they may want to die on their own terms, at their own time, and believe that the laws of the land have no right to tell them they can't. There is also a strong component of compassion and mercy motivating those who support the right to die. They see terminally ill individuals enduring meaningless suffering waiting for a natural death when they could easily be helped to have a peaceful death. As many note, suffering animals are treated more humanely.

Those opposed to changing the laws to accommodate euthanasia or assisted suicide argue, however, that even if a convincing case can be made to allow a competent, terminally ill
individual to obtain help to die from a willing doctor, the law
prohibiting such an action must be kept on the books to protect
vulnerable individuals who do not want to die from others who
think they would be better off dead. As Dr. Elizabeth Latimer, a
Hamilton palliative care physician, warned the Senate hearings,
"Once we decide on any basis that euthanasia is good for some
people, it would be very difficult to say that it was also not good
for others. There are many frail and incapacitated people, who,
in some people's eyes, are serving no purpose in our society. . . .
The continued safety and protection of large numbers of frail
people depends on the maintenance of the law the way it is."
In fact, the recent trial against Saskatchewan farmer Robert
Latimer, who admitted killing his disabled daughter, Tracy, to
put her out of her pain and suffering, and the widespread support for his actions from the public, confirmed many euthanasia
opponents' worst fears that euthanasia would grow to encompass those who do not request it.

That erosion from the principle of a voluntary, uncoerced
request to die has been dubbed "the slippery slope" and is the
most frequently cited reason against changing the laws. The
slippery slope argument is that once the law is changed it will
put in motion a series of changes in our society that we will be
unable to stop. Concerns are that a choice for death will cause
a devaluation of all human life and will reduce society's prohibition against killing; it will result in subtle pressure being
placed on individuals who are dying or disabled to end their
lives and it may even result in the killing of individuals against
their will; it will remove the commitment from governments
and the medical system to provide for good palliative care or to
search for new cures and therapies to help terminal illness; it
will destroy the doctor-patient relationship.

Those who support change in the law agree that slippery slope concerns need to be heeded — no one wants individuals manipulated or killed against their will. They believe society is better protected from unwanted acts of assisted death by writing clear legislation that circumscribes, in definite terms, the appropriate actions. As Dr. Tom Preston, a Seattle cardiologist notes, "There is no real slippery slope; as a society we can stop when we want to stop. We can even go back if we need to. Some people associate the slippery slope with any social change. What we need to do is to ensure we keep asking the question, in terms of individual people, are we making society worse or making it better?"

Both sides agree that even if the law were changed only a small percentage of dying people would actually ask for euthanasia or assisted suicide, perhaps less than 5 per cent of the 190,000 Canadians and two million Americans who die each year. Fortunately, most people die either quickly or peacefully. Their discomfort is eased by drugs and expert medical care; their anguish is soothed by the love of family and friends, by their spiritual beliefs, or by caring professionals. Even among those individuals whose dying is not peaceful — the 15 per cent who suffer unrelieved symptoms such as relentless vomiting, nausea or breathlessness, uncontrolled pain, or physical indignity, or like Bill Davies the paltry choice of either remaining lucid and enduring pain, or being comfortable but sedated — the majority of those people also would not opt for an assisted death because they are eager to hang on to every last moment of life. The question before us, therefore, is whether as a society we can allow individuals like Bill Davies and Sue Rodriguez to determine the manner and timing of their own deaths without changing our society in a way we would regret.

2

DECADE
OF DEATH

Ⓘ N 1968, Gallup pollsters first asked Canadians the following question:

> When a person has an incurable disease that causes great
> suffering, do you think that competent doctors should be
> allowed by law to end the patient's life, if the patient has
> made a formal request in writing?

Back then, less than half of those Canadians polled answered
yes. But it was never to be so low again. Over the last twenty-
five years the percentage in favour has climbed up and up — so
much so that by 1992, when Sue Rodriguez came on the scene,
a full 78 per cent of Canadians felt she should legally be able to
have a doctor help her die. The Canadian population is hardly
unique. The U.S.A., Britain, New Zealand and Australia all
show the same upward trend in public opinion over the same
period of time. The exact numbers vary only slightly. Australia,
where the world's first right-to-die legislation was passed into
law in the spring of 1995, leads with 79 per cent of its population
favouring the choice; Britain mirrors Canada while the U.S. is
slightly behind at 73 per cent. The result is that roughly three

out of every four people in almost all English-speaking countries now believe that, under certain circumstances such as hopeless terminal illness with untreatable suffering, an individual should be able to ask for and receive euthanasia or assisted suicide.

A similar trend has occurred in Japan, Israel and the European nations. A comprehensive survey of European beliefs and morals, called the European Values Survey, was conducted in fourteen nations in 1981 and repeated in 1990, polling more than 50,000 Europeans on a wide range of issues, including euthanasia. The same increasing trend of acceptance was found in almost all of Europe's industrialized nations: France, Sweden, Norway, Denmark, Belgium, Iceland, Switzerland, Germany and the Netherlands, and even strongly Catholic nations, like Italy and Spain, showed that a majority of the population could envisage situations where euthanasia would be morally justified. Ireland was the only country where the philosophical acceptance of euthanasia was still in the minority, but even there, the position had gained some percentage points in the nine years between the polls.

Why is the acceptance of euthanasia gaining ground? What is giving such tremendous momentum to the right to die? The answer comes from the convergence of a number of distinct circumstances at the end of the twentieth century: a rapidly aging population, widespread disillusionment with medical technology, the decline of medical paternalism, the decline of religious beliefs and the rise of individual rights. Each one is a powerful force on its own, but when combined, they create an unrelenting pressure to give individuals the power to choose the time and manner of their deaths.

Never before in the history of human life on earth has the number of elderly people in the population been so high — and the numbers are going to grow even greater in the next few decades. In 1996, the first of the Baby Boom generation will turn fifty and the percentage of elderly in most Western populations will steadily increase to more than 20 per cent of the population through to 2030, when the last of the Baby Boomers turn sixty-five. As people age, it is inevitable that they begin to think of illness, disability and death and what, as individuals, they can do to ease their own passage. While critics of euthanasia often predict that vulnerable elderly people could be harmed by any liberalization of euthanasia laws, it has often been the elderly themselves who have been the strongest lobbyists in favour of a choice to die. Indeed, the majority of members in the more than 120 right-to-die organizations to emerge in the world over the last decade are in late middle age or in their senior years. These right-to-die advocacy groups, which include Toronto's Dying With Dignity, the Victoria-based Right To Die Society of Canada, or the Hemlock Society in the United States, have almost single-handedly kept the issues in the public eye for the past decade. As U.S. writer Anne Fadiman notes, meetings of the Hemlock Society during the 1980s tended to be "a genteel sorority of seniors" with educated, elderly women outnumbering elderly men or younger people of both sexes.

The relentless aging of the population means that in future years the debate over choices at the end of life is only going to increase. Just as Baby Boomers focused their attention on sex, then on birth and parenthood, then on middle age and menopause, the Baby Boom generation will become obsessed with the process of dying as the reality of their own death looms closer, giving even more momentum to the issues of the right to die. Indeed, many people are already having to face difficult medical dilemmas. A loved one is in an intensive care unit on a respirator with no hope of recovery — should doctors be asked to remove the machine? Mother has Alzheimer's and has developed pneumonia, should she be treated with antibiotics? Granny is eighty and frail but in otherwise good health when she goes into hospital for elective surgery — should she request that a "do not resuscitate" order be placed on her chart in case she has a heart attack on the ward? Should high levels of pain killers be given to a loved one dying of AIDS or cancer which will dull his pain but at the same time cloud his brain and hasten his death? These decisions are already being made hundreds of times each day in Canadian hospitals. Yet advancing age might not be a big enough factor to push the issue of choice in dying on its own. It becomes a compelling force when an aging population is coupled with the phenomenal change in medicine over the last fifty years, and how that change, in turn, has transformed the process of dying.

In 1922, when an epidemic of diphtheria was sweeping central Canada, my paternal grandmother sat by the beds of three of her young children, begging God to save their lives. Prayer was all she had. Back then, as it had been for centuries, infectious and parasitic disease were the biggest threats to human life, especially young life. The challenge of staying alive made the question of a "good death" a moot one. Death was a constant visitor and half of all deaths occurred in childhood. My grandmother knew that reality too well. By the time of the diphtheria epidemic she had already lost two children to infectious disease. Willy, her second child, had died of whooping cough in 1910 at only six months of age. In 1918, Gerald, then five, had cut his foot on the blade of an ice skate. Within a few days his foot had become swollen and red and the infection soon spread through his body. Without antibiotics to stem the spread of the bacteria, Gerald slipped into a coma and died of blood poisoning, septicemia, within two weeks of the innocent cut. Helen, Reg and Rita became sick with diphtheria, a disease that was the scourge of childhood and every mother's fear. The two older children had been lucky and received a new diphtheria anti-toxin inoculation at school, and they recovered. But Rita was only four and too young for school; she hadn't been inoculated. Six weeks later Rita died of heart failure. As if the toll of three dead children wasn't enough, my grandmother was to lose two more before the dawn of the Second World War. In 1929, eight-year-old Dorothy died of meningitis in Toronto's Sick Children's Hospital. Jack, her eldest son, was lucky and lived past childhood, but he died at age thirty-five of a lung abscess that today would be treated by antibiotics. William, her husband, died suddenly, too, at forty-five of what was probably chronic asthma. His death came two weeks after she gave birth to their tenth child, my father. My grandmother then developed tuberculosis in 1930 and spent two years in a sanatorium while her children were dispersed to relatives' care. It never surprised me, with such a family history, that my father chose to become not only a doctor but a surgeon, an area of medicine in which physicians have the greatest sense of power and control over the outcome of a treatment or a disease.

While such a litany of grief and tragedy in one family — all caused by what are now treatable or preventable illnesses — seems almost inconceivable to modern ears, sixty years ago such a story was commonplace. Families almost expected to lose a child or two, especially if they were poor. In 1921, for every 1000 children born in Canada, eighty-eight died before they reached their first birthday. By 1985, just 7.9 of 1000 children would fail to reach that milestone. Dr. Lewis Thomas, a U.S. physician and essayist, described in his medical memoirs, "The Youngest Science," how much medicine had changed during his own lifetime as a doctor. "When I was an intern on the wards of the Boston City Hospital the major threats to human life were tuberculosis, tetanus, syphilis, rheumatic fever, pneumonia, meningitis, polio and septicemia of all sorts. These things worried us then the way cancer, heart disease and stroke worry us today. The big problems of the 1930s and 1940s have literally vanished." They vanished in less than thirty years through a combination of improved nutrition and sanitation, immunization of children, and the discovery of truly effective drugs, particularly penicillin, widely available by the end of World War II. By the 1950s, public optimism about what medicine could do had soared. Hospitals, which in previous centuries had been avoided and or held in suspicion, were now almost temples of worship and the doctors the deities who performed miracles. Those miracles seemed all the greater with the birth of "rescue medicine." One after another in the 1950s, machines were perfected that could stave off death by temporarily doing the work of the lungs, the kidneys and the heart. These technologies pulled patients back from the brink of death until the organs could resume their function.

In the scheme of right-to-die cases in the 1970s and 1980s, the development of the modern respirator in the mid-1950s was the most significant technological development. Respiratory failure, particularly the paralysis of the muscles of the lungs caused by epidemics of poliomyelitis, had long been an agonizing problem for physicians and families. In the 1920s, one U.S. physician, Dr. James Wilson, had written as quoted in the writing of Philip Drinker and Louis Shaw, the inventors of the iron lung:

> Of all the experiences the physician must undergo, none can be more distressing than to watch respiratory paralysis in a child with poliomyelitis — to watch him become more and more dyspneic [breathless] using with increasing vigour every available accessory muscle of the neck, shoulder, and chin — silent, wasting no breath for speech, wide-eyed, frightened, conscious to almost the last breath.

The iron lung, which encapsulated the patient in a steel cylinder with the head exposed, had been invented by the Boston scientists in 1928 and its technology rapidly spread around the world. Pumps raised and lowered the pressure within the chamber which in turn forced the lungs to contract and expand. It saved numerous lives, but the problems of the technology became increasingly apparent: it was ineffective for the most severe form of polio; in an epidemic there were never enough iron lungs to go around creating ethical dilemmas about who should have access to one; regular turning and nursing of the patients was difficult if not impossible creating a problem of bed sores; and many of those sustained by the machines could not be weaned from them, becoming imprisoned by the very technology that had saved their lives.

A devastating polio epidemic in Denmark in 1952 proved the impetus for a better method to be found. When the twenty-eighth patient admitted with polio to Copenhagen's Blegdam Hospital died of respiratory paralysis, the head epidemiologist implored the head anesthetist to try to sustain the mounting number of patients by manually forcing air into their lungs with a ventilation bag, a method commonly used for short durations during surgery. It worked even better than the iron lung but it was extraordinarily labour intensive. During the Copenhagen epidemic seventy-five patients were kept alive during their acute medical crisis by teams of 250 medical students doing round-the-clock manual bagging, 260 nurses providing bedside care, and twenty-seven technicians looking after the equipment. Within a year of the Copenhagen group's report in *The Lancet*, companies around the world were coming out with a positive pressure, electrically-driven ventilator that would replace the manual bagging with a reliable machine. The respirator was born, and it was soon discovered that this little piece of technology could keep a person alive almost indefinitely, even when they were in a persistent coma or irreversible respiratory failure.

At about the same time, other groups of scientists were looking for ways to rescue a flagging heart. Before the 1950s, there was little that could be done if a person's heart went into cardiac arrest, its muscles no longer pumping blood through the body in a steady rhythm but quivering and twitching ineffectively in a state called ventricular fibrillation. Nor could much be done if a blood clot threatened to block important vessels, or if coronary artery disease was slowly strangling the blood supply. External cardiopulmonary resuscitation was unknown. Back then, the only known technique to restart a fibrillating heart was to open the patient's chest and grab the wriggling mass of muscle by hand, give it a series of forceful squeezes in the hope the heart would return to a steady beat. Understandably, the method enjoyed a dismal success rate. In the early 1950s, however, Dr. Paul Zoll learned of some Russian research in which an electric current had been applied on the outside of the chest wall to correct a fibrillating heart. Zoll did animal experiments and then in 1952 applied a series of shocks to two patients in ventricular fibrillation. One died but the other recovered. Cardiac defibrillation was born, another of the rescue technologies that could stave off what before was certain death. Further help for diseased hearts came one year later, in 1953, when it became possible to temporarily by-pass the heart and let a machine take over circulation and aeration of the blood, for the first time enabling surgeons to operate on a motionless heart. The heart-lung bypass machine suddenly opened up a whole area of cardiac surgery, paving the way for cardiac by-pass and cardiac transplants in the late 1960s.

Effective medical rescue of the kidneys came on stream by the early 1960s. Earlier attempts to get a machine to do the job of filtering the metabolic waste products from the blood failed largely because medical scientists didn't know how to prevent the blood from clotting or what medium to use for filtration. In 1940s Holland, Dutch physician William Kolff produced the first successful dialysis machine using the drug heparin to prevent clots and cellophane as the dialysis membrane. His first sixteen patients in acute renal failure died, but the seventeenth was sustained for eleven hours until her own kidneys recovered. Continued problems with blood clotting, filter medium, and methods to attach the patient to the machine slowed the widespread use of dialysis in the 1950s. But in 1960, a Seattle scientist introduced a Teflon tube that could be inserted permanently in a patient's vein, enabling him or her to be readily connected and disconnected to the machine for the three or four sessions of blood cleansing needed each week. Dialysis then became a realistic method to sustain lives of patients in renal failure. Thus, at the beginning of the 1960s, all the rescue technologies were essentially in place. Intensive care units were created in hospitals to concentrate these machines, the skilled staff needed to monitor them, and the very sick people who needed to use them. Patients, who just years earlier would have died, could now be saved, many to resume an active life. It was miraculous; but over the next few years it began to dawn on people that miracles can sometimes have a down side.

In one generation, death had been transformed by medical advancement. Compared to the turn of the century, by the 1960s life expectancy in both men and women had jumped an astonishing two decades, the greatest increase in the history of mankind. No longer did the majority of people die of childhood illness, or during birth, or of acute infections and parasitic disease. But they still eventually died. Only now they died of chronic degenerative diseases, at a later age, often after a long, drawn-out illness that was debilitating or painful. Cancer, heart disease, arthritis and neurological disorders like Parkinson's disease or Alzheimer's disease became the modern scourges. The terminally ill, the sick, elderly and the comatose lost "the old man's friend" — a relatively quick and peaceful death by pneumonia as a secondary complication of their underlying disease — because antibiotics could now cure it. Furthermore, rather than being at home among their loved ones, as they had for centuries, the majority of dying patients were now in hospitals surrounded by medical staff who were often determined to fight death to its bitter end, regardless of what that fight might do to the patient. By the 1960s and 1970s, more than 70 per cent of all deaths in Canada and the U.S.A. were taking place in hospital, compared with only 40 per cent before World War II. With the new medical technologies, the dying process could be prolonged long past the time when life had any meaning to the patient or the family.

"The same intervention, applied in one case, has the capacity to pull someone back from severe illness and potential death, yet applied in different circumstances can prolong the process of dying into a torturous affair," says Dr. Tim Quill, a Rochester physician who speaks passionately about right-to-die issues. "With medical advances, we can now keep people alive in vegetative states and in demented states for literally years." It was in the late 1960s when that reality first hit home and individuals began openly questioning the prevailing medical ethic of fighting death at all costs. In Holland in 1968, a physician named Jan van den Berg wrote a book entitled *Medical Power and Medical Ethics*, which criticized the moral consumerism that accepted the progress of medical technology without reflection and without consideration as to whether the technology actually improved patients' lives. In fact, he concluded the technology often made the patient's life worse. This little book, which sold hundreds of thousands of copies in that country, began the debate over withholding or withdrawing treatment and eventually the morality of euthanasia and assisted suicide in the Netherlands, foreshadowing the debate in Britain and North America.

In England, a year earlier, Dame Cicely Saunders who had long fought the medical denial of death, the cold and inhumane treatment of the dying and the abandonment of dying patients, realized a twenty-year-old dream to open a hospice devoted to the comfort care of the dying. Dame Saunders decreed that within the walls of St. Christopher's Hospice, medical technology, when it could no longer cure terminal illness, would be eschewed. In its place, patients would be treated with a gentle touch, a ready ear, spiritual counselling and a liberal approach to pain-relieving drugs to keep them comfortable until they died. Her ground-breaking efforts resulted in the birth of the palliative care movement. In 1969, Dr. Elizabeth Kubler-Ross published her revolutionary book *On Death and Dying: What the dying have to teach doctors, nurses, clergy and their own families*. In it she detailed how the sophisticated machinery of hospitals that is used to keep people alive also made the process of dying a desperately lonely, de-personalizing experience. The modern medical way of death was contributing to the denial of death and the fear of death. In her book, which became an overnight bestseller, she de-mystified death and set out the well-known (if often criticized) five stages of death: shock, denial, bargaining, depression, acceptance.

Not until the mid-1970s, however, did the general public really begin to understand the dark side of medical advancement and what it could mean for some individuals and their families. This understanding came in the form of a young woman named Karen Ann Quinlan. An attractive, athletic, seventeen-year-old girl, Karen made the unfortunate decision at a party on April 14, 1975, to drink a number of gin and tonics after having consumed some tranquillizers. She collapsed and friends carried her to one of the beds. When they realized she had stopped breathing, they gave her mouth-to-mouth resuscitation and called an ambulance. But Karen's brain was permanently destroyed and she never regained consciousness. Instead she was kept alive by the mechanical breathing of a respirator while she remained tightly curled in a fetal position in a New Jersey hospital. Normally one hundred and twenty pounds, her body weight fell to an emaciated sixty pounds. Her parents, devout Catholics, prayed for a miracle, but after months and months when it became clear their daughter would never awaken, they talked to their parish priest, Rev. Thomas Trapasso. "I told them if there was to be a miracle, God didn't need a machine," Trapasso said in media interviews at the time. "If she is restored to her native state, God can either restore her or take her." The doctors, however, refused to remove the respirator and so the Quinlans went to court. Finally, in 1976, the New Jersey Supreme Court sided with the parents. But the doctors, anticipating the judge's ruling, had been working for months to wean her from the machine. When the order to remove the respirator came, Karen could breath on her own. Although she never woke up, she lived in a persistent vegetative state until 1985 when she developed pneumonia and the decision was made not to treat her with antibiotics.

The Quinlan case was a watershed. In his book *Deathright,* U.S. political scientist James Hoefler, notes that prior to Quinlan, only a handful of articles about the right to die appeared each year in medical journals, legal journals and the popular media. After Quinlan the numbers soared. In 1976, the year of the court case, *The New York Times* alone published 100 articles on the right to die. Popular culture picked up on the theme of individuals held captive by medical technology against their wishes. In 1978 the play *Whose Life Is It Anyway?* by British playwright Brian Clark began its long run in London's West End, before moving on to Broadway, and then being made into a feature film with Richard Dreyfus. A number of books told the stories of individuals who had helped their terminally ill loved ones to die, the most famous of which were *Last Wish,* Betty Rollin's account of helping her mother, dying of cancer, achieve a peaceful death, and British journalist Derek Humphry's *Jean's Way*, dealing with his role in helping his wife, who was also dying of cancer, drink a fatal potion.

By 1980 there was a rebirth of interest in voluntary euthanasia organizations such as Britain's Voluntary Euthanasia Society founded in 1935. The U.S. Hemlock Society, founded by Humphry who had settled in Oregon, and Canada's Dying With Dignity (DWD) were formed in 1980. Hemlock and DWD, like many of the world's right-to-die organizations, now numbering in the hundreds, started out to promote living wills, the cessation of treatment, and good palliative care for the dying. Gradually, however, they became more radical, openly advocating voluntary euthanasia laws and assisted suicide by the end of the decade. By the 1990s, DWD's membership numbered 7,000 and other organizations in Canada promoting the right to die had formed, including Vancouver's Goodbye Society, Ottawa's Choice in Dying, and Victoria's Right To Die Society, founded and run by John Hofsess, the motivator behind Sue Rodriguez's court challenge.

In the years following the Quinlan case, one after another, the plights of various individuals trapped between life and death increasingly came to light. As detailed by Hoefler in *Deathright*, more than one hundred cases of a right-to-die nature were heard in various state courts from 1976 until the U.S. Supreme Court heard its first right-to-die case in 1990. That case resulted in the ruling that the family of Nancy Cruzan, in a persistent vegetative state for six years, could have her tube feeding stopped. One case that helped to galvanize public opinion in favour of the right to die was never heard in court. In April 1989, Randy Linares, a Chicago painter walked into the pediatric intensive care unit and holding the staff at gun-point, tearfully unhooked the respirator from his sixteen-month-old son and held him in his arms until the baby died. When Samuel Linares was just nine months old, at a child's birthday party, he inhaled a balloon which got caught in his windpipe. His brain was deprived of oxygen, rendering him comatose but not completely brain-dead. The family requested that the respirator be withdrawn. Though the doctor agreed, the hospital said it was not possible to do so unless the infant showed no brain function or his heart failed. Seven months later, with no change in his son and little prospect for his recovery, Randy Linares committed his desperate act. When the baby died, he handed the gun over to the staff and surrendered. "I did it because I love my son," Linares yelled to reporters as he was led away in handcuffs by police. A few weeks later, a Grand Jury refused to indict him on first degree murder charges.

In Britain, the issue of the right to die was spearheaded by the case of Tony Bland. In 1989, at age seventeen, Tony was in the crowd when the stands of the Hillsborough soccer stadium collapsed. He was crushed and his brain deprived of oxygen. After two years in a persistent coma with no hope of improvement, Bland's parents asked that all of Tony's life support and medical care stop, including his tube feedings and hydration, so their son could die. The problem was that Tony Bland, before his accident, had never told anyone how he would wish to be treated in such a circumstance. In 1993, the British House of Lords finally ruled that, in general, life support treatment could be withdrawn if it was in accordance with the individual's prior wishes, particularly if those wishes have been set out in an advance directive. While that didn't help Tony Bland, the House of Lords also decided that in Bland's case, the feedings were medical treatments that were no longer conferring any benefit to him and therefore the medical profession had no obligation to continue treating him. His feedings stopped and Tony died. The Lords stated that their decision applied only to Bland and in future any cases in which the beneficial nature of a continued treatment was disputed should be adjudicated in court.

In Canada the first well-publicized right-to-die case was that of Nancy B., the pseudonym given a twenty-four-year-old Montreal woman suffering from the neurological disease Guillain-Barré syndrome. Unlike Karen Ann Quinlan who was comatose, Nancy B. was a mentally competent woman who for two years had been paralysed from the neck down and dependent

on a respirator to breathe. Nancy B. asked in late 1991 to have
her respirator removed, saying a life in which all she could do
was watch television had no meaning for her. What made
Nancy B.'s request so controversial was that although her condition was irreversible, she was not facing a terminal illness —
she might live for years in her condition. Many who themselves
were quadriplegic, were dismayed that Nancy B. was saying
that life with such a disability was not worth living. The hospital took her request to court because they were afraid that
under the Criminal Code, they might be charged with murder.
Some in the medico-legal community, however, thought the
case was completely unnecessary because by that time it had
become generally accepted that a competent individual had a
right to refuse medical treatment. After a four-day hearing,
Quebec Superior Court Justice Jacques Dufour gave permission in January of 1992, but ruled the removal would not be
murder because the act would not "cause" her death. It would
simply allow nature to take its course and allow doctors to
follow her competently expressed wishes to refuse treatment.
Sedated by morphine so she did not experience any discomfort, Nancy B. died soon after her respirator was removed in
February, 1992. Seven months later Sue Rodriguez stepped into
the media limelight.

By then, the case law in Canada, Britain and the U.S. had
firmly established the right of individuals or their guardians to
refuse medical treatment or to have medical treatment removed
even if it brought about death — an act that for years had been
called passive euthanasia. Sue Rodriguez, however, wanted to
push the issue one step further: she wanted active euthanasia, or,
if she was still physically capable, assisted suicide. She wanted a
doctor to inject her with a lethal dose or at least set up a device
that she could trigger to bring about her own death. The law
preventing assisted suicide, her lawyer argued, was unconsti-
tutional on three grounds: it discriminated against individuals

who were disabled and could not commit suicide themselves; it interfered with her right to do with her body what she wanted, and it was cruel and unusual punishment. Her case was argued, unsuccessfully, through the Supreme Court of British Columbia, the Court of Appeal of British Columbia and the Supreme Court of Canada. Five of the nine Supreme Court judges refused her petition, saying it was too dangerous to society to allow patients to ask for an injection to bring about death. In the justices' eyes, there was a substantial difference between what Nancy B. wanted and what Sue Rodriguez wanted.

Many Canadians were not so sure. Seeing beyond the judicial language of "intent" and "letting nature take its course," it seemed to many that at heart, Nancy B. and Sue Rodriguez did want the same thing: to be removed from a hopeless situation where medicine could no longer perform a miracle but could only promise a more drawn-out death. They wanted the medical profession, if it couldn't cure them, to furnish a more peaceful death. It was a wish that many individuals could identify with. "I think these cases have really scared people and they are projecting that they, too, or their loved ones, could have a lousy death — that there will be doctors and nurses who will force this upon them," said ethicist Daniel Callahan, the director and co-founder of the Hastings Center, an institute studying biomedical ethics in New York State.

During the past twenty-five years, another striking change has occurred in medicine to give increasing support to the notion that patients should be able to dictate the timing and circumstances of their deaths, namely the decline of medical paternalism and the corresponding growth of patient autonomy. The practice of medicine, by its very nature, encouraged authoritarianism. It is a discipline requiring high intellect, years of study, the acquisition of a complex set of knowledge, the development of highly specialized skills, the ability to weigh facts and to make life-and-death decisions. It is no wonder that for years doctors felt that patients, lacking the training and skills, could not realistically be partners in their own care.

As recently as thirty-five years ago, doctors in Canada, Britain and the U.S. routinely withheld information from patients "for the patient's sake," and made decisions on their care without input from the patient. In 1961, a study reported in the *Journal of the American Medical Association* found that 80 per cent of a cross-section of doctors polled preferred not to tell patients when they had cancer. "The policy is to tell as little as possible in the most general terms consistent with maintaining cooperation with the treatment," Dr. David Oken, the study's author reported. The doctor might say there was a "growth" or a "mass" but would not give full details. "It's for their own good," Oken reports doctors saying to justify withholding the truth, "The news is too devastating." "They would lose hope." Ironically, this prevalent, paternalistic attitude among the medical profession existed at the same time a number of studies were showing that the vast majority of patients wished to be told if they had a serious illness. The doctors Oken surveyed said that they, themselves, would want to know the truth (they, of course, as doctors, could take it) and they would be forthright with another physician. Few people challenged "doctor's orders" and indeed, even though many said they would like to know what was going on, they were relieved to have decision-making taken out of their hands. "You decide, you're the doctor," was a common phrase that even continues into the present day.

Informed consent was just beginning to take hold. Even though a U.S. judge as early as 1914 had established that consent should be obtained for all surgical operations, it wasn't widely adopted into medical practice until rulings in medical negligence cases in the 1970s and 1980s enforced it as a standard of care. U.S. physician and ethicist Howard Brody wrote in his 1992 book, *The Healer's Power* (an examination of the importance of power-relationships in medicine), "practising physicians were first introduced to the concept of informed consent as a legal intrusion on medicine, and not, as ethicists would have had it, as a natural component of a physician-patient relationship." While informing patients of risks and receiving their consent for treatment became required by law in the 1970s, it took longer to acknowledge that patients should be active participants, even equal partners, in medical decision-making, even to the point of being able to make a decision that might lead to their death.

An important step in diminishing the influence of medical hegemony was the birth of medical ethics as a discipline in its own right in the 1960s. Bioethics emerged out of the recognition that the new medical technologies posed such difficult dilemmas that doctors should not be the only people making the decisions. The first hospital medical ethics committee was established in Seattle in the early 1960s as a result of the difficult task of deciding who among the hundreds of patients needing dialysis should get time on the limited number of dialysis machines. Doctors relegated the decision to a committee of lay-people, nicknamed the "God Committee," who would sort through the files of all the patients and decide who would get the life-saving technology. The committee's unenviable job was profiled in a November 1962 article "They Decide Who Lives, Who Dies," in *Life* magazine.

By the end of the 1960s institutes devoted to research and education in bioethics were founded. The first, in 1969, was the Hastings Center in New York State, followed the next year by the Kennedy Center for Ethics in Washington D.C. and over the next few decades similar institutes were being replicated around the world, such as the Centre for Bioethics at the University of Toronto and the McGill Centre for Medicine, Ethics and Law. These institutes became the instigators of debates and discussions about informed consent, patient rights, ethical practices, even the morality of assisted suicide and euthanasia, forcing the medical profession itself to examine these issues and conform its practices to the new ethics.

Another important influence was the women's movement, whose members increasingly refused to allow male doctors to make decisions for women. Instead they sought partnerships in care, often seeking out female physicians or males with a more collaborative approach. Books like *Our Bodies, Ourselves* aimed to give women straightforward, understandable medical information. Many of these became bestsellers and spawned a whole genre of health books aimed to help patients become informed participants in their own care.

The devastation of the AIDS epidemic also spurred demand for more patient autonomy. AIDS protest groups like ACT-UP, railed against the traditional medical model, demanding more shared power in the fight against AIDS. Usually in the prime of life and accustomed to having control of their lives rather than bowing to fate, people with AIDS have been at the forefront demanding the right to determine the circumstances of their deaths.

Along with the social movements, in Canada a series of court cases were influential in establishing the right for Canadian patients to make decisions about their care, no matter how ill-advised that decision might seem to the medical profession. The most important, and one that is credited with also giving living wills their legal validity, was the 1987 Ontario court case of "Malette versus Shulman." Mrs. Malette was a fifty-seven-year-old Jehovah's Witness who in June of 1979 was involved as a passenger in a head-on collision with a truck near Kirkland Lake, Ontario. Her husband died instantly in the crash, but she was rushed to the local hospital where Dr. D.L. Shulman was the attending emergency physician. Semi-conscious and unable to communicate, her face crushed and her nose almost severed from her face, Mrs. Malette was bleeding profusely both internally and externally. Dr. Shulman concluded she was going into shock and needed replacement fluids to restore her lost blood. But a nurse going through her purse found a card, in French, stating "No blood transfusion" and describing Mrs. Malette's religious beliefs. It was signed, but not dated, and therefore it was impossible for the medical staff to know whether it represented her current wishes or was years out of date. The nurse told the doctor of the existence of the card and it was recorded on the chart. Intravenous solutions of glucose were transfused in an attempt to make up the lost blood, but after two hours, Dr. Shulman made the decision that in order to save the patient's life, he must transfuse blood. Taking full responsibility for the decision, he hung the bags himself. When family members arrived, they voiced their objections to the blood and demanded that it be stopped. In court, Mrs. Malette's daughter quoted Dr. Shulman as saying to her: "Don't you care if your mother dies?. . . I am in charge, I am responsible, and I will give blood!"

When the case first came to court eight years later, the judge concluded that Dr. Shulman's actions in administering blood against the instructions on the card and from the family had constituted a battery. Mrs. Malette was not awarded punitive damages — indeed the judge noted that the doctor's actions probably saved her life and were his honest attempt to deal with a complex medical, legal and ethical problem — but she was awarded general damages of $20,000 for mental distress. The ruling was upheld in the appeal court in 1990. Many in the Canadian medical community and general public were shocked, even appalled, at the decision. Here a well-meaning doctor was being punished for actions he had taken, resulting in her surviving to be able to sue him. But an indisputable message had been sent by the courts: doctors could not disregard the patient's desires even if they were doing it for the patient's own good.

While medical paternalism has declined sharply in the last few years it has not been eliminated from the medical system. In fact, its lingering presence is the reason some people are strongly opposed to allowing doctors the legal freedom to perform euthanasia or assisted suicide. They fear that with the attitude "the doctor knows best" still palpable within the medical profession, some patients who are dying, suffering or untreatable may become at risk of an early death because paternalistic doctors may give it to them "for their own good" without the patient asking for it.

Religious beliefs have had an ever-diminishing relevance as a moral force in Western societies over the last three decades. Judeo-Christian religions and Islamic religion have long rejected euthanasia or assisted suicide. The first, fundamental objection in all three religions is that decisions of life and death are God's or Allah's dominion. There can be no such thing as absolute human autonomy because human beings do not own their lives, they are simply stewards of a life that is a gift from God. To decide the circumstances of one's death would be to put oneself above God, to usurp His power. The belief that individuals should be able to control the circumstances of their lives is hubris and one of the lessons of life is to learn to relinquish control to God. Secondly, arguments that euthanasia and assisted suicide should be allowed for compassionate reasons to remove an individual's suffering had little moral suasion in traditional Christian and Jewish belief. A long-standing tenet of Christianity and Judaism has been that through suffering comes salvation and spiritual growth. The suffering of Job, described in the Old Testament as a "perfect and upright man" who endures a litany of trials to test his faith, is held up as an example. Just as Jesus suffered on the cross, Christian belief has been that individuals can achieve spiritual growth or meaning in life through suffering and thus become closer to God. It is important to note, however, that another fundamental tenet of the Christian religion is compassion and the removal of the suffering of others, if it is possible to do so, without actively ending life, which is the philosophy of palliative care. Finally, Judeo-Christian belief opposed an individual taking the life of another individual, even at the latter's request, based on the sixth commandment, "Thou Shalt Not Kill." Life was sacred and for the reasons stated above, an individual could not take it into his own hands to end the suffering of another individual, even if the individual pleaded with him to do it. (It is interesting to note that Christianity does allow some exceptions to the sixth commandment: killing in war, killing in self-defense and, in some cases, capital punishment.)

Thirty years ago, 80 per cent of Canadians polled said they believed in God and attended church or synagogue regularly. The majority of the Canadian population was Christian, with Protestants slightly out-numbering Catholics, and the Jewish religion a distant third. But religious affiliation and service attendance has been steadily declining since the Second World War. Now less than 25 per cent of Canadians attend church or synagogue weekly and each year more people respond to polls with the reply that they have no religion. "The widespread acceptance of the concept of euthanasia today is partly fostered by the de-Christianization of formerly Christian nations," says Dr. Ruud de Moor, sociologist at the Catholic University of Brabant, in Tillburg, Netherlands. As the lead researcher of the European Values Survey, a recurring poll of more than 50,000 Europeans, de Moor has been charting the changing values in Europe since 1981. The polls show that the acceptance of euthanasia increases as the individual holds less, or no, traditional beliefs.

Quite simply, for an increasing number of people in the 1990s, the religious arguments against making a choice for death have lost their plausibility. Perhaps this is why most of the witnesses from religious groups who appeared before the Special Senate Committee on Euthanasia and Assisted Suicide in 1994, focused on euthanasia as a danger to society and social order as the reason they opposed it, not that, in their view, God didn't allow it. In modern democratic societies, one group's religious beliefs are not supposed to influence law or public policy and such an argument, if they made it, would not sway the general public. Yet many advocates for euthanasia and assisted suicide believe that latent religious beliefs still unduly influence Western courts and the medical profession on the issue. According to University of Utah philosopher Margaret Battin, both medicine and law operate within the conceptual framework and assumption about dying that was originally mapped out by religions, even when those institutions appear to be secular enterprises. For example, both modern law and medicine currently hold that it is acceptable to make a decision to stop a feeding tube to allow an individual to die "naturally" even though this may require twelve to fifteen days of starvation before a patient's death. What is rarely scrutinised is why a natural death, even if it induces more suffering, is somehow more proper than one in which humans have a conscious hand. Increasingly, the general public is questioning that long-held assumption.

Such a trend is alarming some religious leaders. In March of 1995, Pope John Paul II issued an encyclical letter, the *Evangelium Vitae* (Gospel of Life), that condemned the growing acceptance of euthanasia as well as abortion. Calling the new ethos a "culture of death" he urged Catholics to resist laws that violate what he called the fundamental right to life. "Such a culture of death," he said "taken as a whole, betrays a completely individualist concept of freedom which ends up by becoming the freedom of the strong against the weak." While many today might disagree with his interpretation of modern forces, there is no doubt he was right that the philosophy of individualism has never been stronger. This leads us to the fifth and final cultural force giving momentum to the right to die.

Over the last century — indeed the roots go back to the French

Revolution — a fundamental shift has been taking place in Western society towards the recognition of the rights of the individual in a just society, replacing the utilitarian concept of the "greatest good for the greatest number." The utilitarian approach sees people as entities whose autonomy and dignity lose out to the good of the majority. Such an approach also encourages paternalism by imposing "an externally defined good on the values of the individual person," explains University of Victoria ethicist Eike Kluge. The philosophy of individualism upholds the belief that people should be free to make their own choices, as long as that choice does not infringe on the rights of others. One of the theories of the process of individualization is that as countries advance economically, the populations increasingly shift in the direction of individual choice. A person's values, beliefs, attitudes and behaviour are less dependent on tradition, social institutions and community norms. Self-development, self-fulfilment and personal happiness become the driving ethic. Under such a philosophy, all religions, governments and social institutions lose their power to dictate the behaviour and beliefs of individuals. That is why, since the Second World War we have seen a liberalisation of attitudes towards divorce, homosexuality and other sexual behaviours, contraception, abortion, as well as suicide and euthanasia that in the past were strictly taboo and condemned by governments, existing laws, community values and religious moral doctrines.

Many social theorists, such as Allan Bloom and Christopher Lasch, see a negative side-effect of individualism: consumerism, rampant capitalism, materialism, hedonism, narcissism, immediate self-gratification, control freaks who are "looking out for number one." Bloom's 1987 book *The Closing of the American Mind,* his observations of American students, blamed individualism for contributing to a moral and intellectual crisis. Lasch, in his 1979 book *The Culture of Narcissism* said the climate of individualism forces each person in society to pursue success and achievement and fosters a decreased interest in public life. "Individualism is linked to unrestrained personal striving with top priority given to personal need fulfilment." A more optimistic view sees increasing individualism as moving society beyond bourgeois, capitalist or materialist values to post-capitalist values which stress freedom, equality, democracy and personal development.

It is interesting to note that people on the left and right of the political spectrum, while both affected by the force of individualization over the last century, have different views about where the line should be drawn between government or institutional interference in individuals' lives. Conservative forces in the U.S. and to a certain extent in Canada, tend to focus their individualism on the removal of government and legal interference in economic issues, business transactions, market forces, gun control and social welfare issues, while they tend to support government keeping a hand in social mores such as limiting abortion or discouraging homosexuality. Those on the left of the spectrum generally want government to let individual choice rule issues like abortion and sexuality, but they want to keep government control of the marketplace and economy and in providing social welfare programs. However, the issues of whether or not the government should allow or prohibit euthanasia or assisted suicide don't fall so neatly into right and left lines. In fact, in Oregon in 1994, card-carrying Republicans and Democrats worked side by side for the first time during the referendum campaign to get a bill passed into law enabling terminally ill patients to ask for physician-assisted suicide. Whether one is on the left or right of the political spectrum when it comes to death, an increasing number of people believe that governments and institutions have no business telling individuals what they can and can't do with their own bodies and lives.

3

OF "SAVAGES"
AND "SAVIOURS"

I N THE SPRING OF 1962, the old chief, Aleak Kolitalik, came down with measles at the age of sixty-nine and it hit him hard: high fever, persistent coughing, terrible sensitivity to light so that the sun reflecting from the snow was almost unbearable, an itchy rash with painful, swollen joints and overwhelming weakness. The measles infection had spread through the northern camp, making everyone sick — women, babies, the strongest hunters. The Inuit had little resistance to disease and a simple infection could fell the mightiest of men. Almost six feet tall — a near-giant among the Inuit, Kolitalik had been the leader for forty years of one of the best Inuit camps in the eastern Arctic, a mentor to the strongest and ablest hunters, a patriarch who saw that his camp adhered to the traditional ways of hunting and fishing. He forbade drinking or scavenging from the military DEW Line outposts and the white settlements. "Kolitalik would have been a leader in any society," wrote Justice Jack Sissons, Canada's first Territorial Court Judge of the Northwest Territories, in his 1968 memoirs *Judge of the Far North*. Through the summer of 1962, Kolitalik was still weak and frail from the measles. By the fall he was no better. He worried about the difficult winter months ahead. He knew he could no longer hunt or contribute his share to the group. In October, he called his relatives around him and told them he wanted to die. He said that they must help him.

Save for a recent case in Nova Scotia in which a woman provided her friend with insulin and syringes, the trial of the three hunters who helped Kolitalik die is the last time that the charge of assisted suicide has been tried, and a guilty verdict found, in Canada. It is a little-known trial, with no court transcript nor court record remaining, except a brief mention in Judge Sissons' memoirs about what occurred both out on the tundra in 1962 and then in a little schoolhouse in Igloolik six months later when the Canadian justice system flew into the tiny community. It remains alive in the memories of Robert Pilot, the arresting RCMP officer and Mark de Weerdt, now a justice at the Supreme Court of the Northwest Territories, who back in 1963 when the case came to trial was crown counsel. Yet the story of Kolitalik, in its bizarre and surreal details, is an unusual window on the age-old practice of assisted death in the Inuit community and what happens when those attitudes clash with the dominant culture's beliefs. For centuries most of Western society has viewed the common Inuit tradition of helping the elderly and sick to die as a cruel and barbaric practice. To the Inuit themselves, however, such a death was noble and honourable, a release for the person from a life that was no longer a pleasure. To them, it was a practical, even essential, approach to the inevitable path of aging and death in a harsh environment, one that kept the respect of the elderly while solving a problem for the community. They believed those who died by their own hand or were assisted by others went to the best spot in the afterworld.

In the 1940s, U.S. anthropologists Charles Hughes and Alexander Leighton reported on the patterns of suicide among the Yuit Eskimos of St. Lawrence Island, situated in the Bering Sea between Alaska and Russia. There, the custom was for the individual who decided she wanted to die to ask her relatives for help at least three times. As a rule the family would not consent at first but try to dissuade her. Only if the person persisted in her request would they comply. The authors asked the Eskimos why they would not originally agree. "Because we love them and we don't want them to go," was the answer. Such was the case with Kolitalik. When the old chief first told his relatives to kill him, they refused. "They didn't want to do it. They were crying and saying no but Kolitalik insisted," recalls Pilot, who has now retired to Ottawa.

Pilot had investigated the case, laid the charge against the three men who helped Kolitalik die, and wrote a thirty-page deposition of the facts, which has been lost over the years. Not only that, but when the case came before Judge Sissons in April of 1963, Pilot was a witness to the good character of Kolitalik and the three hunters as well as the translator of the proceeding into the Inuktitut language so the hunters could understand. What was so interesting about the case, in both Pilot's and de Weerdt's minds, was the methodology of pressure that Kolitalik used to get the young hunters to assist him. By the 1960s most of the Iglulik Inuit had converted to Christianity and they knew that, in their new religion, assisting suicide was forbidden. But over a number of days Kolitalik kept pushing his request on the small camp, threatening that if they didn't help him, his spirit would come back and drive away the game, the seals and the walruses, and they would all starve. "Even though they were Christian, there was still a great belief in the sea spirits and animal spirits. The fear that Kolitalik could put a curse on them was enough for them to eventually give in and do his bidding. He basically intimidated them," Pilot said. De Weerdt agrees: "The accused may have acceded to the old man's wish as much out of fear as out of habit or respect."

In order that no one person carry the burden of Kolitalik's death, the old chief chose the three best hunters, Amah, Avinga and Nangmalik. Amah, his son, was in his thirties. The other two were nephews in their twenties. According to Pilot, on the evening in late October that Kolitalik chose to die, he instructed one to get his .22 rifle, the next to load it with a bullet, and the third to cock the trigger and hand the rifle to him. Then the three men went outside the sod hut where the rest of the camp was wailing and crying. Kolitalik, sitting upright, put the rifle butt between his feet and the muzzle up under his chin and pulled the trigger. The bullet went up through the roof of his mouth and exited through the bridge of his nose. The men heard the shot go off and while Amah stayed outside, Avinga and Nangmalik came back in expecting to find him dead. There was Kolitalik, however, calmly sitting upright bleeding from the bridge of his nose. He asked them to load the rifle again. Kolitalik, Pilot said, fired three more times under his chin. The second bullet exited from his cheek. The third lodged in his forehead. Each time Kolitalik calmly asked his nephews to reload the rifle. At the trial, Kolitalik's son, Amah, said that after the first shot, he didn't hear the subsequent shots, nor was he involved, "because I was crying too hard." "With the fourth shot, I guess Kolitalik figured he had the angle wrong. So he changed it and the fourth bullet lodged in the back of his head, severing a blood vessel," Pilot recalls. Even after four shots to the head with a rifle, Kolitalik did not die. When the men came back, Kolitalik told them they would have to kill him themselves. The young men refused. Instead, they laid him on his bed and covered him with a fur. "At midnight, to everyone's amazement, Kolitalik sat up and asked for a cup of tea and a smoke. And then sometime before the morning he died from loss of blood from the severed vessel," Pilot said.

The three men buried Kolitalik near the sea under a cairn of stones with rifle across his chest, as he had requested. The nature of the death might have remained unknown if a few members of the family, who continued to be troubled by the death, hadn't told an Inuit Anglican lay minister who was one of Kolitalik's relatives. The minister relayed the story to the RCMP. "I remember my district commanding officer and I discussed the case, wondering what the heck we should do about it," says Pilot. "It wasn't that there was a feeling they should be punished. We knew that they had great remorse, that they felt they had done something wrong and that was why they had told the priest. But it was felt that, because the history of the arctic people had many instances of the elderly being helped to die, or being left behind, that a message needed to be sent that this sort of thing couldn't happen any more." De Weerdt adds that in deciding to prosecute, "we also hoped that those in need of medical help would thus be more likely to get it than to be put to death, whether by their own hand or by mere neglect. Kolitalik may have been a shaman, wielding genuine power over the young men because of their belief in his power. By taking them before the Court we hoped they might see that another old man (the judge) did not approve of what Kolitalik had done and thus not feel so likely, in the future, to simply accept the shaman's power and will as final."

The body of Kolitalik was exhumed, taken to the DEW Line doctor at Hall Beach for examination and then brought back and re-buried. Amah, Avinga and Nangmalik were charged with aiding and abetting a suicide under what was then section 224 of the Criminal Code, an offence that carried with it up to a fourteen-year prison sentence. The three hunters were not taken into custody. Pilot simply asked them to please come to Igloolik from their camp in April to meet with "Ekoktoegee" ("He who listens"), the Inuit name for Judge Sissons. In April, Sissons, de Weerdt and Pilot flew in to Igloolik for the trial and the three hunters, of their own accord, came by dog sled from their ice camp eighty kilometres away. The trial was held in the new school house, with the teacher's desk as the judge's bench, and the students' desks for the prosecution and defence. De Weerdt remembers how outside the windows the sun reflected off blinding white snow, making the room inside the school-house seem comparably dark and dim. Pilot remembers how quiet and puzzled the three young men seemed, sitting with wide eyes in the cramped school desks, hands folded in their laps, watching the pomp and circumstance of justice unfold before them in a language they didn't speak. "For some of the legal words there was no word even similar in Inuktitut and I had to try to find some way to explain it to them," Pilot said. "They seemed very mystified."

After the facts of the case had been heard, Judge Sissons found them guilty as charged of assisted suicide and adjourned the court overnight as he decided the sentence. "I remember Judge Sissons calling me into his chambers after the verdict and saying 'Bob, what should I do with them?'" Pilot recalls. The maximum sentence of fourteen years in a federal penitentiary was immediately ruled out as excessive. Sissons suggested that Amah, Avinga and Nangmalik should be placed in Pilot's charge for a year and transferred to Pond Inlet where Pilot was based, but the three men were the leading hunters of their community and their removal would destroy the lives of those left behind. "Here were three men, who were good men, good providers for their families and their community, they were no risk to others. It was decided that justice would be best served by giving them a suspended sentence," Pilot said. He is not sure whether the men felt that with the outcome of the trial their actions had been forgiven. After their day in court they went back to their community. Amah became the leader of the camp, replacing his dead father as Chief; the other two went on to play leadership roles in the community. According to Pilot and de Weerdt, the case did have the deterring effect the Canadian justice system had hoped for. "As far as I know," Pilot said, "after the death of Kolitalik, there was never another Inuit assisted suicide, at least not one that came to the attention of the authorities."

The Inuit were not alone in their practices of assisted death. Among numerous aboriginal societies, abandonment, assisted suicide or homicide of the weak or old was not unusual. Among North American Indian tribes, African tribes, Laplanders, Siberian Natives, South American Indians, South Pacific Islanders and others assisted death was common. The reaction to these practices among white European and North American anthropologists has often been one of shock and dismay. In the context of the societies themselves, however, the practices made perfect sense. Given the fact that it was most common for individuals living in primitive societies to die suddenly and at a young age — in childbirth, of childhood illness, in war, or hunting accidents, or an infectious disease — if a person lived to an old age or lingered with an illness it was generally seen as being better to have life end suddenly than to flicker out by degrees. And if a timely death did not happen naturally, it would be helped along. According to anthropologist Leo Simmons, who in the 1940s conducted the most definitive survey of assisted death practices among aboriginal societies, most often the death was the choice of the elderly or ill person themselves, who asked others to help them. Occasionally, if the elderly or sick person was becoming increasingly enfeebled but was not forthcoming with a request, such a decision might be coerced by neglect of their needs or encouragement from the family. Most rarely, it was imposed against their will. Simmons observed that the more severe a tribe's living environment, and the more voluntary the death by the sick or aged individual, the more noble the death was perceived in the culture.

Not only tribal societies found some honour in choosing one's time of death. The custom was widely embraced by many in both Greek and Roman society. The Greeks gave euthanasia its name meaning simply "a good death" not necessarily a death that someone else, like a physician, helped enact. Roman emperor Caesar Augustus writes that he wishes "euthanasia" for himself and his family but it is clear that he means a peaceful death. It wasn't until the nineteenth century that euthanasia took on the meaning of the merciful death of a suffering patient at the hands of another person. The Greeks and Romans, in their more than 700 years' discussion of the issue, employed numerous terms and expressions to describe a voluntary death or suicide. As Paul Carrick points out in his book *Medical Ethics in Antiquity*: Xenephon used *haireo thanaton* (to seize death); Plato *hekonein haidou* (go voluntarily to Hades); the Stoics, *eulogos exagoge* (sensible removal). In the first and second centuries AD the common terms were *autocheira* (to act by one's own hand); *autoktonia* (self-killing) and *mors voluntaria* (voluntary death). Many of the leading Greek philosophers believed a conscious choice to end one's live could be morally justified under five conditions: terminal illness, debilitating disease, the risk of enslavement, impoverishment, or if one's death could render a service to others.

There were some notable exceptions, however, particularly among followers of sixth-century BC Greek philosopher Pythagoras, who believed life was a sacred gift from the deities. They shunned any human hand in the loss of life, be it assisted suicide, suicide, or abortion. They even eschewed the loss of blood through surgery.

There is some question whether Hippocrates, the Greek father of medicine who lived in the fifth century BC, was himself a Pythagorean. In his famous oath is the line: "I will give no deadly drug to anyone if asked, nor suggest any such counsel, and in like manner I will not give to a woman a pessary to produce an abortion." That clause is the reason some physicians in the twentieth century profess to be opposed to helping patients die. But also in the original oath is the clause: "I will not cut persons labouring under the stone," which means not perform surgery on someone suffering from kidney stones. Renowned Hippocratic scholar Ludwig Edelstein concludes the oath itself was Pythagorean. In fact, Edelstein suggests the oath may not have reflected the beliefs of the entire Hippocratic school of physicians, just a Pythagorean sect of the school. Many scholars, Edelstein included, believe that those who upheld the oath in ancient times were doing so as part of a protest movement. The scholars conclude that the act of helping people die was so common among physicians in Greek and Roman society that physicians in the Pythagorean sect of the Hippocratic school wanted to set themselves apart.

Living at the same time as Hippocrates was Socrates and his pupil Plato. It is difficult to completely separate Socrates' beliefs from that of Plato's as Socrates' dialogues exist only through Plato's writings. Both declare that suicide is morally wrong unless the gods have presented the individual with a situation of necessity, such as occurred most commonly under four conditions: when one is suffering from an incurable illness; when one is disabled; when one takes his life by order of the state like Socrates when he drank hemlock; or when one has committed an irredeemable disgrace. It is clear that Socrates shared the Hippocratic belief that good doctors did not attempt to treat hopelessly ill patients. In *The Republic*, Plato quotes Socrates praising the physician–God Asclepius: "Where the body was diseased through and through, he would not try, by nicely calculated evaluations and doses to prolong a miserable existence. . . . Treatment he thought would be wasted on a man who could not live in his ordinary round of duties and was consequently useless to himself and to society."

What is made evidently clear by this and other writings of the Greeks and Romans is that philosophers in antiquity often made little distinction between what is good for the individual and what is good for the state. Compassion wasn't always the most important factor. Indeed, Plato in *The Republic* presents an ideal society in which individuals make personal sacrifices for the productivity and strength of the community. For a sickly, ill and unproductive person to insist on surviving is seen by Plato as selfish and morally blameworthy behaviour. That is why Socrates, Plato, and Aristotle, Plato's disciple and himself a physician, supported the exposure of sick and disabled newborns — it was seen as being too great a liability to the state for those infants to be reared. Aristotle, however, did not agree with the commonly held views about rational suicide. He saw voluntary death in face of illness or suffering as a sign of moral weakness. In Book Three of *Nicomachean Ethics*, he wrote: "But to seek death as an escape from poverty, love or some other painful experience is to be a coward, rather than a man of courage. For to run away from troubles is softness, and such a man does not endure death because it is noble but because he is fleeing from evil."

The Stoics were the greatest supporters of the view of a chosen death as noble and their beliefs, originating around 300 BC, were widely supported by Roman society until the second century AD. They believed that a human being's ability to consciously depart from life was one of the greatest benefits of being human, because it represented the height of moral freedom. The school's founder, Zeno, born in 334 BC, took his life in old age because of a painful foot injury. Cleanthenes, his successor, began fasting to cure a painful inflammation of his jaw and decided to continue with the fast to end his life. Pomponius Atticus, a Roman of the first century BC who was suffering from what was probably cancer of the colon, also chose to die by starvation after enduring three months of pain. Seneca, born in 3 BC and perhaps the most famous Roman Stoic, killed himself by slashing his wrists when Nero decreed he would otherwise be executed for treason. Seneca's death was considered tremendously noble by the Romans. His writings on suicide make him the Roman most often quoted in the modern era to advocate the right to die. In the following passage, taken from *Epistulae Morales 70*, he refutes the thinking of Pythagoras and Aristotle and offers his own philosophy of voluntary death:

You can find men who have gone so far as to profess wisdom and yet maintain that one should not offer violence to
one's own life, and hold it accursed for man to be the means
of his own destruction; we should wait, they say, for the
ends decreed by nature. But one who says this does not see
that he is shutting off the path to freedom. The best thing
which eternal law ever ordained was that it allowed to us
one entrance into life, but many exits.

Later in the same passage, Seneca seems to indicate, too, that a
voluntary death could be bought, most likely through the services of a physician. Pliny the Younger, in one of his letters
depicting Roman life, seems to confirm that view. He relates
the story of the sick Titius Aristo who gathered his friends
around him, ordering them to question his physician as to the
gravity of his illness. He tells them that if his disease is incurable,
he will exit life with the doctor's poison. To the Stoics like
Pliny, Titius Aristo's calm reflection to decide his death is commendable. For although the Stoics believed individuals should
have the choice to end life, not all suicides were praiseworthy in
their eyes. Noble suicides were only those in which the individual had carefully weighed the pros and cons of his situation so as
to not leave life too recklessly. Part of the Stoic philosophy was
that not only was there an art to living well, but there was an art
to dying well, which was a test of moral character.

Perhaps it was in opposition to the views of their Roman
oppressors that followers of the Jewish and Christian religions
developed an overwhelming abhorrence for suicide. That
abhorrence, however, was not overtly stated in the Old or New
Testament of the Bible. In fact, Biblical scholars and philosophers have pointed out that no direct prohibition of suicide
exists in the Bible; rather the Jewish and Christian condemnation seems to arise from other sources. According to University

of Utah philosopher Margaret Battin, who has made a study of the Judeo-Christian attitudes towards suicide and euthanasia, of the eight cases of suicide in the Old Testament and one in the New Testament, none are condemned. There is the story of the death of King Saul, in Samuel I, who in battle with the Philistines first sees his three sons killed and then becomes wounded in the belly by an arrow. He asks his armour bearer to kill him so that the "uncircumcised brutes" would not "make sport of me." His servant refuses, so Saul falls upon his own sword and kills himself. Seeing his master's actions, the servant falls upon his sword, too. But Saul, a suicide, and his sons, killed in battle, receive the same burial service and monument, which Battin says suggests that, unlike in later centuries, at the time of Saul's death there was no moral difference between suicide and a death in battle. Suicide in the Bible is often depicted as appropriate behaviour, such as when Sampson pulls down the temple killing himself and his Philistine captors, or when Ahithophel, the wise counsellor of Absalom, kills himself after his advice is ignored leading to Absalom's defeat, or Judas, after betraying Jesus to the Romans, hangs himself from a tree. The Bible does offer the stories of individuals who were suffering and who contemplated ending their lives but chose not to — Elijah, Job, Jonah, Sarah — and their forbearance is rewarded. Their consideration of suicide, however, was not condemned.

It is the law-like pronouncements from God rather than the biblical stories of suicide that the Jewish and Christian religions cite for the prohibition against suicide, Battin notes. But despite both religions' common ancestry in the Old Testament, each religion cites different passages for the basis of the prohibition. The Jewish religion cites Genesis 9:5, where God tells Noah that "for your lifeblood I will surely require a reckoning" as being a censure of suicide. But others have interpreted that clause to refer to murder and not specifically suicide. The Christian tradition cites the commandment "Thou Shall Not

Kill," as being the passage that bans suicide. But Battin notes that scholars of Hebrew and Greek have shown the commandment more accurately translates as "Thou shall commit no wrongful killing." If this translation is indeed more accurate, it would better explain the apparent paradox that Christianity condemns suicide but allows killing in war, self-defence and capital punishment. The first reference in the Jewish religion to a repugnance for suicide was in the first century AD when Jewish historian Josephus dissuaded his army from mass suicide against the Roman army at Jotapata arguing that suicide is cowardly, repugnant to nature, and violates the will of God — seemingly echoing the sentiments of Aristotle. Yet it was Josephus who also recorded the story of the mass suicide of Jews at Masada during the same war, which is lauded in Jewish history and is now the site of a shrine. The Jewish censure of suicide arises through the development of the Talmud in the first century AD, a time when the practice was most widely accepted by the Romans.

Battin and other scholars date the absolute Christian censure of suicide to Saint Augustine in the fifth century AD. The bishop of Hippo in North Africa, Saint Augustine's influence on the shape of Christianity through his writing and pronouncements is regarded as second only to Saint Paul. He was the first Christian to call suicide a "detestable and damnable wickedness" and to set in place the subsequent religious law that spread through all of Christian Europe, denying a Christian burial to suicides and condemning them to hell's fires. Augustine declared that suicide was an eternal sin for four reasons: it was against the commandment thou shall not kill; it deprived the individual of penitence and salvation before the suicide death; it usurped God's authority by putting death in the hands of the individual; and it was an act of cowardice.

Battin asserts that Augustine was forced to create a stringent prohibition because without the prohibition, suicide might be appealing to the pious because in Christianity the afterlife is seen as being superior to the present world; after death one is reunited with one's deceased loved ones; and self-sacrifice for the good of others or martyrdom for the faith is commended. According to Battin, by the fifth century suicide among Christians attempting to obtain martyrdom or enter heaven as early as possible was becoming epidemic, particularly where Augustine presided. A sect of Christians in North Africa, the Donatists, preached suicide after confession and the absolution of their sins so they could enter heaven sin-free. Augustine brought down the religious law against suicide out of the need to stop these deaths and the decimation of Christian believers which would harm the spread of the faith. Salvation, he declared, could not be obtained this way.

Many other world religions proscribe suicide, self-willed death or euthanasia. The Islamic religion believes that to bring about one's own death for personal reasons, such as to escape illness or despair, is usurping the will of God. The devout Moslem places his or her fate in the hands of Allah and if it is Allah's will that one should die of a painful disease three months hence, so be it. One must surrender oneself to his mercy. To die in God's name by self-sacrifice in a Jihad, a holy war, however, is commendable and guarantees a swift entrance into paradise.

In Buddhist belief, suicide is also generally condemned, although there is evidence that some Chinese Buddhists allowed self-willed death for debilitating age or illness. The teachings of Buddha, however, state that one of the four noble truths is that existence is suffering and that people cannot avoid it by taking their lives because their suffering, or karma, follows them into the next life. To take one's life is seen as a wasted opportunity to change one's karma and achieve enlightenment.

For many centuries in India, voluntary death was widely practised among some Hindus and Jains. In Jainist belief, an individual who was elderly, sick or disabled could announce his intention of being liberated through a self-willed death and then usually fast until he died. Once the intention had been declared, others could help him achieve his goal. Though criticism of the practice mounted from the tenth century onward it wasn't until the eighteenth century, under the British Raj, that self-willed death was outlawed.

In the Christian world, the condemnation of suicide spread widely and by the eleventh century secular laws in many countries had fortified the prohibition. In Britain, a suicide not only was refused a Christian burial in consecrated ground, but his property was forfeited to the crown and his body displayed at a crossroad with a stake driven through his heart. This practice was observed in Britain until as late as 1823.

Saint Thomas Aquinas in the thirteenth century reaffirmed Augustine's prohibition for the same theological reasons and solidified the Catholic opposition to the practice. Against this backdrop, it is quite remarkable that another canonized Catholic, Saint Thomas More, wrote (in *Utopia*) in favour of assisted death for those suffering from terminal illness:

> If the disease be not only incurable, but also full of continual pain and anguish, then the priests and the magistrates exhort the man, seeing he is not able to do any duty of life, and by outliving his own death is noisome and irksome to others and grievous to himself, that he will determine with himself no longer to cherish that pestilent and painful disease. And seeing his life is to him but a torment, that he will not be unwilling to die, but rather take a good hope to him and either despatch himself out of that painful life, as out of a prison, or a rack of torment or else suffer himself willingly to be rid of it by others. And in so doing they tell him he shall do wisely, seeing by his death he shall lose no commodity but end his pain . . . But they cause none to die against his will, nor do they use no less diligence and attendance about him, believing this to be an honourable death.

More's description of such a death, of course, was widely criticized at the time, but with the dawn of the Renaissance and the
rediscovery of Greek and Roman thought, others after him
began to re-evaluate the religious prohibitions against suicide.
The sixteenth-century philosopher Francis Bacon advocated a
painless death for the terminally ill. His contemporary, poet
John Donne, a Protestant who became Dean of Saint Paul's,
wrote in work published after his death that suicide, in some situations, might be justified. In 1777, Scottish philosopher David
Hume published his essay "On Suicide" in which he declared
that a person committing suicide did not do evil, he just ceased
to do good. Although centuries away from the consequences of
modern medicine, Hume stated: "If shortening our lives inter-
feres with Providence, medical services are already interfering
by lengthening them."

In France, it was the writings of Voltaire, Diderot and Mon-
tesquieu and the championing of the rights of the individual in
the French revolution that led to the decriminalization of suicide in 1790. Germany had decriminalized it as early as 1751. In
contrast, suicide was not decriminalized in Britain until 1961 and
1972 in Canada. During the nineteenth century, an increasing
number of writers and thinkers found that a rational choice to
die could be justified under certain conditions. The Romantic
poet, John Keats, who had studied as a surgeon, even begged his
friend, Joseph Severn, to give him a vial of laudanum as he was
dying of tuberculosis at the age of twenty-five. Severn refused
and Keats was furious, claiming it was his right to have it. French
Romantic composer, Louis-Hector Berlioz, wrote movingly in
his memoirs about his sister's lingering death and reflected on
the practices of other societies mentioned earlier in this chapter:

> I have lost my eldest sister. She died of cancer of the breast
> after six months of horrible suffering which drew heart
> rending screams from her day and night. My other sister,

who did not leave her side till the end, all but died from the fatigue and the painful impressions caused by this slow agony. Not a doctor dared to have the humanity to put an end to this martyrdom by making my sister inhale a bottle of chloroform. This is done to save a patient the pain of a surgical operation which lasts only a quarter of a minute, and yet it is not had recourse to in order to deliver one from a torture lasting six months . . . We must be barbarous or stupid, or both at once, not to use the sure and easy means now at our disposal to bring it to an end. Savages are more intelligent and more humane.

Napoleon, however, didn't agree, believing that everyone must live out their allotted destiny. While exiled on Elba he told Lord Ebrington the story of the battlefield death of his friend Duroc, "who when his bowels were falling out before my eyes repeatedly cried to me to have him put out of his misery. I told him, I pity you, my friend, but there is no remedy. You must suffer to the end."

Euthanasia, in its modern day meaning of a doctor helping a suffering patient to die, first came into use in the 1870s. In 1872, British physician S.D. Williams was the first to use the term and he stated in an essay that "in cases of incurable and painful illness, the doctors should be allowed, with the patient's consent and taking all the necessary safeguards, to administer so strong an anesthetic as to render all future anesthetics superfluous; in short, there should be a sort of legalized suicide by proxy." The next year British philosopher Lionel Tollemache took up the cause, quoted Williams, and defended voluntary euthanasia in an article called "The New Cure of Incurables" in the *Fortnightly Review.* Tollemache wrote, "Any of us may one day have to bear — many of us certainly will have to witness — either cancer, creeping paralysis . . . or a mortally wounded soldier who wished to die . . . So even from the most selfish point of view we all have an interest that this question be speedily discussed." Dismissing concerns that there might be abuses if euthanasia was allowed, Tollemache stated: "If we rejected all reforms which might lead to contingent and remote evil, no reform would ever be passed . . ." Tollemache and others only promoted a practice of euthanasia at the request of the patient, but in 1901 a more sinister development arose when British physician Charles Goddard proposed to the Willesdon Medical Society that not only should euthanasia be available for incurables who wanted relief from suffering, but that a committee of experts should decide the fate of "imbeciles and monstrosities" who were "absolutely incapable of improvement." The suggestion is chillingly reminiscent of what actually occurred in Nazi Germany less than forty years later.

Not until 1931, however, did the voluntary euthanasia movement get its first real boost. In Britain Dr. Killick Millard gave an address to the Society of Medical Officers of Health in which he advocated euthanasia for adults suffering from incurable, fatal, painful disease and outlined an elaborate set of regulations to oversee the practice. Millard's proposal was published in a book along with a draft bill. In 1935 the Euthanasia Society was established in Britain, led by Millard and other leading physicians and citizens to help usher the bill through parliament but when it was debated in 1936 the bill was defeated, mostly because opponents thought it too stringent. Ironically, one of the Lords who spoke against it was Lord Dawson of Penn, the personal physician to King George V, a past president of the Royal College of Physicians and two-time head of the British Medical Association. Lord Dawson said the bill was unnecessary because a "good" physician already knew how to help his patients die. It was only revealed in 1994, when Dawson's diary was opened fifty years after his death, that he spoke from experience. In January of 1936 as King George was dying from cardio-respiratory failure, Dawson recorded in his diary how on January 20th he had been summoned to the Royal estate at Sandringham by Queen Mary. He wrote that at about 11:00 p.m., seeing that the King might linger in the final semi-conscious state for a number of hours, "I therefore decided to determine the end and injected (myself) morphia gr. 1/2 and shortly afterwards cocaine gr. 1 into the distended jugular vein." Dawson admitted in the diary he had taken the action because he felt the announcement of the King's death should first appear in *The Times*, and not in the lowly afternoon papers.

In Canada in the 1920s and 1930s, the discussion of euthanasia in medical journals was primarily limited to reports of what was taking place in Britain and reprints of the draft euthanasia bill. In the U.S., however, a group of New York intellectuals led by Rev. Charles Potter, inspired by the British Euthanasia Society, established the Euthanasia Society of America in 1938. As in Britain, they tried to put a similar bill before the New York State Legislature but were unsuccessful. Another bill that came before the Nebraska legislature in 1938 was also defeated. Despite the fact that the movement to allow voluntary euthanasia was beginning to gather force around the world, there was to be a forty-year hiatus because of the horror of what happened in the name of euthanasia in Nazi Germany. Between 1939 and 1945, along with the more than six million Jews, Gypsies, homosexuals and dissidents killed by the Nazi regime, some 275,000 adults and children who were chronically sick, mentally ill, physically or mentally disabled were put to death under the Third Reich's euthanasia program.

To understand how such a program of mass killing could occur, it is necessary to look back to the end of World War I when the seeds for an involuntary euthanasia program were sown in the deprivation, financial hardship and social unrest in Germany following the war. There began to emerge the attitude that the individual was insignificant compared to the needs of the state. In 1920 Alfred Hoche, a physician, and Karl Binding, a lawyer, published a pamphlet, "The Sanctioning of the Destruction of Life Unworthy of Living." In it the authors urged that scant resources should not be wasted on people who were sick and suffering. They preached the "unimportance of the individual" and the need for Germany to revitalize its people by eliminating its weak elements. According to many historical sources, over the next two decades, the medical profession increasingly saw its role not as the guardians of the well-being and health of individual patients, but as the gate-keepers of the health of the nation. The medical profession became obsessed with how much butter or meat might be saved for every "useless eater" destroyed. This attitude contributed not only to involuntary euthanasia, but the philosophy behind the programs of forced sterilization to prevent "genetic inferiors" from reproducing and the implementation of eugenic policies that led to the extermination of the Jews.

According to Dr. Leo Alexander, U.S. medical consultant at the Nuremberg War Crimes office, when the first direct order for euthanasia came from Hitler in 1939, German doctors were so indoctrinated with the need to strengthen the nation they broke oaths of confidentiality and informed on their patients. The doctors notified the state through a standardized questionnaire of their sick and disabled patients who were past rehabilitation or unable to work. Writing in a 1949 article in the *New England Journal of Medicine*, Alexander said the forms were sent to Berlin where a team of doctors sorted through them, deciding which patients would live and which would die. Patients were then carted away from institutions and hospitals by the truck-load and taken to extermination centres.

For modern-day Germans, that history has made the discussion of voluntary euthanasia impossible. Foreign speakers who have come to lead debates about voluntary euthanasia have been prevented from speaking by angry crowds. But ironically,

while Germany will not even tolerate the discussion of euthanasia, it permits assisted suicide, as long as the assistance is not
given by a physician. Assisting suicide is not a crime, providing
the person committing suicide is capable of exercising control
over his actions and is doing it from a position of informed
choice. That kind of suicide is called *Frietod*, literally "free
death," and is seen as a positive, even noble action, Utah philosopher Margaret Battin observes. Suicide that is the result of
angst, depression or mental illness is called either *Selbstmord* or
Suizid, which have negative connotations. Aiding a depressed,
disturbed or demented person to commit *Selbstmord* is not permitted under German law. Physician-assisted suicide, of either
type, is never permitted because German law also imposes an
obligation on physicians to rescue suicides in progress. That law
is not likely to change because the German public's distrust of
physicians remains extraordinarily high, even fifty years after
their involvement in Nazi euthanasia campaigns.

The spectre of Nazi Germany doesn't just haunt the debate
in Germany itself. The horror that occurred in the name of
euthanasia is continually raised in all countries as one of the predominant reasons why voluntary euthanasia must not be allowed:
it might open the door to a similar campaign of killing the mentally ill, disabled and infirm who don't want to be killed. Those
in favour of right-to-die legislation protest that the authori-
tarian actions of the Nazis bears absolutely no resemblance to
euthanasia firmly rooted in individual rights and personal freedoms. "[The Nazis] decided from the perspective of *their* interests, not from the perspective of the human beings they killed,
that the lives of the latter were of no value. It was nothing
but a cynically disguised program of murder," said Reinhard
Merkel, of the Institute For Criminal Law, Criminology and
Philosophy of Law, at the University of Kiel, near Hamburg.

Yet, the horrific episode of human brutality and utilitarianism-
run-amok has invaluable lessons for the euthanasia debate of

today, says Dr. Hermann Pohlmeier, a psychiatrist and director of the Institute of Medical Psychology at the University of Gottingen. Pohlmeier was the founder of the German Association for Suicide Prevention and now heads the German Society for Humane Dying, a right-to-die organization. "The discussion of the Nazi past is important, because it is everything that euthanasia should not be: involuntary, imposed by the state and the medical profession against the wishes or interests of the individual, with no concept of the right of individuals to make choices for themselves," Pohlmeier said. The Nazi practice of euthanasia, so far removed from the modern-day concept which is based on the primacy of the individual, shouldn't be called by the same name, Pohlmeier says. He and many other right-to-die advocates in Germany refer to the Nazi murder of patients as "T4 actions," which was the code name the Nazis used for the campaign. It was derived from the building in Berlin, Tiergartenstrasse 4, where the team of thirty medical consultants reviewed the stacks of patient forms sent in from doctors.

Unlike Germany, with its long history of authoritarianism, the Netherlands enjoys a four-hundred-year history of respect for personal autonomy and individual rights. When the Nazis occupied the Netherlands the Dutch medical profession refused to comply with German threats to inform on their sick and disabled patients, even at considerable risk to themselves or their families, because Dutch doctors did not believe that the state should come before the individual. Dutch society is rightfully proud of the doctors' actions during the difficult years of occupation. Perhaps that history is the reason why the Dutch medical profession and their patients have had the confidence to be the first society in the world allowed to practise voluntary euthanasia that is grounded in individual choice.

This short history of euthanasia, suicide and assisted suicide throughout the various centuries and various cultures illustrates that in many societies it was widely accepted that the sick or the elderly would choose their time to die. Anthropologists who have studied the practices among the Inuit note that often the individual decision to die would benefit the group as well. Yet the practice rarely turned into outright murder to achieve the same ends because of a number of strict social and cultural proscriptions. Almost always, the decision was voluntary. The fact that usually a relative, often a dutiful child, assisted with the killing reinforced kinship bonds and removed the need for blood vengeance or retributive killing should an unrelated person assist in the death. Beforehand there would usually be a feast, or a speech in which the elderly or sick person would pass on their wisdom. After the death, there was often a strict period of solitary confinement and dietary restrictions for the person (or persons) who had helped with the death, a form of penance as such, thus ensuring that the relative who helped did not do so lightly. These traditions acted as a form of safeguard, a way of reconciling the needs of the individual against the needs of the group, trying to keep them in balance. In most cases the balance struck was such that the individual believed it was best to seek death at that time and the tribe agreed.

Reconciling the needs of the individual against the needs of society is at the heart of the debate over euthanasia and assisted suicide. History shows us that balance has, at times, slipped out of whack so that either the individual or the society is harmed by the prevailing cultural attitude toward death. In Greek times, physician-assisted suicide was so common that the prohibition in the Hippocratic Oath was probably a protest against it. The Christian condemnation of suicide, too, was probably born out of the need to stop individuals from having an over-zealous pursuit of death which was seen as being harmful to society by the premature loss of contributing people and Christian believers.

At other times, most notably in Nazi Germany, the balance

has shifted so that what is good for the individual becomes completely overshadowed by what is perceived as being good for society. Individuals became unimportant — indeed, they were no longer relevant.

Applying these historical lessons to the modern debate, it is easy to see that the risk of abuse is always present in deliberate death. Adhere too stringently to the idea of individual choice and there is the risk that individuals who are not sick, not dying, who are merely depressed or avoiding whatever lies in the future may court death and end their lives prematurely. Go too far the other way by putting the needs of society first and the individual, their hopes, desires and needs, become insignificant. And when the individual doesn't matter, that is when even greater abuses occur. People can be killed against their will where it benefits society, as in Nazi Germany. Or, as occurs today, people can be kept alive when they long to die.

4

A QUESTION
OF CONTROL

In DECEMBER OF 1986, while getting out of the shower, Gayle Stelter noticed something unusual about her reflection in the mirror. In the upper area of her left breast was a strange thickening, a curious irregularity in the texture of the skin. She was forty-six then, the mother of two teenagers, the wife of Ray, an RCMP officer with whom she'd shared her life for twenty-two years. After moving almost every three years because of his career, they were settled now in the small coastal community of Sechelt, British Columbia. Gayle was feeling healthy and fit. Ever since her mid-thirties she had made a conscious effort to keep physically active, taking up jogging and aerobics, learning how to ski and play tennis. She became quite proficient at those sports, too, even though she had always thought of herself as being slightly clumsy and uncoordinated. As she looked at the thickening over the breast in the mirror she wondered if it had something to do with the recent push-ups she'd been doing in her aerobics class. "I rationalized that with my poor coordination I had somehow managed to build more muscle on one side than the other," she was to later write in an essay about living with cancer.

In those early days of December, 1986 there was no lump

that she could feel. Nevertheless she feared cancer. The big "C" had stalked her family for years. Her father had died of cancer. Three of her four siblings, the three eldest girls, had already been diagnosed with it. Carol had been just twenty-nine when a lump in her breast was found — fortunately she had been treated and cured; Anne was still fighting colon cancer; and Kay had died in 1977 of breast cancer, too, a rapid and painful death that still haunted Gayle. "Don't panic," she told herself as she examined the skin and tissue around the breast, "it is probably nothing." For a few weeks Gayle tried to ignore that odd little change to her breast. Even though she was working as a clerk in a medical clinic, she had no family doctor of her own. With the frequent moves in the last few decades she'd never developed a long-standing relationship with a doctor and she had rarely needed to consult one for a medical problem. As Christmas approached, however, Gayle's concern was such that she went to see the wife of the doctor she worked for, who was a physician herself. Dr. M. thought that a surgical biopsy was required. It was an anxious, fearful time as Gayle and Ray awaited the appointment with the specialist in Vancouver, then the few days more until Gayle's biopsy, and then the more than ten days for results. What made it particularly difficult was that they had family visiting over Christmas and Gayle and Ray were keeping their concerns to themselves, at least until the results came back. When the news came just before New Year's that the biopsy was negative Gayle and Ray were elated. Come back in three months for a mammogram, Gayle was told.

When I met Gayle in 1994 she was remarkably calm and accepting of the fact that the initial tests failed to pick up her cancer. Only after the mammogram in March and a set of fine wire surgical biopsies in April of 1987 was it diagnosed. With more delays because of bed shortages, it wasn't until May of that year she finally underwent the radical mastectomy. "A few months were lost in the process, but in the long run it probably didn't make any difference," she said. "At the time, however, I must admit I was a bit bitter." An expressive woman with an artistic flare to almost everything she did, Gayle had always dreamed of being a writer. She would sit at a desk by the front window of the home that she had lovingly decorated in country pine, quilts and folk art, writing in her journal, corresponding with her many close friends, writing to the CBC, trying her hand at essays, articles and short stories that she hoped someday might be published. "The desire of my life has always been to write something that mattered," she wrote in one essay. In that same essay she describes the doctor's phone call with the pathology results after her radical mastectomy:

> Extensive...Aggressive...Previously such innocuous adjectives...hearing these words by telephone, passed somewhat in the polite, impersonal manner in which one might be informed that one's account has been overlooked, one cannot believe the power wielded. Surely if it is all so sane, so matter-of-fact, so down-to-earth, there can be no menace? Yet the menace is there. Couple those adjectives with equally innocuous nouns — extensive involvement, aggressive therapy — the great bloody grim reaper looms...

The pathology report showed twelve lymph nodes were affected — a bleak finding. Gayle went through six months of aggressive chemotherapy coupled with a cycle of radiation. She lost her hair. "The funniest things happen to you when you lose your hair. Losing your bosom is one thing, women look around and compare bosoms all the time. But after I lost my hair I have never seen so much beautiful hair in all my life. I saw beautiful hair everywhere and I'd want to say, put on a scarf, you hussy." The aggressive treatment was to no avail. The following year (1988) tests revealed that cancer had spread to her bones. Gayle feared she would follow in her sister's path and rapidly decline to death, but her journey was different. Her cancer seemed to progress slowly. She read books about positive healing and the mind/body connection, she meditated and ate healthy food. She worked on boosting her immune system and basked in the love and support of her family, sisters and friends. Still the cancer never went away, it was always detectable in her blood, a "malevolent entity," as she called it, lying in wait.

I met Gayle after she had written a moving, eloquent letter to a local CBC radio station shortly after Sue Rodriguez's death about what it was like to be dying of cancer. In her letter she expressed the hope that a doctor, like the one who reportedly helped Sue to die, would be there for her, too:

> For almost seven years I have lived with cancer, living most joyfully and gratefully, but gradually seeing the disease encroaching relentlessly upon my once healthy body. Through these years — more years than I expected to have — I have thought long and hard about death and I have discovered that it is not death itself that is so frightening to me, but rather the process of dying.
>
> Although Sue Rodriguez did not win her battle in our courts, she won ultimately in that her death occurred on her terms . . . For those of us who may choose to leave while there is still an element of control, of coherence, may we too, be fortunate in our friends and in our family physicians.

In the summer and fall of 1993, everything seemed to hit at once. Tumours growing on her ovaries began to block her ureter, forcing an operation to put in a stent to keep the passage open. More lumps were growing in her remaining breast. Through the fall the tumour markers in her blood, which her doctor had been using to track her disease, had begun to climb.

When we talked on the phone her voice was warm and appealing. There was a gentle quality to it yet the words had strength and conviction. I pictured a small, delicate woman. When we finally met in person, a few months later in Vancouver when she was hospitalized, I realized my image was wrong. Even though she was lying weak and thin in a bed at the Cancer Control Agency, you could see Gayle was tall, with a strong bone structure — more a Katharine Hepburn than the Audrey Hepburn I imagined. We sat and held hands as platelets were transfused through an intravenous line. Oddly, it was Gayle, despite her terminal illness, who seemed to comfort me. I was the one who was anxious talking about death and dying. I was afraid I would say something wrong or stupid. With her forthright and gentle manner she put me at ease as we tread this sensitive area of life and death that is so primal yet rarely talked about. To go out of her way to make another person feel comfortable was just like Gayle, Ray says. "She was always looking after other people and their needs."

Ray, her husband, is a tall, lean man of few words, "the strong, silent type" he says. Gayle wrote of him: "He is my best friend, I am his. If life has given me nothing else, I am rich to have someone who accepts me and loves me — totally, not just the more attractive aspect of my chequered character. I treasure this relationship; I treasure this dearest person. I don't want to leave." Gayle knew that she was dying, yet she was intent on living as fully as she could. She'd started piano lessons — she had always wanted to play a musical instrument — and she would sit and play the simple studies and songs at the keyboard. She would climb to the top of a rocky outcrop in the middle of their property, called Gayle's Rock by the family, and sit taking in the view of green trees and rolling landscape. She spent time with Ray and her two children and with friends. As her health deteriorated she began to give back to her many women friends the presents that over the years for Christmas and birthdays they had given to her. "Somehow this illness and knowing that my days are numbered has given me the freedom to be myself, to be a nutcase when I want to be a nutcase and to trust my friends to love me anyway . . ."

In the back of her mind she began to think about how she wanted to die. It was no obsession, no crusade. She simply wanted to have some control over her dying process; she wanted the option to say when she'd had enough and to go. She had assurances from her doctor that she would receive the best of palliative care, but he did not tell her that he would end her life when she asked. She was very low-key about her desire to have some sense of control over her dying; in fact few of her friends and relatives would have known that she was even thinking about it. Ray, even as a former RCMP officer, said he would have helped her, but that Gayle didn't specifically ask. "She knew that I would be there for her," said Ray. "I was her ace in the hole, but I think she was protective of me and didn't want to have to ask me to do it. Maybe she thought I couldn't do it."

She mentioned it to both her sisters, Anne, who was a nurse in Toronto, and Carol, whose breast cancer had been cured thirty years earlier. Both told her they would be there for her if she needed it. "I said yes before I really knew what was involved," said Carol. "I said yes out of love for her. I would have wanted her to do it for me. But I found it a tremendous weight to carry, to know that she might call on me to do it." Carol took the request seriously, buying *Final Exit*, and collecting information about how she would help if Gayle asked. She found the responsibility stressful, a feeling intensified by her inability to speak openly with anyone about her promise. As a social worker, Carol knew that one of the best remedies for stress is to talk to others about it, but she felt unable to tell even her closest friends about the plans to help her sister die. As Gayle's health deteriorated, Carol became increasingly concerned about how to do it if Gayle asked for help. The right-to-die literature recommended stockpiling an overdose of sleeping pills, mixing them in applesauce, and spoon-feeding them to the patient, but Gayle was feeling nauseated and vomiting regularly. How would she keep it down? One day, when a phone call from a friend came in the midst of some anxious worrying, Carol cried out in near desperation, "I have to kill my sister and I don't know how to do it!" She and her friend never mentioned the outburst again.

For Gayle, the details didn't matter. Just knowing that Carol or Anne had assured her they would be there for her, if she needed it, gave her a sense of peace, a sense of personal control. She could relax and put the issue behind her. "I have to tell you that for all this time when I am frightened and looking ahead, to think that I might have this option makes all the difference in the world to me. It enables me to have the courage to look ahead. It removes my fear."

A desire to be in control of our lives and the environment around us is born in each one of us. Alfred Adler, the Viennese psychiatrist, said the need for individuals to attempt to control their personal environment "is an intrinsic necessity of life itself." Numerous studies over the last thirty years have constantly reaffirmed that individuals who feel some sense of control over their environment — whether or not that control is real — fare better than others. In a classic early-1970s psychological study of feelings of control, two social psychologists examined two groups of students and their ability to perform a complex task while an irritating noise played in the background. One group of students had the ability to turn down the noise. The second group were told they had no control over the noise. The result? Those with a feeling of control over the noise, even if they didn't use it, performed the task better. Perceptions of risk and fear are reduced when one feels a sense of control — even if our perceptions are misguided. The chance of dying in a car accident is far greater than the chance of dying in an airplane crash, yet people are much less frightened about getting behind the wheel of a car than they are about taxiing down the runway for take-off. In part, that feeling of confidence comes from the belief that as the driver of the car they have far more control over whether an accident happens. With skill and attention, they believe they can avoid a crash. The passenger in an airplane must put faith and fate in the skill and attentiveness of the pilot, someone they have never seen and whom they know nothing about. Statistically their perceptions of risk may be wrong, but they feel better about being in a car because of a belief in personal control.

Studies have shown that pain sensations, too, seem to be diminished if individuals feel they have some control over the relief of the pain. Take the case of an individual recovering from surgery. Until recently it has been common for doctors and nurses to dole out the morphine and other pain-relievers sparingly, following a rigid schedule that often left patient crying out for relief, but at the mercy of the schedule. The worry was that patients would become addicted or would over-drug themselves if they were given as much as they wanted. But recently it has been learned that patient-controlled analgesia, or PCA, is far more effective in combating pain. Using a self-administered pump that is strapped to their hands, patients are free to press a button and give themselves a dose of morphine or another drug whenever they feel the need, up to a maximum dose an hour set by the doctor. Doctors have found that, instead of greedily giving themselves as much drug as they can, patients using PCA actually use less drug than the doctor allows. Much of the improved pain relief comes from the quick administration of the drug before the pain builds to an intensity where it is much harder to douse. But patients also report a greater feeling of satisfaction when they have control themselves.

A feeling of personal control also seems to improve one's health, sociability and mortality. One of the most striking demonstrations of this phenomenon came in a 1978 study of residents in a New England nursing home conducted by psychologists Ellen Langer and Judith Rodin, of Harvard and Yale universities, respectively. Their hypothesis was that many elderly people in institutions become debilitated, senile and helpless because they are placed in an environment where decisions are made for them and personal control is removed from them. With the co-operation of staff at the nursing home, Langer and Rodin devised a study where residents on two floors of the home would receive two different messages about the amount of control and responsibility they could exercise. One floor was told not to worry, the staff would look after them and make decisions for them. They were given a plant but told the staff would water it. They were told they could see a movie but the staff would pick the film and the time it played. In contrast, residents on the second floor were given messages that stressed their personal responsibility and the choices that were available to them, such as arranging the furniture in their rooms or choosing their daily activities. They were also given a plant, but they were allowed to pick the plant they wanted and told they were responsible for looking after it. They were allowed to choose from a selection of movies and a choice of times for the film to play. The staff encouraged them to lodge complaints or make suggestions to improve their living arrangements.

When the residents were questioned three weeks later, the ones who had received messages stressing their control were significantly happier, more active and more sociable than those who had been made to feel more dependent and "cared for." When Langer and Rodin returned eighteen months later the group whose power to make choices had been emphasized not only continued to be happier and more active, they were also rated by doctors as being in better mental and physical health. Most striking, more of them were still alive! Both groups had been almost identical in the range of ages and infirmities, but after eighteen months, 30 per cent of the residents who had been given a message stressing their dependence had died compared with 15 per cent of the other group. In the years following that landmark experiment numerous studies have shown that seniors who maintain personal control over their lives fare better than those who don't.

Why is it found in public health studies that those who are wealthy or possess the most education consistently enjoy the longest life, the best health and the most active years? It is not, researchers say, simply because more money and more education afford them comforts and material luxuries others don't have. Rather the difference seems to relate more to the personal control those well-off individuals feel and wield.

Of course, individuals vary in the extent of the control they want and believe is possible. Some individuals who have a strong belief in God, or fate, are content to let events unfold without trying too much to shape the outcome. Others may feel their destiny is all of their own making. And still others may have a mix of beliefs, feeling that some events they can control, and should, and others they must leave up to fate.

Psychological studies show that when individuals experience a feeling of loss of control one of two things happen, either they rebel or they give up and adopt a position of helplessness. When an individual feels he should be able to make a choice and such decision-making is forbidden or restricted, the matter often takes on greater appeal than if it were freely available. When people experience a sudden loss of control in their personal life, one of the most common results is a feeling of depression. Unemployment, sudden illness, natural disasters, economic downturns all cause depression not just because they are negative events but because the individuals most involved often feel little power to control the outcome. When a person endures repeated experiences of little or no control, he or she develops what psychologists call "learned helplessness." Youths in inner-city ghettos in the U.S., the elderly living in nursing homes and patients in hospitals have all been shown to become so accustomed to an inability to exert any control in their environment, they did not even attempt to do so when they could.

At the heart of the desire to time or plan the manner of one's death is the desire to retain some control of the dying process — itself rife with loss of control. First, there is the shock the individual feels at the diagnosis of a terminal disease. As the disease progresses, body functions she has taken for granted begin to deteriorate. The bowels may back up, the bladder may leak, the stomach may reject foods, the lungs may fail. The feelings of powerlessness intensify as she moves through the health care system and through society. She waits for doctors too busy to honour appointment times, or for the results of tests that portend her fate. If she is admitted to hospital, meals with set menus come at prescribed times whether she is hungry or not. Visitors are welcome only during the hours the hospital specifies. Her pain medication may be dispensed on the nurses' schedule, not when she feels the need of it. The acts of taking a bath, going to the toilet, perhaps even brushing her hair may have to wait until a nurse is free to help.

Family, friends and strangers may even begin to treat the sick individual as delicate or powerless, talking to the patient like a child or as if he or she weren't there, even if the patient's mental faculties are entirely intact. During the research of this book, countless numbers of individuals with terminal illness or severe disability told me their personal stories of how doctors, nurses or even friends had ignored them to talk to the healthy person in their midst. This tendency was dramatically illustrated to me one day before Christmas in 1993 when I took Sue Rodriguez Christmas shopping. As I pushed her wheelchair around the seaside town of Sidney, British Columbia, helping her to find gifts for her homecare workers and her son's teachers, well-meaning individuals would stop to talk to us. Their comments, however, were most often addressed to me. "How's she doing?" they would ask, or "Keep up the fight!" they would say, but more often than not they looked at me, not her. Few people spoke to Sue herself, even though mentally she was as bright and clear as ever. Even those who simply smiled and nodded in recognition would more often aim their smiles at me. When I remarked on the phenomenon in the car on the way home, Sue nodded and smiled ruefully. "Yes, it is one of the hardest things about being sick." Gayle Stelter made the same observation, "Once you become ill you feel like you have lost your place in healthy society and you are just one of the shadow people."

As a society, we have come to expect the sick and dying to accept a loss of control as being a function of the dying process. Even the words we use to describe serious illness reflect this traditional expectation of powerlessness. Someone who is sick is called an invalid, meaning without force, not valid. Often we speak of people with illness as being victims of their disease, such as "cancer victims" or "AIDS victims" a word that connotes the individual as pawn in the course of their disease, a hostage to fortune. We seem to expect them to acquiesce choices to the care and expertise of others such as doctors or palliative care experts. Even the word patient, as applied to individuals under medical care, has traditionally implied that once entering into the medical model they are expected to bear their pain or trials without complaint. To be fair, many people who are sick want to adopt that role, to let others make decisions for them. It feels right, it feels comfortable. Many modern doctors, who are endeavouring to work in partnership with patients to decide issues of care, have told me how frustrating it is to have a patient who cedes all decision-making to the doctor, not wanting to talk about options or even the disease itself. "You decide, you're the doctor," the patient says as a way of relinquishing any responsibility for the choices made.

An increasing number of sick individuals, however, particularly those with AIDS, are now rebelling against those traditional roles. A passive role does not feel right. From the start
they have been fighting the traditional yoke of powerlessness
and loss of control that comes through illness. They refused
to be called AIDS "victims." I remember when I first started
reporting on the epidemic in the early 1980s, AIDS activists
made a point of telling me the correct term of reference was
"person with AIDS" or "PWA," not "victim." Any editor or
reporter who let "victim" slip into copy or a headline could
expect an admonishing phone call the next day. Groups like
ACT-UP, an AIDS activist organization that spread across North
America in the 1980s, astounded the medical establishment
with their demand to have more control over AIDS treatment,
AIDS research, and the AIDS budget, and with their refusal to
adopt the docile, compliant role of patient. ACT-UP demanded
a say in how medical experiments were run, which drugs were
studied, even the composition of speakers at medical conven-
tions. They would not sit back quietly and allow the medical
profession to talk "over" them about issues that affected their
health. Their slogan was "Silence = Death" and they were
never silent. At the International AIDS Conference in Montreal
in 1987, which I covered as a medical reporter, ACT-UP members heckled speakers, rushed the stage, lay down in the corri-
dors, and otherwise disrupted proceedings, all to the horror and
bewilderment of the medical profession who had never in their
lives seen people faced with the threat of terminal illness act this
way. Where were the submissive, appreciative patients grateful
for whatever tidbit of research came their way? I remembered
thinking at the time, as I watched the motley group of ACT-UP
protestors heckle a flustered, innocent speaker, "Why don't
you just sit down and listen! Can't you see you're alienating the
people who are trying to help you?" And yet I began to understand that they were trying, in the only way they knew how,

to exert some power in the face of powerlessness. Despite the destructiveness of their first efforts, they did manage to make the medical establishment take notice, to include patient's perspectives in their deliberations and meetings, to take their concerns seriously. Over the years AIDS activists' tactics have evolved into more mutual co-operation rather than confrontation with the medical profession, in some places even becoming part of the AIDS medical establishment they were originally trying to destroy. The question must be asked, however, if not for their initial disruptive show of power, would they have eventually entered into the circle of decision-makers?

The first reaction when someone learns they have a serious or potentially fatal illness is to try to do something personally to alter the outcome of the disease. Many turn to meditation, imagery, bio-feedback, positive healing techniques, self-help groups, massage, acupuncture, special diets, vitamins, herbs and medicinals, special clinics — anything that gives them a positive feeling of taking control of the disease process. Sue Rodriguez, before she sought the right to die, spent months and thousands of dollars visiting naturopaths, acupuncturists and a host of new-age therapists. She even flew to Colorado and spent $10,000 having all her amalgam fillings removed in the hope it might alter the course of her disease. Gayle Stelter attended workshops on harnessing hope and using positive imagery to boost the immune system. When attempts to change the course of the disease have failed and death begins to loom as a certainty, as it did for Gayle and Sue, the focus of control naturally turns to the desire to have death come on one's own terms.

Studies that show that when a choice is forbidden it often takes on a greater appeal than if it were freely available raise a fundamental question about euthanasia and/or assisted suicide: are these options seen as being desirable for many dying Canadians, in part, because the government, laws and medical establishment in Canada have forbidden either as a choice to be legally made? In the Netherlands only 3 per cent of dying individuals eventually choose euthanasia despite reports that 80 per cent of the population supports it and 25,000 terminally ill patients each year at some point in their illness discuss it as a possibility with their doctor. "To me, the real value of euthanasia is not the act itself, but the ability for the doctor and patient to speak openly about it," Dutch general practitioner Dr. Gerrit Kimsma told me. "It gives patients the feeling that they have some control over the dying process and, in their last few months of life, frees them to concentrate on other more important things."

Many mental health experts contend, however, that a patient's desire for an assisted death may be a result of the depression that so often accompanies terminal illness. New York suicide expert Dr. Herbert Hendin believes that this frequent association of depression should be one of the reasons euthanasia should *not* be allowed. But let's look at the depression in another way: what if it arises from a feeling of a loss of control over the dying process, just as other instances of loss of control precipitate depression? In that case, prohibiting choice in dying could actually be making the depression worse and its solution would be to give more control, not less. The British parliamentarian Lord Joseph Kagan, who was born and raised in Lithuania, described during a 1986 debate on euthanasia in the House of Lords the prevalent feeling among inmates in the Nazi concentration camp he was held captive in for more than a year:

> The most fervent prayer in the camp was to achieve the death of one's own choosing, and in the manner of one's own choosing. This became the ultimate liberation and the greatest prize. To achieve this in the camp one was prepared for any sacrifice and to submit to any deprivation. Having it proved to be a great comfort . . . it did not encourage people to use it. It gave one strength to carry on fighting

because one felt one had the means, ultimately, not to buy
or extend survival at any price.

Social worker Russel Ogden, who studied the assisted suicide deaths among thirty-four individuals with AIDS in British
Columbia, found that those who chose the timing of their
deaths weren't driven by inadequate medical services, lack of
palliative care options, feelings of depression, or lack of love or
support from friends or family. "Rather it appeared to have
more to do with a desire to be in control of one's death — a
desire to die in a manner consistent with one's moral beliefs and
values and not necessarily with those of the caregivers." Dr.
Marcel Boisvert, a palliative care physician at Montreal's Royal
Victoria Hospital has made similar observations. One of the
few Canadian palliative care physicians who openly supports
choice in dying, Boisvert told the Special Senate Committee on
Euthanasia and Assisted Suicide, "The most common requests I
get for euthanasia on demand or assisted suicide are not from
people with severe pain; are not from people who are aban-
doned; are not from people who are in what I would call distressing physical symptoms. They are from people . . . who
were masters of their destiny until their illness struck, and [to
have no control] is to them totally unacceptable." In two years
of interviewing individuals on the topic of death and dying,
I have been told by all but a handful of the more than eighty I
interviewed facing eventual death, they would have peace of
mind if they knew the option of assisted death would be available for them if they really needed it. Those few who told me
they would not want or need it, without exception, possessed
strong religious beliefs that gave them an alternative sense of
comfort in the face of their approaching death.

Having a feeling of control doesn't mean one will ultimately
exert that control. Gayle Stelter never called on her sisters to
end her life — a considerable relief to Carol. Instead, through

the spring of 1994, Gayle became progressively weaker and needed more morphine to control her pain. When we last spoke, Gayle stressed to me how it didn't really matter to her, in the end, whether she had help to die. "I almost hope I don't need it. That would be best, I think. But I can't tell you how comforting it is to know that I have a plan."

According to Ray, "As she became sicker, she became more concerned with living for as long as she could." Carol described Gayle in the final weeks as "clinging to life," eager for one more day, one more hour with her husband and children, one more moment in the world. Able to stay in her own home, she began to sleep more, waking for fewer and fewer periods. Gayle slipped into unconsciousness and died peacefully, surrounded by family, on June 22nd, 1994.

Many opponents of euthanasia believe the wish for control of death is proof of an unhealthy, immature outlook on life, the vestige of a "control freak." We all know people who fit the term. They are demanding, unreasonable people whose presence drains us of energy, who make a confrontation out of the simplest interaction, who force others to capitulate rather than budge a fraction themselves. They are domineering and manipulative. Where is the line between a desire for reasonable, healthy personal control, and the desire for excessive control? When Vancouver AIDS activist David Lewis announced in 1990 that over the previous nine years he had helped eight people with AIDS to die and was planning his own death, angry letters came into *The Vancouver Sun* condemning his philosophy of having control to the end: "It should be recognized," wrote one male reader from Surrey, British Columbia, "that his position follows naturally from the nihilism and hedonism that sadly characterizes so many [homosexual men with AIDS]. David Lewis's approach to dying . . . is the expression of a philosophy that has to be in control even beyond death." The same criticism was lobbed at Sue Rodriguez by health professionals, particularly after her biography by Lisa Hobbs-Birnie was published. "It was obvious," one palliative care physician said to me, "Sue had an obsessive need for control!"

Many of those who oppose allowing euthanasia or assisted suicide do so, in part, because of a fundamental belief that the desire for control in death is fundamentally unrealistic. We cannot control when or whether we are born, so why attempt to control when we die? For many this position reflects an underlying religious point of view that to desire control is to be spiritually bereft, to have not learned human beings' place in the universe. It is a sign of hubris. If individuals persist in seeking control they miss out on the spiritual growth that comes with relinquishing control to a higher being. "One of the lessons of life is that some things are beyond your power to control and you have to let go. As a society, as individuals, we all try to control too much. It is healthy, I think, to come to a peaceful acceptance that maybe we can't control everything," said Dr. Robert Pankratz, president of Canadian Physicians For Life. U.S. bio-ethicist, Daniel Callahan, agrees: "We all know people whose lives, day in and day out, are dominated by a desire to be in charge of themselves, to have life fully under control . . . I can see in those who live differently, whose lives are not an endless drive for control, a better possibility."

For dying individuals, there is much truth in the fact that giving up unrealistic control can bring peace of mind. Gayle Stelter acknowledged so herself: "Having cancer has forced me to make life changes. I am not in control — though for most of my life I have striven for control. Yet somehow I am stronger. I am somewhat at the mercy of my body and so I have learned humility. I have learned the meaning of thanksgiving. I have learned a capacity for joy. I have learned the value of simply being, rather than doing." Despite learning that relinquishing control felt good, Gayle still wanted the option to control the timing of her death. Was that a sign that she was still striving for control? Was it instead a sign that she was attempting to make a realistic distinction between what was impossible to control, such as the fact she was dying, and what could be controlled, such as the hour and the manner in which she died?

There is a philosophical problem, however, around the issue of personal control and that is whether individual decision-making, pure self-determination, is even theoretically possible. Behaviourists such as B.F. Skinner acknowledge that all organisms, even amoebas, act to control their environments, but that real control is in fact a myth. The amoeba is so shaped and conditioned by its environment that it is simply reacting to stimuli. As human beings, this philosophical viewpoint is that we are so much a product of our environment, our families, our religious upbringings, our community, our cultures, the rewards and punishments we may receive, that we are simply reacting to what is around us. Free will is an illusion. When applied to the argument about euthanasia and assisted suicide the argument might work like this: an elderly woman with ovarian cancer is considering euthanasia and believes it is a choice she is making freely. She lives in a nursing home where three of her closest friends have already undergone euthanasia. She has watched a video on the television that depicted a beautiful death by euthanasia. Her son and her daughter have both told her that to them such a choice is the most rational and noble choice to make — they themselves would do the same. If she decides in favour of euthanasia how much is her decision her own and how much is it a product of the current favourable trend and of the environment she lives in?

In fact, this question was made of Sue Rodriguez's position by many of her critics. They pointed to her relationship with a cold and distant family, and her relationship with her estranged husband who still shared her house, as being environmental factors that negated any possibility her choice to die was truly one reflecting her free will and unmeditated self-determination. Even her biographer, who did not support assisted suicide, asked Sue at the climax of the book: "If you were surrounded by love, by a family that hugged and kissed you and brought you hot soup, and a husband that held you precious, brought you flowers, rubbed your back, Sweet Suzie, would you be doing this?" "'I don't know . . . I don't know,'" Sue replies, "hardly able to breathe for grief," Hobbs-Birnie writes. Did Sue's environment negate the possibility that she was making a rational, self-determined choice to die? Sue Rodriguez knew there was nothing she could do about having a terminal illness, nothing she could do to repair the past or remove the hurt of her failed relationship. The only part of her life she could exert any control over at all was how she died. That's why she fought so hard to have that right.

In the past twenty years, many people have compared the euthanasia debate to the abortion debate: both elicit the same extreme polarization of views, the same political reluctance to handle the issue, the same arguments of sanctity of life pitted against the right to choose. But there are, in fact, even stronger parallels between the controversy over euthanasia and the recent 150-year-long controversy over whether men and women had a right to use *any* form of birth control, not just to have access to abortion. Today, although there are still pockets of resistance, the majority of Western society has finally arrived at a consensus on the issues of birth control and abortion. Regarding abortion, even if one has no religious objection to it, one can't help but experience some disquiet with the procedure. To many it represents an unfortunate failure of contraception; in a perfect world, it would be best if most abortions could be avoided by the consistent and responsible use of safe and effective birth control. But in our messy, imperfect world the majority of us realize that we must keep abortion open, accessible, safe and in women's reach. It is an issue of personal control that if usurped would make an unfortunate situation much, much worse.

In the 1990s there is almost a unanimous consensus that whether or not a couple decides to have children, how many children they have, and when they have them is nobody's business but their own. Today, the majority of Canadian men and women would be astounded if our government or the medical profession declared that for the good of society couples were forbidden using a diaphragm, a condom, the birth control pill or surgical sterilization to prevent conception. Yet as little as sixty years ago, the right for women and men to control the timing and circumstances of births was as factious as the right for women and men to control the timing and circumstances of their deaths is today. The political reluctance to deal with the issue resulted in laws *against* birth control staying on the books until 1965 in some U.S. states and in Canada until 1969, long after the laws had lost all meaning.

Just like the control of death, the desire to control fertility is as old as human society. Archaeologic evidence shows pre-literate societies attempted to control the timing of births or limit the number of offspring in numerous ways: withdrawal of the penis before ejaculation, medicinal suppositories or barrier-like objects placed in the vagina to prevent conception; the use of botanical concoctions to induce abortions. If a birth couldn't be prevented, many societies used infanticide to ensure that only the strongest children, who could contribute to the welfare of the group, would survive. Birth control was largely accepted in ancient Egypt, Greece and Rome, only to become forbidden in the West with the rise of Christianity and the belief in an all-powerful God who determined how and when life is created. The rationale behind government laws against contraception was that if sex were separated from procreation there would be disastrous consequences to human morality and the fabric of society. This belief is identical to the "slippery slope" argument of euthanasia. Just as there are those who argue today that it is too dangerous for society to allow individuals to control the timing of their deaths, for centuries the belief about contraception was that it was too harmful to the structure of society to control the timing of births.

By the Industrial Revolution, however, it was becoming clear to many that unrestrained childbearing was causing a great deal of suffering, ill health and poverty for individuals, as well as causing population and health problems for society. From the mid-nineteenth century, upper class women and their male partners — with the help of birth control bootleggers — became increasingly knowledgeable about controlling the timing of births. Author James Reed, in his definitive survey of the birth control movement since the 1830s, credits the increased interest in birth control in the mid-nineteenth century to a corresponding rise in education, literacy and technological progress which imparted to individuals the sense they had some control over their environment. "They were more confident than their fathers of the individual's ability to control nature and his own life," Reed said. Unfortunately, however, little information trickled down to the lower, uneducated classes. Countless women died in pregnancy or during childbirth, often labouring to bring forth a child they did not want, or were physically unable to deliver. Other women, worn out and debilitated by successive pregnancies, became increasingly ill with each conception until they succumbed to disease. Some women, so desperate not to have another child, would attempt to induce an abortion themselves with knitting needles or other objects, or to seek back-alley jobs, often causing horrendous trauma or their own deaths as well. Yet few doctors would tell any of them how to stop conceiving. U.S. birth control advocate Margaret Sanger, in her biography, wrote of women pleading "for the secret that rich women have."

Children suffered, born into families who didn't want them, couldn't feed them, clothe them or sometimes even love them because of the competing interests of too many other children. Birth control advocates pleaded that access to contraception would improve maternal and child health, marital relations and family welfare. While convincing cases could be made for individual access to contraception, and even if some benefits could be glimpsed for society as a whole, it was seen as being too risky to change the laws and open the doors to widespread use. The theories were varied and dramatic. Woman's monthly menstruation was proof that her allotted role was to bear children and anything that diverted her from her primary purpose would be socially wrong. Contraception would cause the desire for children to diminish or disappear. Women *en masse* would forego motherhood, and the human race would come to an end. Women would join the work force and the economy would be destroyed. If contraception was widely available, wealthy, educated women would decide not to bear children while the uneducated lower classes would breed freely, leading to what was dubbed "race suicide."

The impact of contraception on men's behaviour was also feared. If men no longer had to be concerned about the risks of pregnancy, there would be nothing to keep a lid on their sexuality. Men's respect and concern for a woman's well-being would diminish. Wives and daughters would be degraded and defiled. If men were no longer required to provide for a family, there would be nothing to keep them dutiful, stable, contributing members of society. The loss of sexual mores, the removal of a cost to sexual pleasure would breed wantonness, promiscuity and licentiousness in both sexes. In short, contraception would throw society into structural chaos; into a Sodom and Gomorrah of carnal wickedness. It was variations of those concerns that persuaded the U.S. government in 1873 to pass the Comstock Laws, named for the moral crusader Anthony

Comstock, preventing the distribution of obscene material including birth control information. In Canada in 1892 under the Criminal Code, contraception information and devices became obscene, "tending to corrupt the morals," and anyone attempting the dissemination or provision of contraception became liable for a two-year prison sentence.

While the medical profession might have shared many of the religious and government views against contraception, more often their arguments against it were couched in terms of the perceived impact for human health and the consequences for the medical profession itself, just as the medical arguments against euthanasia are often expressed today. Some of the medical concerns were bonafide, such as the fear that contraception might aid the spread of syphilis, a dreaded disease in the era before antibiotics. Other concerns were less realistic, such as the common belief that birth control would cause uterine disease or infertility either by training the uterus not to bear children or by diminishing the enjoyment of sex. "Repeated coitus interruptus and other contraception lead to sterility because there is not the fulfilment of sexual pleasure. It is only right that women be told the risk they run when interfering with Nature's laws," Dr. Robert Gibbon, a Canadian gynecologist, wrote in his 1923 gynecological text.

Almost parroting the modern-day medical concern that desire for euthanasia is actually an individual's misplaced fear of dying, in the nineteenth century the desire for birth control was often interpreted by the medical profession as being woman's misplaced fear of giving birth, and her weak character for hardship. "She will not endure the seclusion and deprivations necessarily connected with the pregnant condition, but resorts to means to destroy the life within herself," gynecologist David Storer, a professor at Harvard, wrote in 1855. Storer's writing against birth control remained highly influential among the medical profession into the twentieth century. The medical establishment also opposed contraception because they believed it would undermine their discipline's professionalism. During the late nineteenth and early twentieth centuries, leading doctors were greatly concerned with establishing organized medicine as a scientific discipline, with improving medical education and qualification and suppressing medical quackery. Around the mid-1800s, questionable contraception techniques such as items referred to as "Uterine Tonics," "Ladies' Devices" and "Dr. Root's Female Wash" had been advertised in the penny press, in flyers handed from street corners and at carnival side-shows. These "techniques" were associated with the seedy side of life, with quacks and prostitutes. The medical profession wanted no truck with such company.

In much the same way many in the medical establishment today fear that medical involvement in euthanasia might harm the profession's image as healers, up until the late 1930s the medical establishment feared that involvement with contraception might harm their image as scientists and clinicians. Medical articles stressed there was "no 100 per cent method" of birth control and that no method was "physiologically, psychologically and biologically sound." Other criticisms were that contraception was often promoted by the radical lay reformers, like Margaret Sanger and Britain's Marie Stopes, who "had little conception of the medical aspects involved," just as euthanasia and assisted suicide is promoted by non-medical right-to-die groups today. In 1913, when Sanger began her crusade for birth control, she spent six months searching the leading U.S. libraries for practical medical information. She knew there *was* information. She knew some doctors were offering advice, but she found nothing. "Why was it so difficult to find practical information on this subject? Why would no one discuss it openly? Why was it so hidden?" she wrote in her 1931 autobiography.

Canadian historian Mary Bishop described the situation in Canada towards birth control in the 1920s but she might as well

be describing 1990s attitudes towards assisted suicide or euthanasia: "Politicians quoted the law to evade the issue, but scattered groups of determined volunteers made referrals to a few
courageous physicians or provided information themselves." In
another arresting similarity, the Netherlands was the first place
in the world to decide that the control of conception and birth
was entirely a personal decision. They opened their first contraceptive clinic in Amsterdam in 1878, more than forty years
ahead of clinics in the U.S. and Britain, and fifty-four years ahead
of Canada. They developed the first reliable female method of
contraception, the diaphragm, which was given the popular
name "the Dutch Cap." Just as euthanasia advocates and opponents flock to the Netherlands today to garner information
about their methods of handling choice in death, birth control
advocates early in this century made pilgrimages to Holland to
learn more about the provisions of birth control. The parallels
continue: self-help contraceptive pamphlets and books were
the *Final Exit* equivalents of the 1920s, receiving wide and controversial distribution. Newsletters and advocacy groups sprang
up, such as Planned Parenthood Federation, just as right-to-die
advocacy groups have formed today.

By the 1920s and 1930s, many doctors were quietly beginning to doubt the medical association's insistence that doctors
should not be involved in the provision of contraception, just as
many doctors today quietly believe that in some cases euthanasia could be justified. In 1925 Dr. Joseph Cooper was hired by
Margaret Sanger to help bring doctors on side for the fight for
contraception. For two years he criss-crossed the U.S. and gathered the names of 20,000 doctors sympathetic to the cause, but
he found only a handful in each region who were brave enough
to attend public meetings. Even eight years after Cooper collected his huge roster of names, Morris Ernst, a lawyer trying to
mount a challenge to the U.S. federal law on behalf of Sanger
and her group, had a hard time finding nine reputable doctors

in the United States willing to face the glare of publicity and take the stand in support of contraception. The nine doctors were to testify that contraception was sometimes necessary to save the lives of women suffering from a variety of illnesses. On the eve of the case in January, 1936, three doctors dropped out, fearful they would lose their hospital privileges for their vocal stance. Nevertheless, the judge's ruling sided in their favour, stating doctors must not be prevented by government laws to use articles that might save their patient's lives. Contraception could be imported and doctors could prescribe it if the woman's life was at risk.

That same year in Canada, Dorothea Palmer, a field worker for the Parent's Information Bureau, a foundation started by rich Kitchener philanthropist A.R. Kaufman, was arrested for handing out birth control information in a lower-class French-speaking suburb of Ottawa. Her lawyers successfully argued her work was not for profit but "for the public good" and won her an acquittal, opening the way for birth control counselling in Canada. In February of 1937, after more than ten years of rancorous debate, a committee of the American Medical Association finally recommended that techniques of contraception should be researched and standardized, that methods should be instructed in medical schools, and advice should be given by physicians "largely on the needs and judgement of individual patients." The Canadian Medical Association, emboldened by contraception's acceptance by the American and British medical profession, announced in March of 1937 that "properly controlled contraception has become part of preventative medicine." It was a watershed.

However, it took twenty-eight years for the U.S. Supreme Court to strike down the last remaining state prohibition, in Connecticut, against birth control, saying there was a constitutionally protected zone of individual privacy. In Canada in 1967, Justice Minister Pierre Elliott Trudeau announced his intention to remove the law from the Criminal Code, saying "The state has no business in the bedrooms of the nation." By 1969 the law prohibiting contraception was taken off the books with little protest. Such a move no longer had much meaning — couples, with the help of doctors, had been using contraceptives for years.

It would seem that the current debate over the control of death is where the debate over the control of birth was during the early 1930s. The majority of the public say they want it. Some doctors, on the sly, are providing it to a select group of patients. The medical associations, while debating it, have not yet reached a consensus. The courts, by narrow margins, are upholding the existing laws but more court challenges are expected. An increasing number of individuals and groups are being vocal in their support. The governments, however, are reluctant to change the laws because of the religious protest it would bring and the fear of the repercussions on society. Hints are in the air that the balance of power is starting to tip towards individual choice regarding the control of death. Four of the nine judges of the Supreme Court of Canada, including the chief justice, ruled in favour of individual choice for Sue Rodriguez. Three out of seven senators on the Special Senate Committee on Euthanasia and Assisted Suicide came out in support of assisted suicide. There is a growing reluctance to enforce the existing law, aptly illustrated five times in 1994 and 1995 when Canadian judges gave suspended sentences to individuals who had clearly admitted they helped loved ones die. The ethics committee of the Canadian Medical Association in 1994 recommended doctors follow their own conscience in euthanasia issues, but that resolution was narrowly defeated.

In May of 1994, a Washington State judge ruled that just as with birth control and abortion there is a constitutionally protected zone of privacy that extends to decisions about death.

Judge Barbara Rothstein quoted from the 1990 decision "Planned Parenthood versus Casey," that stated at the heart of liberty is "the right to define one's own concept of existence, of meaning, of the universe and of the mystery of human life," and struck down the Washington State law forbidding assisted suicide. The case was immediately appealed by pro-life groups and was reversed by appeal court judges in 1995. It may eventually reach the U.S. Supreme Court in a few years. We are in a watershed position right now in the developmental history of our attitudes about the control of death. Assisted suicide and euthanasia will become increasingly common, if still covert. Individuals like Gayle Stelter and Sue Rodriguez will increasingly call on loved ones, or allies in the medical profession, to help them at the end of their lives. The issue will increasingly come before courts, and legislatures and professional bodies will have to decide what their stand should be.

What can we learn from the history of the birth control movement that can help us in our deliberations about euthanasia and assisted suicide? What warnings can be sounded to help us find the right balance between individual choice, the role of government in protecting or influencing choice, the level of medical involvement and the required legal protection? There is no question that over the last fifty years, the ability for individuals to use contraception has greatly changed the lives of women and men. As with any change, there have been some bad consequences with the good, but almost all would agree there can be no better start to a child's life than to enter the world being wanted. At times, however, the control of contraception and birth has been taken out of individuals' hands and used by states and institutions to further their own aims, without regard to whether it benefited the individual involved. It has been used to advance the cause of eugenics. In the 1930s birth control became respectable not primarily because it finally dawned on people that women and men should have the right to control their fertility but rather because people with power and money saw it as a way to control the untrammelled reproduction of "weaker" undesirable elements of society. The poor would be less of a tax burden on society if their numbers could be controlled. The mentally deranged or chronically sick would be prevented from passing on their unhealthy genes.

When birth control was taken out of an individual's hands it was abused. Six months after Adolf Hitler became chancellor of Germany in 1933, his regime introduced a sterilization law to ensure that only the "healthy" became parents. Included among the "hereditarily sick" who were to be surgically sterilized were people with manic depression, schizophrenia, epilepsy, hereditary blindness, hereditary deafness, low IQs and hereditary alcoholism. Some 300,000 individuals were sterilized in Germany in the 1930s, paving the way for the atrocities of the Holocaust. The U.S., however, had been arbitrarily sterilizing individuals for a number of years before Germany started to. By 1920, laws providing for the compulsory sterilization of the criminally insane and "mentally defective" had been enacted in twenty-five states. In Canada, many of the doctors who opposed allowing "fit" parents access to contraception argued for the forced sterilization of "the unfit" or "feeble-minded." Alberta and British Columbia, caught up in the eugenic craze sweeping the Western world, passed laws in the 1930s that allowed for the surgical sterilization of the mentally ill and mentally disabled. Alberta's law wasn't repealed until 1972. During its years in force some 3,000 children and teenagers were rendered sterile while in government care, many of whom were of normal to low-normal intelligence but who came from abusing homes. Thirteen such individuals in 1995 sued the Alberta government for compensation.

Birth control programs have been forced on whole groups of people or populations in efforts to achieve zero population

growth and demographic control without regard for the individuals involved. China's laws for years have forced couples
by sanctions and punishment to have only one child; India's
coercive contraceptive programs of mass sterilizations traded
toasters, among other things, for vasectomies in the 1970s. For
decades, population control programs around the world have
been exercises that attempted to force individuals to adopt contraceptive practices, not for their own good but for the good
of society. It was only in 1994, at the UN World Population
Conference in Cairo, that it was finally agreed that a top-down
approach had been wrong. It was time to try a new tack: put the
needs of the individual woman first. With education, empow-
erment, realistic options, women would naturally and willingly
use contraception because it meets their own needs of personal
control of their life. Astonishingly, in 1994, newspaper editorials
were calling this "a radical new approach."

Applied to assisted death, the lessons of contraception become
quite clear: when the control of the decision of whether to use
it is kept in an individual's hands, its benefits vastly outweigh
abuses; when the power for the decision is placed in others'
hands and imposed on individuals, even if a convincing case can
be made that it is for their own good, it can quickly devolve
into abuse. Just as it is wrong to sterilize a woman against her
will or without her knowledge on the rationalization she or
society would be better off, it will be wrong for anyone but the
individual himself to decide if he, or society, would be better off
if he were dead. We must always remain on guard for this form
of paternalism in even its most subtle form.

5

THE DUTCH
WAY OF DEATH

IN THE LIVING ROOM of a small townhouse, in the suburb of Koog aande Zaan outside Amsterdam, Dr. Gerrit Kimsma listens intently to his female patient who is dying of ovarian cancer. Leaning forward in his chair, he cradles his chin with his hands and trains his undivided attention on the seventy-year-old patient. "There are two things I don't want — to be in pain, and to be bed-ridden all day," Jeanne Verheijen says determinedly as her husband, Jan, nods in agreement on the couch beside her. "My mother died a horrible death and I won't go that way."

Sitting as she does next to her husband, a tall, healthy man of sixty-eight, Jeanne seems tiny, withering in comparison. She has lost more than fifty pounds since her cancer was diagnosed six months earlier. Her skin has the fragile, dry, parchment look of someone who is dying, yet she has taken care with her appearance for the doctor's visit. "Suppose you don't have to be in pain — we can control the pain — would that change the situation?" Kimsma asks gently, his eyes never leaving her face. Her husband and doctor await the response, both watching her carefully. "I'm not sure," she says. "We'll just have to see." It is a cool, windy day in May of 1994 and it is the couple's first discussion with their doctor about euthanasia.

As Canada considers whether to change its laws to allow euthanasia or assisted suicide, it is essential to examine the experience of the Netherlands, the only country in the world where both practices are permitted under specific guidelines. Since the 1970s, in a compassionate yet flawed compromise the Netherlands has evolved a system for helping patients who request to die. Euthanasia and assisted suicide are still technically illegal — crimes punishable by a maximum imprisonment of twelve years and three years respectively — yet doctors can be reasonably sure they will not be prosecuted if they can ensure the "rules of carefulness" have been met, the most important of which are 1) that the patient has made a voluntary and durable request for help in death, and 2) the patient's suffering is thorough and unrelenting.

The remarks of witnesses before Canada's Special Senate Committee on Euthanasia and Assisted Suicide in 1994 are a good example of the sort of pendulum-swing of information about euthanasia in the Netherlands that is being touted as fact in other countries. Some witnesses urged Canada to follow the Netherlands' model. Other witnesses described the approach as being akin to Nazi Germany's extermination programs. Some of those who presented Dutch horror stories to the Committee were people who hold positions of authority and respect in Canada. Newfoundland palliative care physician, Dr. Margaret Scott, speaking on behalf of the Canadian Cancer Society, told the Senate committee: "Ninety-five per cent of the nursing home inhabitants in Holland are afraid. . . . Citizens in Holland now carry cards in their wallets when they reach sixty saying they do not want euthanasia. That is the effect." Dr. Scott never quoted her sources for these alarming figures and acknowledged that she, herself, had never been to Holland. Nevertheless her words conveyed a chilling effect on all who listened: she seemed to offer convincing evidence that euthanasia had changed Holland from a caring place to one where individuals lived in fear. But were her statements — and ones like them that

I heard repeated but unsourced many times in my research about euthanasia — in fact true? I went to the Netherlands in 1994 to find out, to discern fact from fiction in the euthanasia tales of the Netherlands.

In May 1994, my husband, my two young children, my mother-in-law and I moved to Amsterdam for six weeks. We didn't move into a hotel to live among other tourists. We exchanged homes with a retired Dutch doctor, who came to live in our house, while we moved into her modest three bedroom apartment near the Amstel River in the heart of Amsterdam. We lived like the Dutch among the Dutch. We shopped in the local shops. We played with our children in the park across the street, talking with parents and grandparents as we watched our children play. Across the street from our apartment was a retirement home that housed one hundred elderly people between the ages of sixty-five and 102, with an average age of eighty-four. When I looked out our front window, I could see into the dining room of the Tabitha Care Centre, where the residents were eating dinner, playing cards or having coffee with friends. When I walked by the windows with the children, as I did almost every day after work on our way to the playground, the residents would smile and wave to ten-month-old Madeline perched on my shoulders in the backpack and three-year-old Kate in the stroller. At night we could see festive candles flickering on the tables where residents still socialized with friends.

During the six weeks I visited hospitals, nursing homes, doctors' offices and two hospices; I spoke with individuals whose loved ones had euthanasia and other individuals who would never ask for euthanasia. I sat as a silent observer as Dr. Kimsma discussed euthanasia with Jeanne Verheijen that cold windy day in May. "Our reality is different from the often heard horror stories, but that doesn't mean I am entirely happy with our present reality," said Kimsma, a family doctor who also teaches family practice medicine at Amsterdam's Free University. That

opinion was common among the many individuals I interviewed. Most pointed out they thought the Dutch were doing
the best they could with a vague, ill-defined legal situation and
its attempts to regulate a complex, emotional and philosophical
issue. All felt the situation could be greatly improved — particularly if politicians grasped the nettle and wrote straightforward
legislation to replace the current ambiguous "illegal-yet-allowed"
approach. The present system, while compassionately allowing
individuals choice in death, also seems to impart an atmosphere
of confusion and uncertainty about what is and what is not
allowed around decisions at the end of life. Many of those interviewed stressed that Canada has the opportunity to draft a better
model than that of the Netherlands. They warn that their
flawed compromise evolved because of political inability to deal
effectively with a controversial issue that increasingly faced doctors, the courts and the public. Its policy evolved out of court
decisions, not through definitive legislation. It is a course, however, that many see Canada already embarking on as more and
more cases have come before Canadian courts in which individuals out of compassion have killed others who were suffering,
and the courts have given minimal to non-existent punishment.
Unless Canada's Parliament can step in to set definitive rules, *de
facto* euthanasia may evolve through court decisions, just as it
did in the Netherlands. Despite the presence of flaws in their
system, public acceptance of euthanasia in the Netherlands is
extraordinarily high and has been since the 1970s. In 1980 a poll
showed 70 per cent of the public in favour; by 1986 that figure
had climbed to 76 per cent; and by 1991 it was 81 per cent. The
19 per cent who stated they were against euthanasia did so on
religious grounds and were also, for that reason, opposed to
choice regarding abortion.

The Netherlands is one of the most densely-populated nations
of the world, with 15.5 million people living in a triangular

landmass that would fit in the bottom corner of Southern Ontario. Over its four-hundred-year history it has developed a robust respect for personal autonomy with the result that a wide range of individual behaviour is tolerated as long as it does not infringe on the rights of others. The Netherlands' very existence was born out of a fight against religious oppression. In the 1500s and 1600s, Holland's promise of freedom of conscience attracted religious refugees from all over Europe and strengthened what was at the time a burgeoning state. Lutherans, Anabaptists, Calvinists such as the French Huguenots, and Spanish and Portuguese Jews fleeing the Spanish Inquisition, all flowed into the Netherlands, bringing with them their skills, education and wealth. This flood of immigrants spurred immense prosperity in the Netherlands, and fuelled the seventeenth-century Golden Age when the Dutch dominated European art, culture, commerce and seafaring. Tolerance, the Netherlands learned early in its history, could be highly profitable and good for everyone.

In Holland's Golden Age an individual with talent, skill and ambition could move through the classes, up from the lowest rung to become a leading civic official, member of the clergy or wealthy merchant. Humanist writers and thinkers, such as Descartes (1596–1650), emigrated to the Netherlands because of the freedoms it promised for the individual. The parents of Dutch humanist Spinoza were Spanish Jews fleeing persecution. Out of their writings, and those of another famous Dutch humanist, Erasmus, that emerged during the Dutch Golden Age, many of the foundations of modern democratic society were created, including freedom of religion, freedom of speech and freedom of the press. In the centuries since the Golden Age, the Netherlands has often attempted to conduct a delicate balancing act between individual freedoms and collective well-being as can be seen in its liberal approach to drug use, sexuality and contraception.

John Griffiths, an ex-patriot American who for eighteen years has been a professor of the sociology of law at the University of Groningen, makes the following observation: "What I find most striking about the Dutch is that they function on the basis that nothing exists that can't be discussed openly or dealt with in some manner. They feel if they can bring difficult issues out in the open, they will be better able to regulate them."

The Netherlands' response to the AIDS epidemic is typical of its approach to difficult social issues. When public health experts in Canada and the U.S. were still timidly exploring whether ads could be shown that used the words "safe sex," "condom" and "penis," without incurring the wrath of members of the public, buses in Amsterdam were sporting a graphic depiction of an erect phallus sheathed in a protective rubber. To deal with the spread of HIV in the drug-using population, the Netherlands was the first to realize that lecturing to drug addicts to change their behaviour wasn't going to work; what was needed was to make drug use less likely to contribute to the spread of AIDS. They set up the world's first needle exchange program, which offered drug users a new clean needle, a cup of coffee and a pastry in exchange for turning in an old needle and listening to a little talk about safe sex. As a result, the spread of HIV through drug users in Holland has been at a much slower rate than in North America, where needle exchange programs were fought by many who saw it as inherently condoning IV drug use.

As noted earlier, the Dutch were the first to believe the use of contraception was the right of the individual woman and so therefore established birth control clinics more than forty years prior to any other country. To this day, its contraceptive policies are more open and comprehensive than most other nations. Its abortion law is the most liberal in Europe and yet it has the lowest abortion rate and lowest teen pregnancy rate of any western nation. In Canada, for example, fifty-nine out of every 1,000 teenage girls become pregnant; in Holland, only twelve in 1,000 do. When I asked Dutch officials why this might be so, the typical response was: "In countries like Canada, many people seem to be afraid that talking about sex with teenagers encourages them to experiment with sex. We assume that teenagers are going to experiment with sex no matter what, so our goal is to make sure they do so safely." Sexuality issues are taught openly from earliest grade school, and contraceptives are free with a doctor's prescription. Given the Dutch attitude about many issues of individual behaviour, it is easy to see that their approach to euthanasia is far from aberrant. Rather it is an extension of a long legacy of respecting the needs of the individual and attempting to balance them against the needs of society.

Central to the overwhelming public support in the Netherlands for the availability of euthanasia is the fact that the population maintains tremendous trust and respect for its medical profession. The doctor-patient bond is particularly strong. Unlike Canada and the U.S. there are few medical malpractice suits lodged against doctors. In part, that trust arises from the exemplary manner in which Dutch physicians behaved during the German occupation in the Second World War. While German doctors informed Nazi authorities of their sick and disabled patients — who were then rounded up and either sterilized or killed under the Nazi programs — the Dutch refused to collaborate. "It is to the everlasting honour of the medical profession of Holland that they recognized the earliest and most subtle phases of German requests for cooperation," said Dr. Leo Alexander, consultant to the U.S. Secretary of War for the Nuremberg War Crimes office, in his 1949 *New England Journal of Medicine* article, "Medical Science Under Dictatorship."

According to Alexander, when Arthur Seyss-Inquart, the German Reich Commissioner of Occupied Netherlands, wanted to draw Dutch doctors into the orbit of the German master plan to rid society of its weak elements, he did not tell them "You must send your chronic patients to death factories;" instead, the order was couched in the most subtle and superficially acceptable terms. One of the paragraphs of an order in December of 1941 read:

> It is the duty of the doctor, through advice and effort, conscientiously and to his best ability, to assist as helper the person entrusted to his care in the maintenance, improvement and re-establishment of his vitality, physical efficiency and health. The accomplishment of this duty is a public task.

The Dutch doctors, to their credit, saw it for what it really was: a request to forsake patient confidentiality and to identify their sick patients to authorities to help "rehabilitate" them for useful labour. They refused *en masse* to comply with the request. Seyss-Inquart threatened the removal of their licences; the doctors sent their licences in, removed their shingles and saw their patients secretly. Seyss-Inquart ordered the round up of 100 physicians at random and sent them to death camps; the medical profession took care of the widows and orphans and still held firm. "Thus it came about that not a single euthanasia or non-therapeutic sterilization was recommended or participated in by Dutch doctors," Alexander wrote.

Some opponents of Dutch euthanasia express dismay that Dutch doctors in modern times have apparently turned their backs on what is a noble past to now allow the killing of patients. "How did a society change from a people resisting submission to the German Nazi principles of health care to a nation accepting euthanasia in less than fifty-five years?" asks Dr. Joop Van Rijn, the vice-president of the World Federation of Doctors Who Respect Human Life. Van Rijn is on the board of the Dutch Physicians' League, a group of six hundred doctors who oppose euthanasia and abortion and who broke with the Royal

Dutch Medical Association (RDMA) over its tolerant stand towards those procedures. Yet when both the doctors' actions during the occupation and the present euthanasia policy are examined in the light of the Netherlands' long history of respect for individual autonomy, they seem remarkably consistent. Doctors in the 1940s would not put the needs of the state as expressed by their occupiers ahead of the needs of individual patients. Dutch doctors in the 1980s and 1990s will not let arguments of euthanasia's risk to society or its risks to the principle of sanctity of life to be given more weight than the needs of the suffering patient who asks for help in dying.

Euthanasia has not always been accepted in Holland; rather the acceptance grew gradually over the last twenty years. Dutch doctors in the late 1960s started to debate whether it could ever be justified to help a patient die at the patient's request. Highly influential in the debate was a little book written in 1968 by Dr. Jan van den Berg called *Medical Power and Medical Ethics*, in which he lamented that medical ethics had not kept pace with the advances in medical science and that much of what was considered medical progress actually made patients' lives worse. He suggested that small committees be made to decide these matters, a suggestion that was rejected then and is still rejected by those who favour euthanasia. This book, however, spurred the debate, selling more than 200,000 copies in twenty-two editions. At first, the majority of the Dutch medical profession, including the board of the RDMA which represents the Netherlands' 30,000 doctors, was not in favour of the euthanasia. But through the 1970s and early 1980s more and more doctors were faced with difficult situations regarding dying patients. A few doctors began to openly defy the law prohibiting consensual killing to help their patients die. When the doctors were prosecuted, the judges sympathized with the doctors' predicament and passed minimal or non-existent sentences.

The first case came to court in 1971. A female doctor gave her mother an injection of 200 mg of morphine after the elderly woman had repeatedly begged to die because she could not endure her pain or her meaningless life in a nursing home. Eighteen other doctors in the community, the people of her village, and ten Mennonite ministers all supported the doctor in her actions. Two years later, the court found the doctor guilty — because the law left no choice — but gave her a one-week suspended jail sentence. The ruling spurred the formation of at least three groups in Holland dedicated to promoting the legal and moral right to voluntary euthanasia. Newspapers and magazines and professional journals were filled with the subject. During the late 1970s and early 1980s a series of similar permissive court rulings (including a lenient Supreme Court ruling in 1984) established the defense of "*force majeure*" for doctors performing euthanasia — meaning the doctor was placed in a conflict of duties between obeying the law and honouring the needs of the patient. Euthanasia was still illegal, but doctors could now plead a defense of their actions if certain conditions were found to have occurred.

In 1984, in response to both a government committee studying euthanasia and to conditions set forth by the courts, the Royal Dutch Medical Association re-examined its position on euthanasia and issued an ethical position paper. In a radical departure from other medical associations, the RDMA reenforced the court rulings and stated that, as a medical body, it agreed that under certain circumstances, euthanasia could be justified. It set out its own rules for carefulness that would establish a medically justified act of euthanasia:

- The patient has made a persistent, voluntary, competent and durable request.
- The patient's suffering is thorough and unrelenting, with no prospect of improvement.

- The patient has full information on his or her condition.
- Any alternative treatments are both known and are found wanting.
- The euthanasia is performed only by a physician after a consultation with a second physician who confirms the decision.
- The case is documented in writing and no certificate of natural death is issued.

Unlike some who claim euthanasia is any deliberate act that causes the death of the patient, the RDMA accepts only one meaning for the word euthanasia: the deliberate termination of the patient's life *at the patient's explicit request.* I have emphasized the final phrase of the above sentence because some critics lump together any deliberate actions, including removing life support, or giving pain relief at a level that may hasten death, and call them euthanasia. That is why estimates of the number of "euthanasias" in Holland can vary greatly, because different groups use different definitions.

With the medical profession, in essence, giving its blessing to acts of euthanasia under specific conditions, the door was finally opened. Even if the law against it was still on the books the possibility of euthanasia became a *de facto* arrangement between dying patient and attending physician because the doctor knew that if he performed it properly, he would no longer fear censure from his colleagues. From 1984 until 1990, however, the practice of euthanasia in the Netherlands occurred with little scrutiny or follow-up by either the government or the medical profession. The number of euthanasias performed each year was unknown because the majority of doctors never reported the acts to the authorities. Observers say the low rate of reporting occurred because euthanasia was still illegal and subject to police investigation. Doctors wanted to protect grieving families and

themselves from heavy-handed police interrogations immediately after the death. The police process, doctors felt, treated
the participants like criminals. It was common for a doctor and
patient to decide, usually with the agreement of the family, to
keep the act their own little secret to avoid dealing with law
enforcement officials. The lack of firm data fuelled international
rumours of as many as 20,000 people a year dying by euthanasia.
One of the most influential and inflammatory reports was written by Dutch pro-life cardiologist Dr. Richard Fenigsen, in a
1989 Hastings Centre Report. The article, which compared
Dutch acceptance of euthanasia to the Nazi ideology of ridding
society of its weak elements, was roundly condemned and dis-
credited by the Dutch themselves, but had a tremendous impact
on the international view of the Dutch situation.

In order to get a handle on the real number of euthanasias
the government and the RDMA changed the reporting procedure in 1990 to remove the police interrogation and instead
have doctors report to the coroner, who then passes on the
information to the local prosecutor. That same year the government also ordered a commission of inquiry, headed by Prof. Jan
Remmelink, Attorney General of the Supreme Court to investigate euthanasia and assisted suicide in order to prepare the
Dutch legislature for possible euthanasia legislation. As part of
the Remmelink study, the committee ordered the first scientific
study of all medical decisions at the end of life, giving doctors
immunity from prosecution from any information revealed
through the research. The study, headed by Dr. Paul van der
Maas and his colleagues at Erasmus University, finally made
clear that euthanasia as the Dutch define it — a doctor causing
the death of a patient who has made a repeated voluntary
request — happens only 2,300 times a year among the country's
130,000 deaths. Assisted suicides, in which the doctor provides
a lethal drug which the patient takes himself, happens just
400 times a year. But the study did reveal irrefutable evidence

that there were problems with the Dutch situation that needed to be addressed, particularly the existence of some cases in which deaths had been hastened without the explicit request of the patient.

I met with and interviewed a number of doctors during my stay in the Netherlands, but it was Dr. Gerrit Kimsma, a family doctor and professor of family medicine at Amsterdam's Free University, who took me under his wing to ensure that I gained an accurate look at euthanasia in the Netherlands. Kimsma, in his late forties, holds a Masters degree in philosophy as well as his medical degree, and he is a board member of the European Society for the Philosophy of Medicine. Kimsma has been a practising "huisarts" for sixteen years. The word "huisarts" translates directly as "house doctor" and as such it is an accurate description of the family doctor's close and strong relationship to the patients he cares for. The relationship is usually long-standing, often includes frequent house calls, particularly if the patient has a terminal illness. Seeing the patient in her home, surrounded by her family, in the midst of her living environment, helps the doctor to better assess the situation, particularly those involving requests for euthanasia, Kimsma notes. Acceptance of euthanasia among the public and medical profession is also bolstered by the fact all Dutch citizens have comprehensive medical care and the cost of long-term terminal illness is completely covered by the state. Doctors in Holland are paid through a combination of salary and fees, not a strictly fee-for-service system like Canada's, so the performance of euthanasia is not a billable item. "Receiving a fee for euthanasia would be a vulgarity," said Kimsma.

From our earliest correspondence, long before we met, Kimsma stressed to me that euthanasia is a process, not a single act. "It is a decision that is forged over time. One that emerges as other options diminish," he said. Among his practice of 1,500 patients, he has helped six patients to die by euthanasia or assisted suicide since 1984. "As a physician it is a most intimate window on life and death. It is astonishing in its intensity. It is so moving that when I come home I cannot even speak to my wife about it. But the families of the people I have been involved with in this process, we bond for life."

Kimsma cares passionately that euthanasia is done well, with thought, care, thoroughness and accountability. With his colleagues at Free University's medical faculty, he has set up the country's first medical course in grief, dying, and euthanasia. It is now a compulsory course for all doctors in that school training to be family physicians. Teaching the details about how and when to administer euthanasia correctly and ethically is just one part of the twelve-week course. Just as important is the information taught about the care and management of the dying process. The students role-play to practise how to deliver bad news, talk to dying patients, and how to help individuals and their families with grief and mourning. The students sit in small groups and discuss their own experiences with grief and death as well as their own attitudes about euthanasia. They are also presented with a variety of problematic cases of euthanasia: one with undue pressure from the family, one where the patient's request is vague and needs further clarification. In working through these cases, the goal is to teach the student the careful step-by-step process of "a euthanasia decision-tree," as Kimsma calls it, in order to ensure that the euthanasia request is durable, informed, uncoerced and necessary.

Months before Kimsma's patient Jeanne Verheijen discussed euthanasia with him on that day in May, even before she had been diagnosed with ovarian cancer, she let Kimsma know that she supported euthanasia. In fact, she and Jan had both handed Kimsma a signed and witnessed declaration for euthanasia as part of a living will when the couple first became his patients eighteen months earlier. So now that Jeanne is dying from stage four ovarian cancer, it isn't a surprise to him that they wanted to talk about euthanasia. He asks them if he can bring a Canadian journalist along to observe the euthanasia decision-making process. They agree. I take the commuter train from Amsterdam to a suburb about twenty-five minutes northwest of the city. Kimsma picks me up at the station and as we drive to the couple's small townhouse, a few kilometres away, he says: "I have been expecting this discussion." The couple welcome us warmly at the door and invite us into the small living-room.

Six months earlier, after Jeanne's inexplicable weight loss, the invasive cancer had been diagnosed. Jeanne spent four months of the winter in hospital hovering on the brink of death, and then, when spring came, a sudden turn for the better made it possible for her to return home. It is now early May, 1994. A large mechanical hospital bed, which they have rented, takes up most of the living-room. "Jeanne has been having a hard time getting up and down the stairs," says Jan, nodding to the bed, "so we thought it would be easier to have her stay down here."

Kimsma sits leaning forward, forearms resting on his knees, on a chair directly across from the couple on the couch. "Tell me what is on your mind," he says. Jan picks up a clipboard and pen he has waiting beside him and begins to go through an itemized list. "First, we want to know why her energy level seems to vary from one day to the next. Some days, when we walk, she can go for half a kilometre, the next day she can hardly get out of the car," begins Jan. Kimsma assures them this is a normal part of the disease process — she will have good days and bad days. For the next forty-five minutes they spend most of the time talking about her symptoms and discomfort: how to improve her sleep and energy, what could be done about her diminished appetite and nausea at the smell of food, if there is any hope in attempting a trial of the drug Taxol. Her husband does most of the talking while Jeanne sits with her hands calmly folded in her lap, nodding her head in agreement as her husband ticks items off the list on the clipboard, one by one, as they are discussed.

Then, as the final item on the list, the talk turns to euthanasia. For the first time, Jan falls silent and Jeanne takes over. This is an important change — something that Kimsma looks for, he says later. Who asks for euthanasia? The patient or the partner? The RDMA, in a briefing paper on euthanasia, makes the same point: "Although it may not always be possible to be completely sure whether the request was influenced — the doctor must keep an eye out for the internal relationship and communication patterns . . . he must pay attention to who does the talking or takes the initiative." Jeanne speaks forcefully now, while Jan nods his head in agreement and puts the clipboard aside. She says she doesn't want to be racked with pain or captive in bed, unable to move. She describes how her mother, who died of cancer fifteen years earlier, had been force-fed with a tube and her hands had been tied to prevent her from pulling out the tubing. When Jeanne had pleaded with the staff to stop the feedings they "treated me as if I'd asked her to be murdered."

Her fear is that she may face a similar end. Kimsma knows that the desire for euthanasia is often a result of a particular fear over some part of the dying process. The RDMA, in its briefing paper noted: "In view of the fact that the request for euthanasia is often found to be an expression of fear — fear of pain, deterioration, loneliness — the physician should take into consideration that these fears are playing into the request and try to dispel these fears." Kimsma reassures her she will not need to be admitted to hospital, she will be able to stay at home and no one will force-feed her, nor will pain likely be a problem. His words seem to comfort her, but she is still adamant that if her suffering is too much, she wants to go. He says he understands. At the end of a casual, wide-ranging, discussion about life and death, the only commitment made is that if Verheijen really believes she cannot go on and needs euthanasia, Kimsma will be prepared to help her. "You've got a long way to go before we need to consider that," he tells her. The doctor's relaxed visit ends with a handshake from Jan and a hug and kiss on both cheeks from Jeanne. She is smiling.

Studies show that some 25,000 patients in the Netherlands each year discuss euthanasia with their doctors and 9,000 make an initial request. Fewer than 3,000 go on to receive it. The rest either felt they didn't need it or changed their minds. Such was the case with Jeanne Verheijen. In the end, she didn't need it. In her final weeks, Kimsma adjusted her pain medication and gave her morphine in low doses to keep her comfortable. She remained lucid throughout. On the morning of July 29, 1994, she told her husband she did not feel well. He carried her to her bed, where, a little while later, she passed away silently in his arms. "She is one of my patients for whom I am convinced the understanding and agreement we had on an active ending of her life made her anxiety less: she could concentrate on day to day worries without fearing an ugly death. Her disease called her before the ugliness intervened." Kimsma feels that by discussing euthanasia with her and reassuring her that he would see her through whatever her dying might bring, Verheijen's fear of death was eased. She was given the confidence that she could cope with her dying because she had a way out if she needed it. "To me, the real value of euthanasia comes not from the act itself, but the ability for the doctor and the patient to speak openly about it," Kimsma said.

The story of Jan Smit illustrates how in Holland euthanasia or physician-assisted suicide is usually a decision that evolves over time. Jan was dying for years before he opted for assisted suicide; even then it took him eight months to finally decide on the date to go ahead with it. I never met Jan; he died four months before I arrived in the Netherlands, but I met his attractive and articu- late widow, Hélène Swierstra-Smit. The Netherlands Voluntary

Euthanasia Society put me in touch with her soon after I arrived in Amsterdam. I was the first journalist she had spoken to about her husband's death and near the end of May, 1994, I went to her apartment on the outskirts of Amsterdam to hear the story of Jan's life and death. Hélène's English was almost flawless, even down to the idioms. We talked for five hours. Jan had been just fifty-nine when on January 10, 1994, he drank a fatal glass of drugs mixed with orange juice and slipped into a coma as his wife and doctor sat by his side. But his story is not that of a person who had given up the will to live, but of someone who clung to every hope that medical technology could offer, until it could offer no more. Medical science put him in a predicament of a living death; he needed medical help to set him free.

The two of them had met and married twenty years earlier when he taught the history of philosophy and she taught art at an Amsterdam teachers college. Seven years later, when he was a strong, healthy man of just forty-seven he had suddenly been struck with a mysterious virus that infected his heart and destroyed his valves. Despite a valve replacement, the years that followed his infection were marked by a slow and steady decline: months off work, increasing tiredness and infirmity, repeated hospitalizations, reluctant retirement at fifty-one and an ever-diminishing ability to do the things he loved, like walking his golden retriever or gardening at their vacation home. "It was so terrible. It all went so slowly, slowly, slowly. He never had pain, he was just so tired, so weak. It was so frustrating for him."

An accomplished painter and sculptor, Hélène's art during Jan's thirteen years of illness seemed to feature a recurring theme of individuals held captive, confined in tight boxes, birds held by chains. That was what his illness was like for both of them, a prison of infirmity, she said. Finally in 1991 his doctors told him that his only hope for life was to undergo a heart transplant in

Utrecht. "We thought a new heart would mean a new life," says Hélène.

First, however, he had to be hospitalized for three months while he fought off a bacterial infection. Then he had to endure six weeks of tests and screening to ensure he was fit to be a transplant candidate. Worst of all for him, he was told he had to give up his dog because she might pass on an infection in his weakened state. "When he was told that the dog must go, he was grief stricken. That was almost too much to bear." He passed the screening and was accepted into the transplant program. And then he had to wait and wait and wait. Unable to exert himself in the slightest, he lay on the couch with a beeper on his belt that would ring once a donor had been found. The call finally came six months later in June, 1992. They were both full of optimism that their life was about to change. They were soon to realize, however, that the new heart did not release Jan from the prison of his infirmity. Instead, it was the instigator of a whole new series of calamities.

His weakened arteries caused him to haemorrhage after the operation, necessitating a second, emergency operation to stem the bleeding. During the second operation the new heart was likely damaged. For days he struggled for life in the intensive care unit. Just when it appeared his condition was stabilizing, tests showed his immune system was rejecting his new heart. For the next eight months they struggled to control the rejection with up to fourteen medications a day. Every two weeks he had to return to the hospital for a heart biopsy, a painful procedure he absolutely detested, in which a catheter was threaded under local anesthetic through his veins to his unanesthetized heart. There tiny samples of tissue would be snipped from five different places for analysis in the lab. He underwent twenty biopsies during the year. Each snip of tissue would make his heart jerk, as if it was exploding into his chest wall. Eight months after the transplant, while lying on the couch he hardly ever left, he had a stroke that put him back in the hospital for six weeks and left him partially paralysed. Wheel-chair bound and dependent on his wife for all his care, Jan told a shocked transplant team he would undergo no more biopsies and was dropping out of the program. "He'd had enough. He'd been struggling for ten years and he had finally had enough." In April of 1993, Smit told his wife to get the forms for euthanasia from the Netherlands Voluntary Euthanasia Society. "Life had lost all enjoyment for him. He could no longer read, which was his great love, and all he could do was watch videos. He was so smart, but in the end he couldn't even follow the plots of the videos. For months he had death in his eyes."

Still, Jan deliberated for eight months over whether he should opt for euthanasia, discussing it at length with his wife and Dr. Frits Schmidt, his doctor for seventeen years. "He didn't want to die, he only wanted peace," Hélène said with tears coming to her eyes. Schmidt suggested that Jan speak with a humanist minister to work out any conflicts he might be feeling. The minister came to the apartment a number of times in the fall to conduct intensive counselling. "He was the same age as Jan and very intelligent. Jan would really enjoy his visits. They would sit in the den and talk about philosophers, and history, and writing, and Jan's life. I think Jan found it very helpful to pull his life together, to see it in perspective.

In October of 1993, the transplant team's cardiologist and social worker visited him to see if they could persuade him to go back into the program. Smit would not budge. They told him he didn't need euthanasia — they could keep him comfortable with morphine and help ease his passage. No, he said, if he was going to die he wanted to make the decisive act himself. Hélène still harbours anger towards the transplant team for what they did next. Having learned that Jan was considering euthanasia they approached his family doctor to ask Jan for his body after his death. They wanted to study it to find out why the new heart had been rejected. "That made Jan so angry. He'd been involved with them for two years, here they had visited him and they didn't even have the guts to ask him to his face for his body. He felt it was just more proof of their whole technological approach to him, never seeing him for who he was, just seeing him as a disease that would be interesting to study." He refused their request. He also refused to lie in bed, even though he was no longer able to walk or do anything for himself. Each day Hélène would help him get up and get dressed so he could sit on the couch or in a favourite chair to watch television. In the last few months it could take two hours to get him dressed, she said.

"He was worried about me, what his illness was doing to me. He would ask me, 'Do you think I should do it?' and I would say, Jan, I will be here for you, no matter what, but I can't make that decision for you, only you can." Not wanting to mar the family's Christmas, nor their twentieth wedding anniversary at the end of December, he decided on January 4th that he would have physician-assisted suicide on January 10th. His two daughters from his first marriage who lived in Switzerland and Israel were called to come home. Hélène's two daughters and Jan's brother who lived in Amsterdam were also informed of the date. His brother, whom Jan had been close to all his life, had the hardest time with his decision. He didn't want him to do it. When he knew Jan was determined and would not be swayed, he wanted to spend all his time with Jan in his last days. He came by the Saturday night, three days before Jan's planned death and he told Jan he would be there the next morning. "He told him, No, Henk, you cannot come, I want Sunday alone for Hélène and me." For Jan's daughters and relatives, the most painful yet significant moment was when he said goodbye to each one of them individually and alone, sharing an intimacy with them and giving each one something to remember him by. "When you die like this you have to talk about everything. We were sad, of course, but no one felt guilty that they hadn't said something they wanted to say. It was really very beautiful," Hélène said.

The night before his death, Hélène could not sleep, but Jan "slept like a baby." When they awoke that morning, for the first time in his years of illness Jan told Hélène not to dress him, he would stay in his pyjamas. They watched the video of the film *Amadeus* because Jan was "crazy for Mozart" and then a soccer game because he was "crazy for football." Jan was calm and happy. Hélène was tense and anxious. Not knowing what to do, at one point during the day she found herself making an apple pie in the kitchen. "It seems so odd to be making a pie when your husband is going to die, but I felt I must do something with my hands."

This was to be Schmidt's twenty-third case of assisted suicide or euthanasia in his seventeen years of practice and by now he had established an effective routine. At noon, Schmidt came to give Jan some anti-nausea pills to settle his stomach to ensure he wouldn't vomit the overdose. Jan was told not to eat anything that day as the medication works best on an empty stomach. Later that afternoon, Schmidt personally picked up a specially prepared dose of nine grams of phenobarbital from the pharmacist and delivered it to the apartment at 7:00 p.m. He asked Jan for a final time if he was sure he wanted to go ahead with it. Jan said yes with no hesitation. With his brother and Hélène's eldest daughter in the living room, the doctor, Hélène, and Jan retired to his small office off the front hall. "It was terribly hard for them in the living-room, they paced back and forth."

Jan wanted to take the drug himself, not to be injected by the doctor, but just in case the fatal glass of drugs did not work or Jan vomited the medication, Schmidt carried a syringe filled with curare in a pouch around his waist. As he mixed the phenobarbital in a glass of juice, Jan held Hélène's hand, telling her how much he loved her. As the doctor handed him the drink, Jan smiled at his wife and said, "You will be fine. You can do everything." He drank the liquid down, but even the orange juice didn't hide the barbiturates's bitter taste. "Next time, I want more orange juice," Jan joked to the doctor with a straight face.

Within two minutes he fell asleep; less than forty minutes later he stopped breathing. Hélène leaned over, kissed him, did up the top button of his pyjamas and closed his mouth and eyes. She hugged Schmidt and called his brother and her daughter in from the living-room. They came, with tears in their eyes and kissed his still-warm cheek. The doctor then called the coroner who arrived at the apartment by midnight. He collected a questionnaire Dr. Schmidt had completed and verified the facts of this "unnatural death" to pass on to the public prosecutor. Less than an hour later, the undertaker arrived and set up a refrigerated casket in the den. There Jan laid for three days as family and friends paid their respects, until his funeral and cremation ceremony at the end of the week. Three months after the death, Hélène received a letter in the mail from the public prosecutor stating that Jan's death had met the euthanasia guidelines and no further investigation or charges would be necessary.

"I will miss him forever. I did not want to lose him, but your heart twists in pain to see him suffer like that," Hélène said. Although she was still mourning months after his death, she felt the grieving process had been eased by the process of euthanasia. Her friend, she said, had noticed the same thing. Her husband died of euthanasia a few months before Jan after suffering from leukemia, and she had remarked that her grief had been helped by her husband's conscious decision to embrace death. "It's true. When Jan died, I knew it was what he wanted, and I knew he was at peace. That made it easier for me to accept."

In the ten years that Dr. Sven Danner has been director of the Netherlands' largest clinic for the care and treatment of AIDS he has come to accept euthanasia as a compassionate adjunct to his profession. "I feel it is part of my duty not to abandon my patients when I have nothing else to offer them," says Danner, who heads one of Europe's leading research programs to find better drugs and anti-viral agents for the treatment of AIDS. His compact office is on the fifth-floor AIDS ward of the enormous 1,200 bed Academisch Medisch Centrum, or AMC, the Netherlands' largest hospital. The office is piled high with medical journals and modern texts. An exceedingly bright and engaging specialist, Danner is proof positive that one can be a doctor on the cutting edge of medical science, yet still believe there is a place for euthanasia in one's care of patients. "I think the ultimate responsibility of our profession is to serve the well-being of our patients. I think that, in very specific situations, under specific criteria, part of our responsibility is to ease the passage of death."

Danner's attitude corresponds with that of the majority of Dutch doctors. In 1990, the state-commissioned Remmelink study found that 90 per cent of general practitioners and 84 per cent of clinical specialists would be willing, under certain conditions, to comply with a patient's request for euthanasia. Of the 10 per cent of GPs who said they were unwilling to perform euthanasia, only 4 per cent would not refer the patient to another doctor; of the clinical specialists, 8 per cent. In a month of interviews among Dutch doctors, I found a similarly high acceptance of euthanasia. No doctor professed to like it. Many told me how emotionally difficult it was to do, how sad and moved they often felt. In one written report, a doctor described how he burst into uncontrollable tears while driving home after a euthanasia case. In the summer of 1995, the RDMA shifted its position more towards physician-assisted suicide, stating that wherever possible, patients should end their own lives, using drugs provided by a physician. The new emphasis on patient responsibility is recognition that euthanasia takes a tremendous emotional toll on doctors and it is easier on doctors' psyches if patients perform the final act themselves. But, the RDMA is adamant that doctors be the only ones to provide a patient with a fatal dose of a drug to take themselves, or give a patient a fatal injection, or decide to withhold or withdraw treatment: "The physician is the only person capable of answering the questions so crucial to a careful decision process, namely the correct diagnosis and prognosis, the competency of the patient to make a decision, the level of suffering, and the availability of alternatives," the RDMA stated in its position paper.

For most Dutch doctors, euthanasia or assisted suicide is a rare event, even among doctors like Danner who treat AIDS patients. In the ten years the AMC's clinic has been operating, treating more than 600 patients in its fifteen beds or as outpatients, only about twelve have undergone euthanasia. But almost all (numbering more than 1,500) have talked to Danner and the other doctors about the possibility of euthanasia. "Almost 100 per cent mention the subject, just talking about it, early in our contact — not because they want to die, just to know what is our attitude, or the hospital attitude, so they know what to expect," Danner said.

The unit's euthanasia numbers are low, in part, because most of the Dutch AIDS patients prefer to die at home with the help of their family doctor. A study by Dr. Henk-Maarten Laane, an Amsterdam doctor and public health officer, found that 35 per cent of deaths among people with AIDS in Amsterdam were from euthanasia or assisted suicides. That was twelve times higher than the overall incidence of euthanasia in the Netherlands. The Remmelink Report also found that between 20 to 30 per cent of people with AIDS die by euthanasia. But Danner stresses those figures still illustrate that more than 60 per cent of AIDS patients in Holland don't ask for euthanasia, even though they are dying of a devastating, untreatable disease, and even though they live in a country where euthanasia is widely accepted. "I have had so many patients say, when they see a friend or another patient in the final stages of AIDS, 'My God — I'll never get like that. Long before, I will ask for euthanasia.' But then as their disease progresses, their attitude changes. They realize that the decision is irreversible and that life itself has value. . . . And then, well, they cling to life more than they would ever realize," Danner said.

Like the majority of hospitals in the Netherlands, the AMC has developed procedural guidelines under which euthanasia can be performed that mirror the guidelines set by the courts and the RDMA. A 1989 survey of ninety-six hospitals showed that, like the AMC, 65 per cent had developed a policy allowing euthanasia if certain conditions were met, 21 per cent had developed a policy prohibiting euthanasia, usually on religious grounds, and 14 per cent had no policy but left it up to the doctor and patient. The AMC's conditions for euthanasia are as follows, with comments from Danner:

- The doctors must know the patient, who is part of the unit's program. "We do not accept patients from England, or France, or Germany who fax us asking if they can come for euthanasia. That is absolutely out of the question."
- The patient, of their own free will, must ask for it. "Not their lover, not their friend, not their family. Family members often say, 'please can't you give it to him, look how he is suffering?' but the patient is not asking."
- It must be an enduring request. "He can't say one day he absolutely wants to die and then the next day say, well, I'm feeling a bit better today, so maybe later. If he is wavering, up and down, that is not considered a real request."
- The patient must be mentally competent. "That means people who have developed AIDS dementia are no

longer eligible, no matter how devastating that scenario can be."

- There must be no other realistic or acceptable options for treatment and the patient must have unbearable suffering. "This can be difficult for the patient, because they may come into my office and say, 'I can't stand this,' and I will say: 'You went to a movie last night, or you had dinner with friends. I am sorry, in my opinion, you are not suffering enough to justify euthanasia.' If they are angry with me, I say, too bad, you go home and do it yourself. For me to give euthanasia, I must agree."

- An independent doctor, preferably from another hospital with experience in AIDS, will assess the patient. "He must confirm that the patient wants to die, that there is no other treatment possible, and that the suffering is unbearable. And he must write in the file that this is so."

- A full report must be filed with the hospital and the local authorities. "I am strongly against unreported cases of euthanasia. To me that is the real danger of euthanasia, when it is done in secret. We need the prosecutor to examine the case, just to add authority to our decisions."

In all the cases of euthanasia to have occurred among AIDS patients in the hospital, it was clear in every one that the suffering was terrible and there was no realistic alternative that the hospital or doctors could provide, Danner says. He will never forget his very first case of euthanasia because it was "really representative of all the cases that came after it." It was 1984, shortly after the Supreme Court ruling and the RDMA guidelines had been released. The patient was a journalist in his mid-thirties who worked for an Amsterdam newspaper. He was suffering from four or five opportunistic infections, including a mysterious infection of the spine and his central nervous system. "He became paralysed in one leg, then in the other, then incontinent for urine, then incontinent for stool. He would sit in a diaper all day. Then he developed a strange abscess in his stomach, and it ulcerated, opening a fistula between his stomach and intestine. He began to vomit his stool." The doctors tried as best they could to control the vast array of distressing symptoms with naso-gastric tubes, medication and sedation. Danner recalls: "He said to me, 'This is enough. I am in absolutely good mental health and I know this is only going to get worse. I trust you enough to ask you to help me.'

"I had never thought of it that way, as a sign of trust between the patient and the doctor. It took me a week to find out all I needed to know about the regulations and procedure. I talked with the hospital, I phoned the state attorney. I phoned an anaesthetist I knew who had experience to find out how I should do it. I spoke with a professor of health law. At the end of the week I felt comfortable that I could do it." He says he will never become inured to the "strange turmoil" of planning the patient's death — scheduling the time the way one would book surgery, checking the nurses' schedule, arranging so that the family can be there, if they wish. "You say, okay, today is Friday, how about Monday? And the patient agrees, and so you book it for Monday morning at 11:00 a.m. Even though you know you have met all the conditions, it still feels very, very strange." At the appointed hour the patient is asked a final time if he still wants it, and then an overdose of thiopental is run in through an IV line. The patient falls asleep and within forty to fifty minutes the patient is dead. In rare cases, an injection of curare will also be administered when the overdose of barbiturates has not proved fatal. "We feel forty to fifty minutes is the best amount of time. You absolutely don't want to have the patient die, as we say 'on the needle' that is too hard on everyone, particularly the doctor, who feels that he is the hangman. But you don't want to have it take twelve hours either. That is hard on everyone, too."

Many individuals in North America promote legislation that allows assisted suicide but not euthanasia as preventing possible abuse because the act is left in the patient's hands. But Dutch doctors like Danner see this attitude as naive and unrealistic, and suggest that drawing the line at assisted suicide may cause unnecessary suffering and harm to some patients. Dutch studies show that 25 per cent of assisted suicides fail — the patient either vomits the drugs, or the overdose is not enough — and doctors must step in to complete the act with a lethal injection. Without recourse to the lethal injection, many individuals might be brain damaged or rendered comatose but still be left alive. Even though the RDMA has recently suggested to doctors that assisted suicide should be more common than euthanasia, at the AMC AIDS unit, the option for a patient to drink a fatal potion is not allowed. "If it is in the hospital, we want to be in control," said Danner. "I did two assisted suicides in patients' homes but I will never do it again. Too many things can go wrong because these patients are so sick."

Many in the Anglo-American medical professions believe, too, that good research and good palliative care cannot exist in a climate that openly accepts euthanasia. But Danner feels the opposite is true. "As a doctor, to be comfortable with euthanasia, you have to feel that you have looked at all the options. You have to feel you are offering the best of palliative care, or chances for improvement. You must feel that you have no other recourse. That is the only climate in which euthanasia can or should exist."

In recent years there have been some highly controversial cases in the Netherlands, most notably the existence of an estimated 1,000 cases in 1990 in which doctors ended a suffering, dying

patient's life without an explicit request from the patient. These
numbers were extrapolated from 47 cases of unrequested euthanasia found by the Remmelink study. In more than half of the
cases the patient had previously told the doctor they wanted
euthanasia but then became so sick they could no longer make
a formal request. In the remaining 40 per cent, the family or the
doctor decided the patient would be better off with euthanasia. "In all cases it was not a criminal attitude of the doctor but
paternalism — the doctor thinking it was best for the patient,"
said Dr. Gerrit van der Wal, a medical inspector for North
Holland who conducted an independent study that confirmed
the Remmelink findings. "But, that said, it still shouldn't happen." The existence of these cases shocked the Dutch and scan-
dalized the international community, fuelling opposition
criticism that euthanasia was hurtling down the "slippery slope"
in the Netherlands. Dutch officials in the government and the
RDMA, however, are embarrassed and disturbed by the findings
and have acted to try to prevent more cases in the future. In
1993 the government passed an amendment to the burial act
setting down the reporting procedure in law and codifying a
sixty-point questionnaire that doctors file with the coroner. A
statement was released by the RDMA and the government condemning involuntary euthanasia and promoting the use of living wills to ensure patient wishes are being followed when they
become incompetent to make decisions.

Also startling to the Dutch, who pride themselves on their
openness, is that the Remmelink study found that still half of all
doctors performing euthanasia do not report their cases to the
authorities. The predominant reason for not reporting seems to
be that euthanasia is still illegal; doctors are reluctant to self-
incriminate and face a potential criminal conviction. They resent
being treated like criminals, second-guessed by the prosecutors
as to their actions, and having the threat of a lawsuit over their
heads for three months or more until a letter arrives from the

prosecutor saying no charges will be laid. They also want to protect grieving families from the anxiety and threat of a prosecution. Since 1990, reported rates of euthanasia have risen substantially, probably as a result of continued focus by the RDMA and the government on the necessity of reporting. Gerrit Kimsma acknowledges that the process of reporting euthanasia can be a headache. "But considering the frequency of this — perhaps once a year — it seems the least one can do, if it enhances the trust between the public and the profession."

Controversy has also arisen from cases in which the patient's suffering was more mental than physical. Although the Dutch have never stated that patients must have a terminal illness, only unbearable suffering, a few cases have tested the boundaries of that belief. One such case was that of a twenty-five-year-old woman, who suffered from anorexia for fifteen years with repeated unsuccessful hospitalizations and therapies. She begged her doctor repeatedly to help her die, and after making an extensive video tape of her request, he helped her. He was charged with murder and prosecuted but when the court viewed the video tape he was acquitted.

Another recent case involved a psychiatrist, Boudewijn Chabot, whose patient was a fifty-year-old woman with a history of intractable depression following the death of her two sons. She had already attempted suicide by an overdose of prescription drugs when she came into Chabot's care in 1991. She wanted a lethal prescription in order to kill herself. He told her if he was unsuccessful treating her, he would help her to die. Over the course of a month, Chabot held twenty-four hours of therapy sessions with her. There were also sessions with her sister and brother-in-law. She refused his pleas to try antidepressants and he could see no justification for committing a competent individual to an institution for treatment against her will, nor did he believe such an act would help her.

In written letters and discussion with him she clearly and

consistently showed that she understood her situation and the consequences of her decisions. He took her therapy notes to seven other psychiatrists who agreed that if she would not consent to any treatment, there was no prospect of improvement. In September, 1991, Chabot decided to honour her request. He gave her a lethal dose of drugs, which she consumed in the presence of Chabot, her family doctor and her friend. Chabot was completely open about the case, even writing a book about it, and was charged with assisting suicide. He was acquitted by two lower courts but the prosecutors pursued it all the way to the Supreme Court. Three years after the act, in the spring of 1994, the Supreme Court finally ruled on the case. It accepted that Chabot had followed the guidelines to establish his patient was competent, suffering unbearably, and had a voluntary, well-considered and enduring wish to die. But it refused to accept that he had acted under *"force majeure"* because the doctors he consulted had not themselves seen and examined the patient, only the therapy notes. The court found him negligent but gave him a suspended sentence. A year later, the medical disciplinary tribunal was more harsh, saying Chabot was wrong to assist in the suicide. He should have insisted that she be seen by a colleague and he should have done more to insist that she try treatment with antidepressants. He was sternly reprimanded. The tribunal, however, did not fine him or remove his licence.

Euthanasia experts in the Netherlands see the Chabot case as a very important legal landmark to clarify three issues: terminal illness, or the terminal phase of dying, did not have to be present to justify euthanasia; untreatable mental suffering was as legitimate as untreatable physical suffering for a request for euthanasia; and consulting doctors giving second opinions on euthanasia must see the patient themselves. Euthanasia opponents, however, have been outraged that Chabot was not punished, even though he was found negligent. The case is being interpreted as giving a green light to the assisted suicides of healthy but depressed individuals. Others contend that the Chabot case and other controversial rulings are simply setting the margins of what is acceptable — not widening the availability of euthanasia, but narrowing it.

"Many people think that from now on, after Chabot, it is easy for people who have psychiatric suffering, psychological suffering to get help to die. This is not so," says Martine Cornelisse, co-ordinator of member's services for the Netherlands Voluntary Euthanasia Society (NVVE). The NVVE supports the broader availability of assisted suicide for psychological suffering on the basis of personal autonomy, and feels doctors should not be paternalistically protecting individuals from taking their life if the individual has made a well-considered, competent decision to die. "If anything it is now more difficult," Cornelisse says. "Psychiatrists are very wary of this topic and the publicity of Chabot has made them even more wary. His decision was attacked in our most important mental health journal. In psychiatry there is no support for it."

Controversial cases of assisted death don't end with Chabot, however; debate is also raging inside and outside the country over ending the lives of disabled newborns. In recent years, some doctors have admitted giving fatal injections to severely disabled infants shortly after they were born. It is estimated that this occurs four or five times a year, after the parents of the infant have refused life support, surgery, or therapy that might extend the infant's life. Dutch doctors who support such acts say that the decision to withdraw treatment from severely disabled newborns occurs in all western nations. Once that decision has been made they believe it is more humane to help the infant die quickly and peacefully by an injection, rather than to let it linger for days or weeks until "natural death" occurs, as is the practice in other countries, including Canada.

In one such case Dr. Henk Prins, an obstetrician, gave a fatal injection to a four-day-old girl who was born with spina bifida and a partially formed brain. Baby Rianne seemed in severe pain and her disabilities were such that doctors estimated she would live for only a few months at most. There was no possible operation or treatment that might improve her condition. Her parents requested that she be given a lethal injection to let her die and in consultation with other doctors, Prins agreed. The baby died in her mother's arms after Prins injected her with a muscle relaxant. He reported the case and was charged with murder. When the district court ruled on the case in the spring of 1995, the judge found that Prins had committed murder but he refused to punish him, saying that under the situation his actions were justifiable. The judge, Ben Posch, said in the court's view it was permissible to end the life of a newborn if the baby is in unbearable pain which cannot be alleviated by medical care and if the parents repeatedly request for the child's life to be ended.

Prins told reporters at the end of the verdict that the death of baby Rianne had left him "emotionally scarred" but he has no doubt that his act was the correct one. The case is expected to be battled to Supreme Court by prosecutors who want a harsher verdict. The results have also fuelled more criticism by euthanasia opponents. "It shows that once you accept killing as a solution for one problem, you soon find 100 problems for which killing can be regarded as a solution," said Dr. Karl Gunning, of the Dutch Physicians' League. "First you kill at the patient's request, then you kill the comatose patient without their request, then you help a healthy but depressed person to commit suicide, then you kill the handicapped newborn. Where does it stop?"

The RDMA's Dillmann says, however, that the termination of lives of newborns will probably remain highly controversial for years to come in the Netherlands and there is no medical consensus about what the ethics in these difficult cases should be. He adds that such cases of involuntary euthanasia should not be a reason to forbid voluntary euthanasia or to halt the discussion of all the issues. Griffiths shares the same perspective: "The most important conclusion to be drawn is not that there are problems — it is known that it is imperfect. Rather, it is the quality of the discussion that is going on. Nowhere else in the world are these difficult questions being discussed so openly, so systematically, so calmly and thoughtfully, and with such a lack of ideological rigidity as in the Netherlands. Other countries may not follow the Netherlands' example, but they can't fail to learn from their experience."

What about the rumours of elderly people living in fear? Is there any evidence that the tolerance of euthanasia, assisted suicide and other medical decisions at the end of life have made the Dutch elderly feel threatened? A few days after my arrival, Kimsma took me to the Noordse Balk nursing home, a modern, well-kept, low-rise, twenty-five minutes outside of Amsterdam, in the village of Wormerveer. As with all 308 nursing homes in the Netherlands, Noordse Balk is open to all denominations and incomes. People with money are expected to pay a portion of the costs, while the government picks up the full tab for those unable to pay. In the lobby I met Kimsma's former patient, Mrs. Freda Mauer, ninety-two, who has lived at the home since August, 1993, when her advanced breast cancer spread to her spine. Now under the care of the nursing home physicians, she is paralysed in her right leg, confined to a wheelchair and in need of twenty-four-hour care. On continuous morphine as well as five other medications, she is lucid and clear and says that her pain is well controlled. Although she is now unable to look after her own needs it is obvious the nurses on her floor have helped her attend to those personal details so often neglected in busy, short-staffed nursing homes. I ask about the staffing ratios: during day-time hours there are four nurses to every fifteen patients — about three times the standard ratio in Canada. "I like it here, I have many friends here. It is like a home," she says as she gives me a tour of the building, showing me the hydrotherapy room, the chapel, the wheelchair repair room, and the bright and sunny activity room that overlooks one of the gardens. This room is full of similarly well-groomed residents reading books, knitting or crocheting, or working on jigsaw puzzles.

Although about half of Dutch nursing homes have a policy prohibiting euthanasia on their premises either on religious grounds or because all their patients are mentally incompetent and therefore unable to make an informed request, the Noordse Balk home, which looks after predominantly competent elderly individuals in its 130 beds, has a policy allowing requests for euthanasia. Yet Mrs. Mauer, a devote Christian, will never request it. "I had moments when I was very down. I couldn't move, I couldn't drink. But my husband and children went to church and they prayed for me. That night in the hospital I was visited by God and He said, 'What do you do? You cannot work against my wishes.' So I said, Lord, I will not oppose you anymore, my life is in your hands, I ask forgiveness. And then I am not feeling down any more. And I can eat. So God must have a task for me, I am not sure what. But I can help somehow, I can be here." Perhaps because she is philosophically opposed to euthanasia she is one of the rumoured elderly who fear they will be killed against their will?

Puzzlement creases her eyebrows, as if she does not comprehend the question I am asking. We have been speaking mostly in English because, as a teacher for more than forty years, her English is good. She is not sure she has got it right: is she afraid? Of being killed? She turns to Kimsma to have him pose the question again in Dutch just so she is certain she is not mistaken. Kimsma obliges, and explains the North American rumours. As he speaks, she continuously shakes her head, disbelieving. "Nee, nee, nee, nee," she says. "This is not true." She says she knows of no one who has said they are afraid — not her eighty-seven-year-old husband, not members of her church group whom she still sees regularly, none of the other residents whom she speaks with in the nursing home. When I ask Inez Windrich, a nursing home nurse for twenty-five years, about fearful elderly residents the look of utter disbelief is the same. "Is that what people are saying?" she sighs, seeming vexed. Of the hundreds of patients she has looked after over the years, only one has requested and received euthanasia, she says.

A study of euthanasia in nursing homes conducted by Dr. van der Wal, found that fewer than one in ten requests in nursing homes result in the actual administration of euthanasia or assisted suicide because either all the conditions are not met or the patient no longer requires it. The study, published in the June 1994 issue of the *Journal of the American Gerontology Association*, found there had been 300 requests for euthanasia from among the 52,000 patients in Dutch nursing homes, but only twenty-five actual acts of euthanasia each year. Of the country's 713 nursing home physicians, only 12 per cent had ever complied with a request. Van der Wal's study confirmed the results of the Remmelink study that euthanasia among the elderly is rare. Both studies found euthanasia most common between the ages of thirty-five to seventy, with very few cases for people in their eighties or older.

"Our studies have shown that most people who ask for euthanasia have suddenly developed cancer," van der Wal said. "It is speculation, but I believe one of the reasons elderly over seventy don't ask for it so much is that they have already been experiencing a gradual decline and perhaps their disease causes them less suffering than for someone who has gone from being well to being sick quite rapidly." In fact, like nursing homes in Canada, the United States and Britain, it is far more common in Dutch nursing homes for doctors to make the decision, with the family or patient, to stop, or not start treatment, or to give pain relief to alleviate symptoms, even though both actions may hasten the death of the patient. Yet no studies have been carried out in North America to detail how commonly this occurs and under what situations.

I tell Windrich that Canadians are concerned about the availability of euthanasia altering the climate of care in nursing homes and hospitals. Has she seen a change in the way nursing home care is given in the Netherlands in the ten years that euthanasia has been freely available? "Yes, definitely," she says, "It has changed for the better. We listen to the patient more. We used to say: "Now you go to bed. Now you eat this. Now you do that." But now we say, "We have an idea, but what do you think?" There is talk, negotiation, working out what is best for the patient. I don't know whether euthanasia caused that — perhaps the acceptance of euthanasia is more a result of that, of listening to the patient."

Everyone I talked to seems to support the idea of euthanasia if their dying process is too painful or protracted. I worried that maybe I wasn't talking to the right people. After five weeks of watching the Tabitha Care Home across the street from our apartment in central Amsterdam, I decided to pay a visit there. I walked in unannounced to the eight-storey Christian old-age home one day in early June. There, one hundred people between ages sixty-five and 102 live in their own two-room apartments, each one different, each one furnished with their own belongings. Gaily-coloured parasols hung upside down from the common room ceiling; black-and-white photos of Hollywood screen stars adorned the walls. It was 12:00 p.m. and residents streamed down from the elevators to eat a lunch of their choice, of cous-cous or veal cordon bleu, with a selection of soups, salads and desserts. Elderly men and women, still living on their own in the neighbourhood, use Tabitha like a drop-in centre, coming in for a free cup of coffee, to take part in the many activities, or to have an inexpensive meal. A few eat all their meals here while still living at home, says chief administrator

P.J. Dyk. When the time comes for them to need supervised care, they will go there, already feeling at home, Dyk says.

In my thirteen years as a medical and health journalist, during which time I have visited dozens of nursing homes and old-age homes in Canada, I have never seen one as pleasant, well-designed or well-kept as the Tabitha in central Amsterdam, and income is no barrier. Whatever portion of the CAN $2,300 a month an individual can't pay, the government picks up. Nor have I seen a group of elderly in a care home more lively, bright and interactive.

So, what do they think of euthanasia? The question draws the same look of puzzlement, as if it is a strange question for a young Canadian visitor to be asking. "One hopes it never comes to that, but it's reassuring to know it's there," says one woman, while her friends around her shake their heads in agreement. Even as a Christian home, the Tabitha management has no formal policy prohibiting it. "We feel it is a personal choice between a patient and their doctor," said Dyk. "If we knew a patient was considering it, we would see if there were anything we could do to remove the need for it, but in the end, we would never forbid it. This is, after all, their home. It is their own decision."

Where do these rumours of elderly in fear come from? Surely there must be some basis for it? Dr. Paul van der Maas, the lead author of the Remmelink Report and the director of the department of public health, Erasmus University, in Rotterdam, says the rumours of frightened elderly individuals come from a single newspaper report about a survey conducted by the Dutch Physicians' League (NAV). "We were concerned. We asked the [League] for the data, so we could have a look," van der Maas said. "We found that it was a survey of a selected group of their own members and that 2 per cent had responded that they were afraid, not 60 per cent or 90 per cent. It is a very unscientific study."

What about "Do-Not-Kill-Me" cards? Do some Dutch citizens feel it is necessary to carry such declarations in their wallets to ensure they are not killed against their will? In almost six weeks of constant interviews, I did not meet anyone who carries what is called a Life Passport by the Physicians' League and its sister organization, the Patients' Rights Association. "Can you put me in touch with anyone near Amsterdam who has a Life Passport?," I ask Dr. E. Th. Droop, the secretary of the League, on the telephone. "I must speak with someone before I return to Canada." "I don't know about Amsterdam," he says from the association's headquarters in Veenendaal, near Arnhem. "Amsterdam is a very socialist, liberal, un-Christian place."

Through the Patients' Rights Association, which is also located in Veenendaal, and has 60,000 members throughout Holland, I obtain the name of Wim Burggraaff, a KLM account services manager who lives in Hoofddorp, a community about forty minutes outside of Amsterdam near Schipol airport. I arrive at the Burggraaff's tidy townhouse the next evening, a few minutes after the forty-year-old man, his wife and seven children have finished dinner. They are warm and welcoming, even though I am more than two hours late for our scheduled interview on account of a wildcat railway strike. They are eager to share their opposition to euthanasia. As his wife Hélène cleans up the kitchen and gives their youngest children their baths, Wim and I sit in the living room. He has asked a colleague, John, who spent his childhood in the United States, to sit in for the interview in case his English is not adequate to explain his views. Wim tells me he is in perfect health. Hélène looks older than her thirty-seven years, perhaps as a result of having seven children between the ages of one and sixteen.

Wim pulls a folded blue-and-white document from a clear plastic billfold he always carries in his wallet and spreads it out on the coffee table. He points to the document's preamble, which states he is a Christian and does not believe in euthanasia.

"We say that every human has a right to life and that life is not mine to take away. Our Lord will do so," he explains. Various sections detail what he wants in various life threatening situations. The document, for all intents and purposes, looks like an advance directive, known in Canada more commonly as a living will. "We are not saying that we want life at all costs. We say give the necessary care. They can give pain relief to the level that it keeps me comfortable, even if it hastens death. And I don't want senseless operations or experimentation. If I am in the dying stage, and they have spoken with my family, then they can stop the respirator or treatments that are keeping me alive. When it is a person's time to die, it must be possible," Burggraaff says.

Wim tells me his family doctor performs euthanasia. Does he feel he must carry this document or otherwise his doctor might take his life without his request? "Oh, no, I trust him, we have a good relationship. He knows how I feel. But if I were injured in a car accident and taken to hospital unconscious, then I would want those doctors to know how I feel, too. And other people may not be as forceful as I am, the elderly, the sick. I am a strong man, and I speak my views. For them, it is more necessary to carry one." Would he change doctors if one was available who shared his pro-life views? "I don't think so. Our doctor has looked after us for a long time. He's a good doctor." Why does he feel he must carry his Life Passport at all times? "It is a political statement, really. We want to have our beliefs known. We are saying, we do not like what you do." Wim's friend John, who has remained quiet during the interview except to translate where needed, offers to drive me back to Amsterdam and I gladly accept. In the car I ask him whether he shares the Burggraaffs' concerns about euthanasia. He pauses as he diplomatically searches for his response. "I very much respect Wim and his opinions. He is a good person and I know he cares very much about this issue. But I guess I believe it is more a matter of personal choice and I think if I were dying, I might want the option."

I note with interest a few days later that a public service advertisement has begun to run in newspapers and on television throughout the country. Its message: Write out a living will detailing what you would like to happen if you became sick or incompetent. Discuss it with your family and your doctor and carry it in your wallet. Who sponsored it? Remarkably, the pro-life Patients' Rights Association of which Wim Burggraaff is a member *and* the Netherlands' Voluntary Euthanasia Society. The two diametrically opposed groups worked together with the Ethical Advertisers Association to produce the month-long campaign. After more than a month in the Netherlands, it strikes me as a typical example of the Dutch openness and ability to accommodate a range of beliefs. I can't imagine in Canada a pro-life group and an pro-euthanasia group being able to co-operate on a campaign promoting living wills. Martine Cornelisse, of the NVVF, said the co-operation was welcomed: "Of course, we feel there is absolutely no need in Holland to carry a 'Do-Not-Kill-Me' Card because it has been accepted that euthanasia is only done at your own request. But we like the idea that people write down what they want, discuss it with their family, and with their doctor. Whether someone wants euthanasia or whether they want to be treated until the very last moment, the important fact is that they let people know and that wish is respected," she said.

International criticism of the Netherlands often focuses on the Netherlands' provision of palliative care. Unlike Britain, which developed free-standing hospices that administer to the dying in the 1960s, or Canada and the U.S., which have had palliative care programs dating back to the mid-1970s, in the Netherlands palliative care is an emerging specialty. For that reason I am very interested in visiting some of the hospices to have emerged in recent years. One, Stichting Kuria, is on a quiet little plaza near the centre of Amsterdam in a renovated three-storey building. The hospice, run by a Christian charity, occupies two floors of the old building and has room for six patients, each in their own private, bright and sunny rooms. In the two years it has been operating, patients have been evenly divided between cancer and AIDS patients.

I wait for my interview to begin in the office of the hospice director, Jaap Gootjes, while he is looking after the needs of one of the patients. When Gootjes enters a few minutes later, we are both taken aback — we recognize each other. From where? It takes us a few minutes to determine that several weeks earlier we had both been among some fifty international visitors at the renowned St. Christopher's Hospice in London, England, having a tour and brief audience with Dame Cicely Saunders, the founder of palliative care. We compare the intimate, apartment-like Stichting Kuria, with its staff of seven and handful of rooms, to the hospital-like St. Christopher's with it four floors of wards, sixty-two beds and close to one hundred staff, not including its roster of more than 300 volunteers. Gootjes, a nurse by profession, is humble: "This is not St. Christopher's, but we do our best with what we have." To my mind, however, if I were a dying patient, I would greatly prefer to stay in the Dutch hospice's quiet, family-like atmosphere than among the hallowed halls of St. Christopher's. In one of the rooms upstairs, John, a native of Jamaica, has the same feeling. He is dying of AIDS and today he is celebrating his thirty-second birthday. Left-over cake and cards tell of the birthday party that the hospice and his friends threw for him a few hours earlier. "This is like the home I never had. It is wonderful here," he says. He previously lived on the Amsterdam streets. John will stay at the hospice until he dies, whether that is four days from now or four months.

No doctor is on staff at Stichting Kuria, instead the nurses work with the patient's family doctor and the pain team at a nearby hospital to keep the residents comfortable. Gootjes, a Calvinist Christian, says he is fundamentally against euthanasia and he laments that most of Holland embraces it. It is not allowed at Stichting Kuria, and if a patient wants it, he or she must leave. The discussion of euthanasia, however, is welcome. "If they say they want euthanasia, we try to find out the reason, and that can help us give them better care. The discussion is welcome." Gootjes says that many of the sixty patients who have come through their doors are relieved that euthanasia is not an option there — it removes the pressure of a profound decision from them in their dying days. "I think the decision can be very difficult for some people. They feel that if it is available, then they must make a choice and that choice is a very hard one to make. If they want to stay alive, they feel they must justify that. It is more simple for them when they know that choice is not an option here."

A few weeks earlier I had visited Hospice Rozenheuvel, a new Dutch referral centre for the terminally ill, near Arnhem. As I walked up the gravel driveway to the stately white mansion, I could see that staff had wheeled a hospital bed out under the shade of a leafy tree. An emaciated woman, dying of cancer, lay in the bed in the dappled sunlight while a relative held her frail hand. The smell of hyacinth drifted through the spring air. It was the picture of peace and tranquillity. Like Stichting Kuria, no euthanasia is performed at the converted mansion in the wooded suburb of Rozendaal, three kilometres outside of Arnhem. Unlike Stichting Kuria and the other small hospices that have emerged in recent years, Hospice Rozenheuvel has a doctor on staff and was the first to try to work in direct partnership with the local medical profession.

It's founder and medical director, Dr. Zbigniew (Ben) Zylicz sees his mission in life as the prevention of euthanasia through good palliative care. "I want to prevent a crisis situation in which a patient feels they have no choice but to ask for euthanasia," says Zylicz, a Polish-Catholic *emigré*, who trained as an internist and oncologist in Nijmegen. He also holds a Ph.D. in the clinical pharmacology of analgesics, and completed palliative-care training in Britain with Dame Cicely Saunders. At Rozenheuvel, the goal is to work with the family doctor to settle a patient's acute problem, such as uncontrolled pain or vomiting, and to then send the patient home. Zylicz makes it clear he is adamantly opposed to euthanasia. He feels it is his Christian duty to try to prevent as many cases as possible. He is a member of the Dutch Physicians' League (NAV), which split from the Royal Dutch Medical Association over its stand on abortion and euthanasia. But Zylicz disagrees with the NAV's anti-euthanasia tactics, which consist in part of mud-slinging against mainstream Dutch physicians, and the use of questionable research data. The NAV's tactics are "too radical," and only re-enforce the polarized views on the topic, Zylicz said.

Instead Zylicz has chosen to work alongside the region's general practitioners and specialists, acting as a consultant in palliative care, offering his expertise in the management of pain and other symptoms for the dying among the region's populace. Zylicz puts a great deal of emphasis on obtaining standardized clinical data that will not only prove the cost-effectiveness of good palliative care to Dutch health insurance companies, but will show the effectiveness of the techniques in diminishing the requests for euthanasia. Backed by a bequest from a dying patient who shared his vision of integrated palliative care, Zylicz was given the use of a rundown mansion by its Salvation Army owner. After extensive renovations to the home, a year ago Zylicz began to call on local doctors to garner their support for the project.

At first he met with resistance, particularly by some doctors who thought he was implicitly criticizing their care of dying patients. But since the hospice opened in January of 1994, he has received an ever increasing number of calls from doctors with difficult cases. "If a GP has a problem, he can call me and we can talk together about the best way to help the patient — different medications, different delivery. One of the reasons I think euthanasia is seen as a solution is that the GP is working alone. Frequently under the pressure of the family, under the pressure of a difficult dying situation he agrees to euthanasia because he knows of no other way to help the patient," Zylicz said. If a patient's condition cannot be stabilized at home, his or her family doctor can admit him or her to one of the eight beds in Hospice Rozenheuvel where Zylicz and his specialized staff will work to get symptoms under control. Zylicz stresses that even when the patient is in the hospice, it is the family doctor who is in charge of the patient's care, with Zylicz acting as the specialist consultant. When the patient is once again comfortable — usually about two weeks later — he or she returns home.

The common British, American and Canadian criticism that the Netherlands lacks a well-developed network of independent hospices or palliative care units in hospitals, though true, is also simplistic, Zylicz says. "In Britain there is more of a tradition of hospitalization, of institutionalization for the dying. It is different here. Dutch people are used to dying at home," Zylicz said. In Holland statistics show that nearly half of all patients die at home, with fully available home nursing care, compared to only about 20 per cent in Canada and Britain. As well, Zylicz adds, the British system of charitable hospices emerged because of a lack of hospital beds for palliative care. But in the Netherlands, there are too many hospital beds per capita. "To create more institutions will not help. We do not need here in Holland forty or fifty hospices. We need a new way of thinking. We need thirty to fifty consultants on palliative care who can work with the doctors in the community, visit patients in their homes. We need university training programs to teach the advanced methods of pain and symptom control."

Other doctors, even those who favour euthanasia, agree there is always room for improvement in care of the dying. Dr. Paul van der Maas notes that in the last three years, however, pain teams have been set up in every regional hospital and cancer centre in the Netherlands, and pain research now receives designated funding in the health budget, in addition to a comprehensive brochure on pain management having been sent to every physician. Home nursing care is available to all citizens. "I believe this is evidence that care of the dying is getting better in the Netherlands, both as a result of and in conjunction with the availability of euthanasia," Dr. van der Maas said.

Still, Zylicz's dream is that in ten years there will be enough palliative care consultants all over Holland that one will be able to go at any moment to a patient's home, or into a nursing home to ensure optimal care. Despite his opposition to euthanasia, Zylicz said "nearly all" of dying patients coming to the hospice want to talk to him about the prospect of euthanasia. Like Gootjes, he welcomes the discussion. "Euthanasia is not new. It happens everywhere. I think it is important that only in Holland can you talk freely with patients and doctors about it. Nowhere else in the world can you talk so openly and honestly. I think that is good." Zylicz encourages patients to talk about euthanasia, particularly because it helps him put his finger on the patient's fears, concerns and problems, which then helps him better meet their needs.

A case in point, he says, is a woman dying of colon cancer who on her first day in the hospice presented him with a signed and witnessed declaration wanting euthanasia. "I said, 'Okay, let's talk about this, why did you do this'" More than thirty years earlier her father had been dying of the same disease and he suffered horrible pain. The woman and her sister had begged his doctor to give him more morphine, but the doctor refused because it would kill him. She never wanted to be in the same situation. Zylicz promised he would sign a document assuring her he would never deny her pain relief. She has stayed, happy and pain free, with no subsequent request for euthanasia.

While euthanasia will never be conducted on the premises of Rozenheuvel, the patient is free to leave at any time if the care does not meet his or her needs. "I am under no illusion that I can prevent every case of euthanasia. But if we try to prevent most of them we can look and see what is left over. I'm experienced enough to say that some are so complicated and some so horrible. There will be some failures. Perhaps it will be 1 or 2 per cent. I don't know." Zylicz said it is against his conscience to refer such a patient to a colleague who will perform euthanasia, but because the family doctor is in charge, he won't have to refer. It will be up to the family doctor. It is clear, that to Zylicz, such a case would be a personal failure, but to the patient and their family, I am not so sure. It strikes me that in the scheme of dying it is the best of all worlds. A dedicated palliative care physician and his staff will do whatever they can to keep me comfortable until my final days, but if they are unsuccessful, then I can return to my family doctor for euthanasia. I like the sound of that.

To me, the existence of Hospice Rozenheuvel, Stichting Kuria, and other emerging hospices, of individuals who carry living wills saying "no euthanasia" working side-by-side with others who say they want the option, all seem to belie the criticism that in a land of euthanasia, choices for the dying are becoming increasingly limited. If anything, choices seem to be getting better year by year in the Netherlands. Individual patients are increasingly offered a plurality of choice, simply by the divergence of opinion.

Despite the existence of problems, the Dutch seem to be the only ones in the world right now able to openly and systematically discuss these complex issues of medical decisions at the end of life. It strikes me that the Netherlands is not sliding down the "slippery slope," but step by step it is attempting to climb its way to a place where the rights of individual patients, the role of the medical profession, and the needs of society are on an even footing. Other countries are just beginning the climb.

6

MEDICINE
IN TURMOIL

T HE BALLROOM of the Radisson Hotel in Calgary
was filled with doctors from across Canada, gathered for the
annual general meeting of the Canadian Medical Association. It
was August 1993, and the topic of discussion before the General
Council was euthanasia. What policy should be adopted by
Canada's foremost medical organization on this divisive issue?
With Sue Rodriguez's petition before the Supreme Court of
Canada, the issue intensifying more each day, the ethics committee of the association that represents some 45,000 doctors
across Canada needed direction from its members. One after
another, physicians approached the microphones placed
throughout the ballroom and addressed the head table with
grand pronouncements: "We must stick to our principles of
healing and not become killers," said one. "We must not bow
to pressure groups who are peddling state-sanctioned death,"
urged another. "Remember doctors' role in Nazi Germany!"
warned a third.

Toronto physician Ted Boadway couldn't believe his ears.
He was sitting with a group of physicians to one side of the
room, listening with amazement. Moments earlier the association had released the results of a survey stating that 60 per cent

of Canadian doctors, given the cloak of anonymity, had responded that they wanted some liberalization of the law to allow euthanasia or assisted suicide under specific conditions. No one, however, was saying so at this meeting of their peers. "It seemed so unreal. It was this grand session of denial. No one was getting up and telling the truth," Boadway recalls. In the whispered discussion with colleagues around him, Boadway knew it was unlikely anyone was going to stand up and present an opposite point of view. He looked around the room and could see that almost all were practising doctors. With a law on the books that threatens up to fourteen years in prison for anyone assisting suicide, with euthanasia defined as murder, with medical disciplinary boards across the country set to investigate any medically suspicious deaths, what physician in his or her right mind would risk everything by being honest? It was up to him. A general practitioner for thirteen years, Boadway had left his practice ten years earlier to become director of health policy for the Ontario Medical Association (OMA). He was no longer actively involved in seeing patients and thus was far enough removed that he could speak openly. He'd not prepared his words; he just took his place behind the microphone.

"As a profession we need to adopt guidelines and policy. The reality is that this is already happening in Canada and happening on a daily basis, with no records, no discussion, no consultation, no direction, no guidance and no comfort to the public or the profession that it's being done well or correctly." The journalists in the room suddenly took notice of this forty-eight-year-old physician across the room at the far microphone. Canadian doctors in the past had spoken in favour of medically assisted death, but Boadway, as part of the OMA, was the first doctor from the medical hierarchy to acknowledge the practice in Canada. "It is occurring entirely underground. These doctors are operating in fear, in great anxiety, experiencing great moral angst in their own hearts about what they are doing."

When the session broke, Boadway was swamped by journalists putting microphones in his face: "Dr. Boadway, have you ever practised euthanasia?" He refused to say. "If it is happening, why won't doctors go public?" "No one wants to be a test case. It is career destroying, personally destroying. Doctors who have been involved are not prepared to talk about it," he replied. The whole episode left Boadway somewhat amazed; first, because the media called his comments a "bombshell" and featured them for the next twenty-four hours in news reports; and then colleagues in the medical profession reacted to his statement in a pendulum swing of emotions over the next weeks and months.

"I was stunned. A number of doctors in the medical power structure — well known names that you would recognize — quietly told me 'Thank God you said something.' And I was completely taken aback by the ferocity with which some other doctors attacked me, the hostility. They were rabid in their invectives." Some doctors in the medical hierarchy warned him that it would be wise if he just kept quiet about the whole issue. Most startling to Boadway, however, was that almost everywhere he went in the next few years, doctors and nurses would cautiously seek him out to tell him they had done it, or knew colleagues who had. They seemed eager to disclose to him their own personal stories of medically assisted death. "Since I spoke out about assisted suicide, I cannot stop people from talking to me about it, physicians and nurses,'" Boadway told the Special Senate Committee. "I deliberately try to avoid learning anything about the circumstances of the case because I don't want to know. However, I can tell you that it is constant." The senators seemed a bit sceptical: Why, they asked, do some doctors adamantly maintain it isn't happening in Canada and you tell us that it happens all the time?

To Boadway the answer was clear. Disclosing information about euthanasia seems similar to what happens when individuals disclose anything about any taboo issue: they first test the potential person to whom they are disclosing the matter for safety. When Boadway spoke at a medical society meeting in an Ontario community in 1994, for example, one of the community's more prominent doctors berated him for his comments on the frequency of euthanasia and asserted: "Euthanasia or assisted suicide never happens here . . . I would know, people would tell me." But after the meeting six separate physicians approached Boadway and said "We would never disclose to him."

Nowhere is the issue of physician-assisted suicide and euthanasia more controversial than within the medical profession itself. Not a month goes by where there isn't a medical journal somewhere in Canada, Britain or the U.S., publishing an impassioned letter, editorial, commentary or survey promoting or opposing the options. Medical associations around the world have been struggling to map out policy positions, causing rancorous debate among their members. That turmoil is understandable. Doctors as a group are being asked to be agents of an easy death — to write the prescriptions that an individual takes to commit suicide, to give the injection that eases the passage of death — yet many doctors aren't even sure they want the job. The medical profession is full of questions about what would happen to the ethos of the profession, to the emotional lives of individual doctors, to the doctor-patient relationship if they openly had the ability to help their patients die. Would their role as healers be undermined? Would the search for cures and treatments for terminal illnesses lose their urgency? Would the process of ending life dehumanize and numb individual doctors to their patients' pain and suffering? Or would it make them more compassionate? Would patients' trust of doctors be enhanced or diminished should doctors usher in death as part of their job description?

Some doctors, like British Columbia's Scott Wallace, a former provincial politician as well as a family physician, point out that the medical profession ushers in death hundreds of times a day in Canada by actions such as turning off respirators or giving high doses of narcotics to relieve pain and symptoms, which as a side effect may hasten death. These actions, referred to ten years ago as "passive euthanasia" by the medical profession, now receive philosophical support from doctors in most western countries and are called good medical care. Yet a deliberate injection or fatal prescription is denied. "What was the difference between Nancy B. and Sue Rodriguez?" Wallace asks. "Both were women who found their lives to be intolerable and meaningless. Both wanted to die. Nancy B. could have lived for ten years or more on her respirator yet she had the right to have the respirator removed but Sue Rodriguez had nothing to turn off and no right to help. We say one is good medical care and the other is murder. If you ask me it is a bunch of meaningless, philosophical hair-splitting. It is hypocrisy."

The key, according to the medical profession and the law, is the intent behind the actions. The intent behind withdrawing treatment is to remove burdensome medical technology when there is no hope, or to honour a patient's right to refuse medical treatment, letting "nature take its course." The intent behind giving high doses of pain medication is to kill the pain, not the patient, although that may happen, too, because morphine depresses respiration. Many doctors, who oppose euthanasia, acknowledged in interviews with me that they had used morphine "very liberally," to help some dying patients in extreme distress have an easier death. "The medical culture has developed a prevailing mythology that giving high doses of morphine or removing treatment at the end of life is not killing, even though the patient dies as a result, and hence not subject to moral or legal censure," observes Utah philosopher Margaret Battin.

While medical ethicists had been discussing the pros and cons of physicians intentionally assisting a patient's death for

years, the issue for mainstream medicine first emerged into prominence in the winter of 1988 when the *Journal of the American
Medical Association* printed an anonymous letter from a gyne-
cology resident entitled "It's Over, Debbie." It was the account
of a sleepy resident, awakened one night to go to the bedside of
a young woman who was dying of ovarian cancer and who
couldn't sleep for pain and breathlessness. The resident had
never seen her before, and quickly looked at her chart. "Let's get
this over with," Debbie says obliquely, as her mother holds her
hand. The resident deliberately draws up an overdose of morphine and says, "This will let you rest." After the shot, Debbie
closes her eyes, her strained breathing eases, and she dies a few
minutes later.

The story caused nothing less than a sensation. It was the first
time anything like it had appeared in a peer-reviewed medical
journal and the reaction was swift and thunderous. All major
media picked up the story, many of them trying to find the
anonymous doctor or the family of the woman. The public
prosecutor, too, attempted to track down the players in an
intense investigation. Hundreds of letters poured into the journal, the overwhelming majority of them condemning the doctor
for his actions. Even right-to-die groups, like the Hemlock
Society, were appalled by the case because to them it represented
everything the society did *not* want to see occur with legalized
euthanasia: a doctor with no previous relationship with a patient,
hastily and sleepily examines her chart, hears an ambiguous
request which he does not clarify, and makes the decision to end
her life without any consultation with her, her mother or
another physician. Then he uses a euphemism to disguise what
he is actually doing. "The case of Debbie was simply the illegal
and unethical killing of a patient by a resident physician," one
Hemlock director noted.

Even the journal came under attack for giving the letter its
forum, but the editor defended his decision to run the sensational

piece. "Such discussions should not be confined to whispers in doctors' dressing rooms and hallways. . . . The debate needs to be brought into the open." "It's Over, Debbie" did indeed stimulate debate among the medical profession — the letter marks the beginning of a constant stream of articles and opinion pieces that still hasn't ceased.

"Doctors Must Not Kill!" was the title of one of the more persuasive and most frequently cited pieces in response to "Debbie." It was penned by four prominent U.S. physicians and ethicists: Willard Gaylin, Edmund Pellegrino, Mark Seigler and Leon Kass. In it they stated that "the very soul of medicine" is on trial over the issue of assisted suicide and euthanasia:

> This issue touches medicine at its moral center; if this moral center collapses and, if physicians become killers or are even licensed to kill, the profession — and therewith each physician — will never again be worthy of trust and respect as healer and comforter and protector of life in all its frailty.

Others, such as U.S. philosopher Dan Brock, countered that the quartet had it all wrong: at the moral centre of medicine should be two values — respecting patients' self-determination and promoting their well-being — not preserving lives that don't want to be preserved. To put more emphasis on the physicians' role as the guardians of life than on their role as agents of their patients' self-determination and well-being, is like saying, "we respect your life, but we do not respect you."

The impact on patient trust, raised in "Doctors Must Not Kill!" became another recurring theme in the medical literature against assisted death, with many doctors using the same image, even the same quotation, to describe what they feared might occur: "When a doctor comes to the bedside to give them a needle for their pain, patients won't know whether it is to temporarily relieve their suffering or to permanently put them out of their misery." That, too, was countered by others in the medical profession who saw the opposite as likely to occur: patients' trust of doctors would be enhanced if they felt a doctor would openly talk about and honour a wish to die. A study underway by Yale surgeon Charles McKhann is showing precisely that result — patients' trust improves when they feel a physician is open to being approached on assisted suicide.

Yet another objection raised to allowing the medical profession to be agents of voluntary death is the Hippocratic Oath, which states, in part, "I will give no deadly medicine to anyone if asked, nor suggest any such counsel." Critics of that stance, however, say doctors hide behind the 2,400-year-old creed and fail to take the whole oath in context and in its original form, which ordered doctors not to perform abortions, not to perform surgery for kidney stones and not to accept payment for teaching medicine — provisions that have all been dispensed with over the years. In the world of twentieth-century med-icine, with its transplants, chemotherapies, respirators and intensive care units, not only is the oath largely outdated, many medical school graduates in North America no longer even take it.

Other obstacles to the medical profession's acceptance of assisted dying are the profession's highly conservative nature, and its tendency to deny death or see death as a foe to be defeated. According to Dr. Sherwin Nuland, author of the best-selling book, *How We Die*, studies indicate that, of all the professions, medicine is the one most likely to attract people with high personal anxieties about dying. This can lead to denial of death, the over-use of medical technology to stave off death and, when technology fails, the abandonment of the patient in the final weeks or days when the doctor can no longer offer hope or cure. Says Nuland: "We become doctors because our ability to cure gives us power over the death of which we are so afraid and loss of that power poses such a significant threat that we must turn away from it and therefore from the patient who personifies our weakness." Since many in the medical profession see death as the enemy, it is little wonder there is palpable reluctance among many doctors to add assisting death to their job description.

According to Dr. David Roy, director of the Centre for Bioethics at the Clinical Research Institute of Montreal, many excellent physicians are totally hopeless at communicating with dying patients. "It is difficult to carry on a conversation with people to find out where the loneliness is, the hurt, the guilt, the brokenness. To give these doctors legal and social authority to administer death when they do not know how to talk to their patients seems to be a terribly unwise thing to do." Nevertheless, it is the medical profession, more than any other group in society — even more than politicians, judges, lawyers and the general public — who will hold sway on the issue of assisted death in coming years. It is the medical profession's attitude towards the act — whether an agreement is reached that at times it can be medically justified, whether doctors who admit openly to doing it face condemnation or acceptance — which will determine whether or not euthanasia or assisted suicide become options available to suffering patients.

"Until the medical profession gets behind the concept of patient choice in dying, it isn't going to happen," says Dr. Colin Brewer of London, England. That observation is borne out by the experience in the Netherlands. It was Dutch doctors who took the lead on the issue, not the legislators nor the public. The Royal Dutch Medical Association is the only medical body in the world that accepts such practices provided their guidelines are followed. The question is whether the other leading medical associations in years to come will gradually grow to accept the idea that it is proper and professional to end a patient's life when the patient is experiencing unrelieved suffering and clearly and repeatedly asks to die.

For many years the issue and the debate about assisted death within the medical profession has been largely academic. Of course, doctors in the past were known to speed a patient's death, with or without the patient's consent. Sometimes doctors would simply leave a bottle of sleeping pills or extra morphine with the family of a patient during the course of a particularly difficult death, saying obliquely: "This is to help Joe sleep, but be careful, if he takes too much — forty pills would be too much — it could kill him." The next morning or a few days later Joe would be dead, the bottle of pills out of sight, with the family not saying nor the doctor asking what actually happened. Some doctors were more blunt, albeit to a select audience. Ted Boadway remembers as a medical student in the late 1960s a respected clinician taking the young physicians aside on rounds after they'd been at the bedside of a young man dying of Lou Gehrig's disease. "He said, 'You may need to know how to help someone die someday,' and then he told us how to do it. I was absolutely floored. But I will never forget it."

No doctor, however, was openly acknowledging that he had helped a patient to die or was broadcasting to the public that he would do so. Then, in the late 1980s, a pathologist from Royal Oak, Michigan, started making the rounds of talk shows with a machine he called the "Mercitron" — a contraption that allowed patients to press a button to administer a deadly drug. Dr. Jack Kevorkian, for the general public, dramatically focused attention on right-to-die issues, acting as lightning rod for public dissatisfaction with the medical management of death. "The medical profession leads you to the door of death and then drops you off there. Dr. Kevorkian is willing to help you through the door," said Ron Adkins, the husband of Kevorkian's first patient, Janet Adkins. She was just fifty-six and newly diagnosed with Alzheimer's disease when he helped her to die in June of 1990.

While the general public has increasingly viewed Kevorkian

as a hero, the renegade doctor has had no credibility with the medical profession. As a pathologist, Kevorkian's life was in the lab, not dealing directly with patients. Throughout his career he'd been associated with bizarre ideas and obsessions, advocating that prisoners on death row be used for medical experiments or organ transplants; trying to take photographs of individuals at the time of their deaths to see whether there was any similarity in the look in their eyes; creating ghoulish, surreal paintings with titles like "Genocide" or "Death" using his own blood to paint the frames. By the 1980s, Kevorkian was seen as being so weird that no hospital would allow him on their staff. Even when the numbers of individuals Kevorkian had assisted began to steadily climb into the twenties, the medical profession refused to view him as anything but a macabre joke. He hardly posed a challenge to the views of mainstream medicine about a physician's role in openly assisting death.

Then, in March of 1991, a respected Rochester physician named Timothy Quill wrote in *The New England Journal of Medicine* about his agonized decision to give a long-time patient, who was dying of leukemia, a prescription of barbiturates with which she ended her life. The refined and judicious Quill was as different from Kevorkian as a glass of fine burgundy is from a shot of moonshine. Quill was well-versed in palliative care as a former director of the local hospice. He was an associate professor of medicine and psychiatry at the University of Rochester School of Medicine. He advocated end-of-life decisions made in the context of a long-term doctor-patient relationship, in which all options have been weighed, as opposed to Kevorkian's quickie "death on demand." His patient "Diane" was a forty-four-year-old woman who had overcome a number of hardships in her life. When she was told by the doctors that there was a 25 per cent chance that extensive chemotherapy could cure her leukemia, the odds weren't good enough for her when weighed against the rigours of the therapy. Quill first tried to convince her to attempt the treatment, but she continually refused and Quill grew to respect her choice. A few weeks later she phoned him asking for barbiturates "to help her sleep," but he knew that the drugs were the essential ingredient in a *Final Exit* suicide. He asked her to come into the office, where they had a long and open discussion. Quill became convinced that she was not despondent nor overwhelmed by her situation. He made her promise that before she used the drugs she would meet with him to ensure all avenues had been exhausted. "I wrote the prescription with an uneasy feeling about the boundaries I was exploring — spiritual, legal, professional and personal," he wrote in the *NEJM* article. "Yet I also felt strongly that I was setting her free to get the most out of the time she had left, and to maintain dignity and control on her own terms until her death." Three months later Diane used the drugs to have a peaceful death.

Quill wrote and published the article about Diane, he says, as a challenge to the medical profession to take a more personal, in-depth look at end-of-life suffering. "Previously published cases were either anonymous or so extreme, like Kevorkian, that they could be easily dismissed by the medical profession. . . . But as a physician established in the academic mainstream of medicine, I believed my presentation of a real experience could not be so easily dismissed." He was right. The medical profession didn't dismiss it — Quill's article set off a whole new round of debate in the medical press. But the general public and the legal system didn't ignore it either. The column precipitated a personal nightmare for Quill in which he was threatened with the loss of his medical licence, loss of his career, criminal charges and jail. He was hounded by journalists and law enforcement officials who both eventually found the real identity of Diane and then hassled her family. Diane's body was exhumed and an autopsy performed, causing grief to her family. The university and state licensing board conducted their own investigations which hung over Quill's head for months. Criminal charges were considered against him ranging from tampering with public records for the false declaration on her death certificate to manslaughter for causing her death. Quill was brought before a Grand Jury to see whether there was enough evidence against him to warrant charges and a trial. The Grand Jury, however, refused to indict him. "I don't understand," one of the jury members said to him, truly perplexed. "Is your crime that you helped a patient die, or that you wrote about it?"

When he emerged from the crucible almost a year later he had obtained the status of a medical hero. He received more than 2,000 letters from patients and doctors telling him their own stories, commending him for his courage and integrity. Quill has since proposed strict guidelines for physician-assisted suicide, written a book about choices in dying, and now speaks extensively on the medical lecture circuit about how doctors have to listen more to their patients and have to search creatively for the ways to really meet their dying patient's needs.

I spent a day with Quill in January, 1994 when he spoke to doctors in a Bronx, New York hospital, explained his own philosophy of care for the dying and listened to medical students as they presented their difficult cases of dying patients to him. "I have a reputation for helping people die," Quill tells the assembly of doctors at St. Barnabas Hospital, who sit with their arms crossed, stethoscopes around their necks and beepers clipped on their lab coat pockets. "But what I am really about is helping people find their own path, and to make their own decisions that are well-informed. I am willing to look at things with a very open mind." Quill's hour-long impassioned speech is illustrated with stories of dying patients for whom he has helped find paths as varied as hospice care, experimental therapy, cessation of treatment, opting for long-term sedation, or writing a fatal prescription with which a patient could actively end his or her life.

"Sometimes illness takes patients to places that really seem to be worse than death. And if they end up in a state like that, I think we have an obligation as physicians to help them find death." When a patient says to a doctor "I want to die, will you help?" it is both a statement and a query that must be independently understood and explored, says Quill. The doctor's initial response should not be a "yes" or "no" based on the assumption of what the patient is implying, rather the request needs to be acknowledged and explored. Quill recommends doctors say something like this: "Of course, I will try to help you, but first I need to understand your wish and your suffering, and then we can explore how I can help. What is the worst part? What is your biggest fear?"

Quill urges the doctors to struggle every day with the difficult dilemmas in high-tech medicine, to not abandon their patients, but to work with them to the end, and to constantly ask themselves whether they are advocating what is truly best for their patient. "I think the profession of medicine is being undermined by the fact that we are fearful of addressing assisted death in the open, that we pretend that it doesn't exist," Quill said. "We say that there is something wrong with patients that they should want that kind of an option. And, most importantly, the people who are suffering the most we are leaving alone, abandoning them, which I think is a fundamental violation of our duties."

Still, not everyone in the medical profession is receptive to Quill's message. While many of the young doctors at St. Barnabas nod their heads in apparent agreement, many of the senior doctors in the audience pepper him with hostile questions: "What if somebody just says: 'I'm getting old, and life's a bitch, and I don't have any money, and I don't want to eat.' Then they have an incurable condition of starvation — would you help *them* die?" challenges one. Replies Quill, "There is no obligation to assist, but there should be a right to ask. What I have to have,

personally, to assist somebody, is a clear, unequivocal understanding of their condition, and why they find it intolerable,
and what the other choices are and why they reject them. So I
would enter into a long relationship with that elderly person."

When Quill steps down from the podium, medical students
and residents gather around him, eager to ask him questions.
They tell him their stories of challenging and complex cases,
asking his advice. It is clear that Quill is putting a respectable
face on physician assistance with death, to let patients know that
there are physicians out there who will help them, who will listen to them, who won't abandon them in their dying no matter
where it takes them. For dying patients, however, finding such
a physician in their time of need can be impossible.

During the August week in 1993 that Ted Boadway was standing before the Canadian Medical Association in Calgary, and
Tim Quill's eloquent and thoughtful essay "Doctor I want to
die. Will you help me?" appeared in the *Journal of the American
Medical Association*, Doug Miller was in Victoria, madly putting
the finishing touches on a research paper that was the culmina-
tion of the last four years of his life. The forty-year-old scientist
had no idea that in only a few months he and his wife would be
desperately seeking a compassionate, understanding physician
who would help him to die. The research paper was a mathe-
matical model of the visual cortex of the brain — a seminal
work in the study of artificial intelligence, Doug's area of expertise. The work was considered brilliant. Now, he was being
invited to present his paper during the last week of August to an
elite group of scientists in Woods Hole, Massachusetts.

He'd been too busy to pay much attention to his health,
working as he was night and day on the paper. He had always
been fit and healthy anyway, with never any notable sickness
or injury save for a broken leg, years ago while skiing, and a
bout of haemorrhoids two years earlier. But in the last month

he'd been experiencing painful bowel movements. "It feels like a lobster is grabbing my ass with its claws," he told his wife, Louise. Neither of them worried about it much — he was too healthy. He ate right and exercised. Just two months earlier he had been climbing mountains in the Olympic Peninsula of Washington State. It was probably just haemorrhoids again. If it still bothered him when he got back from Woods Hole, he'd see a doctor. Working on the paper he put almost everything else on hold — everything, that is, except Louise. He always had time for her, even when she would come up behind him as he was deep in concentration at the computer, putting her arms around his neck in a big hug. "Want a break?" she'd say. "I'd love one. Just let me finish this paragraph," he'd respond. And then they'd go for a walk along the ocean bluffs of Dallas Road near their small apartment, or make love, or go cycling.

From the moment they'd met, almost six years earlier in Berkeley where Doug had completed his Ph.D., they'd felt they belonged together despite their disparate backgrounds. He was a shy New York Jew, a bit reserved, but with a keen sense of humour and a strong will that pushed him to excel. Louise was petite, voluble and intense, a bilingual French Canadian who wore her emotions on her sleeve. When they had met, Louise was thirty-nine and she had almost given up hope of ever finding her soulmate, until he appeared in the form of Doug, loaning her his computer through a friend. Six months later, they were married. When their wedding photos came back, they were delighted at how in each picture their expressions and gestures matched, tilted head for tilted head, wry smile for wry smile. Here was photographic evidence, they laughed, of their inherent harmony.

After Berkeley they moved to Montreal, where Doug took up post-doctoral research in artificial intelligence. A few years later, Louise landed a job that meant she had to move to Victoria while Doug stayed behind to finish his research work and fulfil his contract as a sessional lecturer at McGill University. They'd spent $10,000 in airfare flying back and forth to visit during that year. Now that he had moved permanently, just three months earlier, they were revelling in simply being together again.

Doug was pleased with his Woods Hole presentation, but a week later when he returned to Victoria his bowel pain had not diminished. He booked an appointment with a physician. During the check-up, Doug mentioned that his father had been diagnosed with colon cancer at age sixty-eight and successfully treated with surgery ten years earlier. "Hmmmm," said the doctor. "At your age, it probably is just haemorrhoids but I'm going to book you for a colonoscopy to make sure." On the couple's fifth wedding anniversary, September 27, 1993, Doug spent the day fasting and taking laxatives. The next day a fibre-optic tube was threaded through his colon so doctors could view the inner surface of the intestinal walls. When he awoke from the sedative, the radiologist showed the couple the tunnel-like pictures. "Here's what healthy tissue looks like," he said, showing the shiny pink, elastic walls of the large intestine. "And here's the spot that concerns us." It was a purple and yellow oozing mass of ulceration. "What is it?" they asked. "It is probably cancer," the radiologist said.

The definitive diagnosis came two days later with the pathology report: invasive carcinoma of the rectum. It was the same day that the Supreme Court of Canada brought down the decision on Sue Rodriguez, but Doug and Louise's world was spinning too fast for them to even notice. In less than a month they had gone from blissful happiness to the devastation of cancer. They felt like they were drowning in the flood of emotion, of medical information, of decisions and change, of powerlessness. Doug was sent for an ultrasound test to find out if the cancer had metastasized to other organs. To the couple's relief, the test results were negative. The tumour, they were told, would be excised in surgery, but its placement meant there would be a permanent colostomy with abdominal-perineal resection — meaning Doug's body waste would hence be excreted into a bag hung on the outside of his abdomen. That news in itself was a devastating shock, an assault on Doug's body image. Also devastating was the high risk of impotence from the operation — overwhelming news for a young couple whose physical relationship had always been treasured.

The day before the operation at the end of October, Doug and Louise sat in the oncologist's office as the doctor went over the statistics about what might be found during surgery. If the tumour was just local, the colostomy would be all that was needed and there was an 80 per cent chance of survival five years later. If the tumour had invaded neighbouring tissue through the intestinal wall, radiation would be added and five-year survival fell to 60 per cent or less. If even a microscopic cancer cell was found in the lymph nodes, then both chemotherapy and radiation would be needed along with the surgical excision and his chance of five-year survival would then fall to 40 per cent. Since the ultrasound test results had been negative, the doctor didn't raise the possibility of a fourth scenario — terminal cancer that had metastasized to other organs. "To us, the worst it could get was needing chemotherapy," recalls Louise.

On the day of the operation, Louise went to work, feeling that she would go crazy if she paced the halls for the four hours or more that Doug would be under anaesthetic. It was almost five hours after the start of the surgery when Louise received a call from the surgeon. Louise believes he must have been deeply shaken by what he had found and therefore had not rehearsed what he would say: "We've done the colostomy and that went fine. However, Doug has a tumour the size of a baseball in the middle of his liver and it's inoperable." "Does that mean he'll need chemotherapy?" asked Louise, her voice trembling. "Well . . . No, in these cases we don't bother." *Don't bother! Don't bother!* When Louise hung up the phone, she staggered from her desk. Her husband, not yet middle-aged, was dying! Her cries of anguish brought colleagues running down the hall. All her hopes and dreams for the future, all their plans, even the simple pleasure of being together were crashing down around her.

As Doug awoke from surgery, Louise was at his bedside, her face tear-streaked, red and puffy. She broke the news to him that his belly was full of cancer. Doug was clear and determined. "I won't go through the final stages. I will commit suicide," he said. When Louise called Doug's relatives and friends later that day with the devastating news, one relative, a retired pediatrician who had been very close to Doug all his life, had the same reaction. "Start stockpiling barbiturates," he told her. "When the time comes, you'll know what to do."

During the hearings of the Special Senate Committee on Euthanasia and Assisted Suicide, Senator Wilbert Keon, a cardiovascular surgeon and head of the Ottawa Heart Institute, expressed an opinion that many doctors share: "What bewilders me about the request for euthanasia is that if a person really does want to die, it is not a complicated act. They simply have to stop eating and drinking and make themselves comfortable with sedation. They will not be around for very long . . . Why do these patients want someone else to take them out?" It was a comment that shocked many advocates of a peaceful, medically assisted death, and one that Keon explained, in later hearings, he hadn't intended to sound callous or unfeeling.

Keon, however, did put his finger on an issue that bothers many in the medical profession: the public is asking doctors to shoulder the responsibility for the profound decision of ending a life. The overwhelming reaction of many doctors to patient demands for an assisted death is "do what you like, but leave me out of it." Vancouver palliative care physician, Dr. Jacqueline Fraser told me: "I believe if someone wants to commit suicide she has a right to do it, but she doesn't have a right to ask me to perform it." Dr. Allison Ferg, my own family doctor whose open, consultative and respectful patient manner drew me to her practice, expressed the same dilemma: "Philosophically, I really support the idea that individuals should be able to make a choice about the timing of their death. But I just don't know whether I, as the doctor, could be the one to do it. Emotionally I would find it so difficult, to end a life. And with the law the way it is, it puts me and my family at risk. I could lose my licence, I could ruin my career, I could go to jail. I could destroy my family. The risk is just too great."

To many doctors it is ironic that the increasing call for euthanasia and assisted suicide is being fostered, in part, by patient backlash against modern medicine and yet euthanasia and assisted suicide are themselves a medicalization of death. Patients, frustrated and disillusioned with the way the medical profession handles death, nevertheless want members of the medical profession to be the ones to kill them. However, doctors in favour of assisted death argue that physicians have a duty not to walk away from patient's needs when modern medicine has, in large part, set them up for an unacceptable way of dying. "Walking away, denying that medicine can do anything to help in the patient's plight, is an immoral abrogation of medical power, especially in cases in which the prior exercise of the medical craft has extended the patient's life and resulted in the complications that have brought the patient to the present state of suffering," says U.S. ethicist Dr. Howard Brody.

Nevertheless, the medical reluctance to be involved led members of the Canadian Medical Association in August of 1994 to propose a different resolution than the one put forward by the CMA ethics committee. The ethics committee, after more than a year of in-depth work that included producing an excellent set of background papers explaining the options, submitted a proposal to delegates at the CMA annual general meeting suggesting the CMA remain neutral on the issues and let doctors act according to their own conscience. Less than 200 of CMA's 45,000 members voted, but the proposal was rejected. Instead delegates passed their own resolution, ninety-three to seventy-four, stating "doctors should specifically exclude participation in euthanasia and assisted suicide." Dr. Daniel MacCarthy, a West Vancouver doctor who proposed the resolution said: "Legislators cannot proceed with granting it or legalizing it under the assumption that physicians will participate."

Do doctors really need to be involved or could euthanasia and assisted suicide be done without them? That question has been pondered by many in the bioethics field and their conclusion seems to be yes, it could be done by others. Just look at Kevorkian — he lost his medical licence and his ability to prescribe drugs after his third assisted death. Technically he is no longer a doctor, yet that hasn't stopped him from rigging a can of carbon monoxide to a mask to help upwards of twenty more people die. Some maintain it should be anybody but the physician so that medical power is not misused — a pastor, a friend, a loved one. In Germany, for example, assisted suicide is legal as long as the person committing suicide is capable of expressing control over his or her actions and is acting freely. Physicians, however, are forbidden from being involved in such acts because the law imposes a duty on them to intervene. A physician can give a prescription for a lethal drug, but once the patient is unconscious, there is an obligation to rescue the suicide in progress. Most ethicists, however, believe that for acts of euthanasia or assisted suicide to be delivered safely, effectively and with quality control, the medical profession must be involved. Doctors have experience assessing competency and impaired judgement, detecting and treating depression, and knowing the other medical options open to the patient. Without their involvement, there is the risk patients may be inadequately informed of their disease and its outcome, and the method used to take their life may be unreliable or inappropriate. This is the view of the Royal Dutch Medical Association. The act of giving a patient a fatal injection, providing a patient with a fatal dose of a drug to take themselves, or deciding to withhold or withdraw treatment must be "emphatically restricted to the physician," the RDMA maintains, "because the physician is the only person capable of answering the questions so crucial to a careful decision process." Those questions include the correct diagnosis and prognosis, the competency of the patient to make a decision, the level of suffering and the availability of alternatives.

In addition, the medical profession is a self-regulating group, with a code of ethics and proscribed behaviour. It is able to set standards, and enforce them through peer pressure and peer review, that would effectively require all physicians to comply with guidelines in the practice of euthanasia or assisted suicide. There is a practical reason, too, why physicians should be involved: they have a relative monopoly on the prescription pad. Medical doctors, along with dentists and veterinarians, are the only people who have access to the pharmaceuticals that can provide an easy death. While it is possible for individuals to kill themselves by other means, jumping off buildings and bridges or shooting themselves, those methods are violent and may traumatize others.

Proposing death by starvation has become a common medical response to the public's calls for assisted suicide and euthanasia. The very week that Keon made his comments in the Senate Committee hearings, a U.S. physician, Dr. David Eddy had described in the *Journal of the American Medical Association* the death of his ailing mother, who made the conscious choice to stop eating and drinking on her eighty-fifth birthday, and died six days later. "Without hoarding pills, without making me a criminal, without putting a bag over her head, and without huddling in a van with a carbon monoxide machine, she had found a way to bring her life gracefully to a close," Eddy wrote.

Starving may indeed be an option for patients who lose their appetite during the dying process, but many terminally ill people retain their appetite. Starvation, for them, may take weeks to lead to death and can be agonizing in the process. "I had a patient, who was over 240 pounds with chronic emphysema, who had a huge need for food," says Marilynne Seguin, a former nurse who is the executive director of Toronto's Dying With Dignity. "I had another patient with AIDS who called me in tears after four days of starving because he had broken down and had a glass of orange juice." Nor does the medical profession always allow patients to stop eating. Quill recalls that one day on medical rounds, he counted five elderly, incompetent patients waiting for a feeding-tube placement because they had all stopped eating. "Nobody had asked whether these individuals would have wanted a feeding tube and whether giving them a feeding tube would have been in their best interests."

Doctors right now, with no change in the law, have the ability to write fatal prescriptions. Doing so, however, puts them at considerable risk of being caught. The prescribing doctor's name is on the bottle of any lethal drug and he or she must trust the patient to keep quiet about the assistance, or to maintain the cover that the pills were only intended to treat insomnia — or to arrange for disposal of the evidence after the death, but the dispensing pharmacy will also have record of the transaction, increasing the doctor's risk of being discovered. U.S. medical ethicist Kenneth Vaux notes that despite the inherent professional risks, many physicians acknowledge that they would defy the law to give their own spouse, one of their parents, or their own child a merciful death if they were suffering horribly. The fact that most physicians would give such a death to their loved ones, but deny it to their patients says something of the moral nature of the act, Vaux states. It shows there is at play an "exception ethic" physicians use so as to assess when personal risk is outweighed by the necessity to act. Besides having a doctor in the family, other conditions make it easier to obtain help in dying: being the patient of the same doctor for numerous years, having doctors as friends who know you in a social setting, or being wealthy and/or well-connected. Writer Andrew Solomon detailed in an elegant article in *The New Yorker* in 1995 the assisted suicide of his mother, a wealthy, educated society woman who had no trouble in finding sympathetic doctors to write the prescriptions. While no one has yet publicly stated that Jackie Kennedy Onassis had a physician-assisted death, the rumour mill in right-to-die circles started buzzing that she, too, had supportive physicians. She checked herself out of hospital when her chemotherapy for leukemia was failing and died the next day at home, with her family around her. Her son, John F. Kennedy Jr., seemed to allude to such an assisted death when, the following morning, he told the press outside his mother's apartment: "My mother died on her own time and on her own terms."

Unfortunately for Louise and Doug Miller they were not well-connected nor the long-term patients of a sympathetic doctor.

Doug didn't want to commit suicide right away, he simply wanted the comfort of knowing he could if the need arose. He wanted to have a peaceful, effective method on hand so he could escape before his dying process became too onerous. How would he do it? Who would they go to? Doug and Louise decided it would be up to Louise to do the research to find the method. The surgeon had told them Doug would probably have four to six months of relatively good health before the onset of his inevitable decline. They decided that when he recovered from the surgery, they would go to Israel. His job, then, was to concentrate on getting back his strength. Louise would do the leg work to obtain the necessary materials and information about assisted suicide so Doug could concentrate on living without having to plan his death.

"I was so naive," says Louise. "I thought all I had to do was ask a doctor for a prescription and a doctor would give it to me." She soon learned it wasn't going to be so simple. When she asked the family doctor outright, he declined. "I will make sure Doug is comfortable, but I could not possibly kill him and I can't know the two of you are planning a suicide." Louise was upfront and direct, not trying to veil her request or use deceit. She asked friends to refer her to doctors — no one knew anyone who would assist a patient they didn't know. She phoned right-to-die organizations, thinking they would have a list of doctors willing to help. Every avenue she tried proved a dead end. "I knew that it was illegal, but I assumed that, like abortion before it was decriminalized, there was an underground one could access. That so-and-so would know someone else, who would know someone else who would help you."

After Doug came home from hospital, there were regular visits from Victoria's Capital Regional District nurses and from home support workers, but Doug hated the continuous trooping in and out of people, a different person almost every day asking the same incessant questions, often in a patronizing tone: "How are your bowel movements? Did you remember to take your laxative? You really ought to take your morphine." Doug did not like to take the oral morphine he'd been prescribed. Both the pills and the syrup made him vomit. Besides, he didn't believe taking morphine was compatible with their travel plans to Israel so he was trying to wean himself completely from the medication. Louise remembers how he rankled at the way the health care workers treated him as if he were a child, not a mature adult with considerable intellect who happened to be dying. There were merciful exceptions, however, like the oncologist from the British Columbia Cancer Centre who sent them medical research papers, discussed options and statistics with them like equals, knowing that they were capable of understanding the scientific language and the complex issues.

Or the nurses from the Royal Jubilee Hospital's Enterostomal Therapy Centre who had a way of dealing with Doug with dignity and humanity despite their job of showing him how to clean and care for his stoma (the new opening into his intestine) and the bag of faeces that hung from his waist.

At the end of November, just five weeks after the operation, Doug was experiencing such high fevers that he had to change his T-shirts every couple of hours, they were so drenched with sweat. He was so weak he couldn't get up to urinate and he was bleeding through his perineal wound. Was an infection raging in his compromised body? He was re-admitted to hospital for CT scans, tests and massive IV doses of antibiotics. When the surgeon palpated his liver to feel for the tumour's growth, his jaw dropped. In less than five weeks the tumour had tripled in size. Metastases had spread to his lungs. It was only later that the couple learned the CT scan showed tumours growing in the lymph nodes at the top of Doug's legs. No one mentioned it to them at the time, perhaps believing there was no point in piling devastating news on top of devastating news. The hoped-for grace period of good health was not to be. A sub-cutaneous tube was attached to Doug's chest so he could receive morphine injections every four hours (or more often if necessary) without needing to have his skin pierced with a needle every time. In early December, Louise took leave from her job to take care of Doug at home.

For Louise, the emotional trauma of knowing her husband and love-of-her-life was dying was compounded by her emerging understanding that she was not the natural caregiver and nurse to Doug that she wanted to be. "Simple things like making meals and serving them to him, I found so difficult. Doug was always the cook in our relationship — I have always been hopeless in the kitchen. I felt totally incompetent looking after him. Nurses have training and at the end of a twelve-hour shift they go home exhausted. I had no training, my shift never ended, and I had a phenomenal emotional involvement with the patient I was tending." Yet, twenty-four hours a day, she cared for him at home, in part because Doug did not want strangers coming into their tiny apartment. The inherent harmony captured by the wedding photos, in sickness became a liability; she would cry when he cried, she would panic when he panicked, and feel nauseated when he was vomiting. Instead of being able to calm and comfort him, they mirrored each other's stress. With each passing day she was finding it harder to cope. She was exhausted from being Doug's primary caregiver, yet she was unable to sleep from her anxiety, worry and grief. At any moment she felt she would snap from her despair over seeing Doug die by inches before her eyes, from her exhaustion, from her feelings of inadequacy and from her fear of what lay ahead.

A colleague at work told Louise about palliative care, but Doug at first refused to have any part of it — that was for patients in the final stages, he said, not him. Louise told Doug about counselling services available to patients. Doug's response was: "The only kind of counselling I'm interested in is how to commit suicide. But if I bring this up with them, they'll just try to talk me out of it." Louise, however, began to attend support group meetings for the partners and families of terminally ill patients, but in a retirement city like Victoria, everyone there was twenty or thirty years her senior. The sessions only intensified her feelings of isolation, of the unfairness of Doug's diagnosis at such a young age, at her own impending loss. Adding to her stress was her inability to obtain a fatal prescription for Doug to have on hand. "With my emotional Gallic personality, I was the worst kind of person Doug could have had as an advocate — particularly in an Anglo-Saxon environment," Louise recounts. "The more desperate I became, the more intense I became, and the less co-operation I obtained. And the less co-operation I obtained, the more desperate I became. I was reacting to Doug's symptoms, but for them it wasn't his symptoms that were the problem, *I* was the problem."

From her years in the litigious U.S. she assumed that doctors' reluctance on this issue was simply fear of being sued by family members who didn't agree with the actions. For that reason she thought it would help their cause if doctors knew she was all in favour of Doug's suicide. Her eagerness only hurt her cause. "They saw the wife doing all the asking, making all the inquiries, doing all the pleading — as if I was the one who wanted my husband dead. From their eyes, I'm sure I looked like a crazy woman. Even if someone had been sympathetic to us, I can see now, why they wouldn't touch us with a ten-foot pole."

Louise turned to books like *Final Exit* and *Departing Drugs*. They suggested entering into a gentle subterfuge with a doctor or two. Go to your doctor, they counselled, and ask for something to help you sleep. The doctor will likely give you a prescription for one of the new generation of sleeping pills, like Ativan or Halcion. A week or two later, go back to the doctor and tell him or her they are not strong enough and ask, instead, for twenty capsules of the barbiturate, Seconal. A few weeks later return again and ask for another twenty, or go to another doctor, tell the same story and get the same prescription. Don't ever say what you are up to and the doctor will never ask, even if he or she has a good idea what you are doing. That way both of you are protected. When you have amassed forty capsules, you have enough. "I couldn't do it," says Louise. "I couldn't lie or pretend, or remain cool and collected. It just wasn't me. Besides, I didn't think we were expecting so much. We weren't requesting anyone to be present at the death; we were merely asking for a prescription."

They had rejected many of the seemingly "obvious" suicide methods because the possibility of a botched suicide terrified them. Violent means were out of the question because of the trauma it would create for others. Carbon monoxide poisoning

was out because they didn't have a car. An overdose of oral
morphine was rejected because Doug was afraid he would
vomit it; sub-cutaneous injections of morphine were imprac-
tical because the numerous shots and large doses meant Doug
could not do it without assistance. An intravenous drip of morphine might have worked — according to self-deliverance literature, intravenous injections can be effective with only one
tenth as much medication as is needed with sub-cutaneous
injections — but the couple lacked the equipment and the
technical know-how for proper intravenous administration.

Each day that passed, however, brought new symptoms.
Doug's belly was swelling with the growth of the cancer. In
mid-December, Doug began to experience terrifying panic
attacks that could last for thirty minutes or more, leaving him
quivering and crying, a shaking wreck. Sometimes he would
crawl along the floor of their apartment as if to escape his
anguish. Sometimes his panic would be fixated on the clock and
the slow passage of time: "Look at the time! Only five minutes
have passed! I can't take another minute!" The panic in his
voice would drive Louise into agitated helplessness and all she
could do would be to hold him as they both cried on the bed.
By the last week of December he began to talk of suicide more
urgently — not as an act that would be considered for the
future, but as something to be done now. He hadn't eaten any
solids for almost a week, he was only drinking fluids. On the
morning of December 29, 1993, when Louise was holding him
in her arms as he cried after another panic attack, he said, "I
can't stand it. I need out now."

Within the medical profession, a disagreement rages over
whether any desire to die can be ever be termed "rational." In
the medical model of suicide, which has arisen out of the specialty of psychiatry, suicidal thoughts and desires, no matter
what the individual circumstances, are always a symptom of

mental illness — untreated or unrecognized depression, deluded thought processes, or severe emotional distress. It is a circular argument: someone who wants to commit suicide must be mentally ill because only people who are severely disturbed would want to kill themselves. Suicide is always a desperate, tragic act, the theory goes, that might have been averted with proper medical attention. "Rational suicide is an oxymoronic statement," says Dr. Kathleen Foley, a neurologist and palliative care expert at New York's Sloan Kettering Cancer Center. "The data accumulated to date indicate that a significant percentage of patients, more than the majority, have significant psychiatric morbidity influencing their requests for death."

In the medical model of suicide those who are suicidal — the troubled teen, the stressed executive, the lonely senior, the terminally ill patient — all share the same background features: an inability to cope with their present situation, a loss of meaning in their lives, feelings of helplessness and hopelessness, and loss of any optimism that circumstances may improve in the future. It is this mode of thinking that has fostered the development of suicide prevention programs, the suicide crisis lines, and suicide counselling services that aim to get the suicidal person into care to treat the underlying depression and hopelessness. Rather than assisting terminally ill people with their wish to die, proponents of this theory claim that the medical profession should be trying to treat their depression, using good palliative care to treat pain and symptoms, and giving counselling and spiritual care to help deal with feelings of meaningless and helplessness. One of the leading U.S. advocates of this view is Dr. Herbert Hendin, a New York psychiatrist and the executive director of the American Suicide Foundation, who has recently turned his gaze to suicidal thoughts in euthanasia and assisted suicide. He believes that, at the root of all terminally ill individuals' desire for an earlier death, is actually a fear of death. The individual displaces the terror on to the conditions of dying, such as pain, loss of independence and loss of bodily functions. What the individual needs, Hendin states, is not a sympathetic physician to write a prescription, but one to help the patient deal with the fear of dying.

Those who support the validity of rational suicide, however, maintain there is a discernible difference between the angst-ridden suicide, which leaves surviving family and friends shaking their heads in grief and dismay, and a careful decision to leave life when the burden of living outweighs its benefits and to which family members usually agree. In a rational suicide the individual possesses a realistic assessment of the situation, the mental processes leading to his decision are unimpaired by psychological illness, and family, friends and uninvolved observers understand the reason behind it. Unlike irrational suicide, in which the feelings of hopelessness arise from delusional thinking, in rational suicide, the hopelessness is real, and everybody else believes the situation is hopeless, too. An increasing number of psychiatrists and medical professionals, even those who specialize in suicide prevention, are coming to believe that some suicides are indeed rational. One such psychiatrist is Dr. Hermann Pohlmeier, the founder of the German Association for Suicide Prevention and its president for seven years. Pohlmeier, a psychiatrist, has been conducting research into suicide, depression and suicide prevention since 1972. Yet in 1993, in a move that surprised his colleagues around the world, he became the head of the German Society for Humane Dying, a German right-to-die organization.

Sitting in his office at the Institute of Medical Psychology, which he heads, at the University of Gottingen, Pohlmeier described how someone like himself, who has devoted his life to the prevention of suicide, should suddenly head an organization devoted to choice in dying: "From my research in suicide I have found that not all suicides are products of mental illness. It is completely possible for a person to be well-informed, not depressed, and decide to leave life after assessing his options. It is an exercise of free will. The importance, for the medical profession, is to be able to determine the difference." No one argues that some terminally ill individuals do indeed become depressed — their sadness, grief and distress at their impending loss of life sends them into a clinical depression that *may* respond to treatment. Pohlmeier maintains that the key for the medical profession is to determine who can or cannot be helped to regain some meaning and enjoyment in life through the use of anti-depressants, counselling, or relief of their pain and symptoms. Those individuals who are not suffering from a treatable depression, who have no realistic alternatives, or no hope of relief of their suffering should be eligible for an assisted death.

If the medical profession accepts that some suicides are reasonable, there are some who fear the social proscription for all suicides will be weakened, leading to an increase in irrational and tragic deaths among populations where suicide has been traditionally high. As Randy Bottle of the Alberta Indian Health Care Commission told the Senate Committee: "We understand the different circumstances facing the terminally ill, yet, many of our young people consider their situation equally desperate. If assisted suicide were legal for the terminally ill, what do we tell a young Native person who sincerely considers his or her circumstances to be utterly hopeless?" This is indeed a realistic concern. But Quill, Pohlmeier, and others present an opposite optimistic scenario if physicians were allowed to legally assist with rational suicides. Irrational patients with suicidal thoughts might seek out medical care: wanting help to die they might arrive at the doctor's office to ask for a prescription and instead get help for their mental pain. Too often, under present regulations, irrational suicides occur without anyone — doctor, family or friends — recognizing the individual's intentions until he or she is found swinging from the rafters or asphyxiated in the garage. Bringing rational suicides into the open will force other suicides to the surface, too, allowing qualified medical help to treat them before it is too late.

"The decision to seek death should be forcefully challenged by the medical profession," says Quill. "Patients' fears should be probed and counselled. Distorted thinking arising from treatable depression or other mental illness must be carefully examined. But as physicians, we must be realistic that for some dying patients, their excruciating suffering is truly hopeless and meaningless." Most people with terminal illness are sad, and in some that sadness may deepen into depression. The majority, however are not clinically depressed and are capable of making a rational choice, Quill maintains. Like his patient Diane, their mental reasoning is "as clear as a bell." Once the medical profession has helped them determine realistic options, outlined a reliable prognosis, dealt with misconceptions about their condition, counselled them about their fears, treated any possible depression, it is up to the patients, he says, to determine whether they can find a reason to carry on.

Agreeing intellectually with suicide in the future is one thing, hearing your spouse say "I want to do it now," is quite another. When Louise heard Doug utter those words that December morning, she wasn't sure she was ready; she wasn't sure that she'd be strong enough on her own. They called Doug's brother and sister-in-law in California, with whom the couple were extremely close. Peter and June, as they will be called here, got on the first available plane. "By the time they arrived the next day, Doug had convinced me that now was the time," Louise recalls. Peter took control, however, calling doctors to ask for something "to give Doug a will to carry on," and to ask for a medical assessment of Doug's condition. Within an hour, the pharmacy delivered a prescription for steroids and an appointment was booked the next day for a palliative care doctor to visit Doug. Almost immediately, the steroids picked up Doug's appetite and gave him more energy, but he still remained intent on suicide. The next afternoon Doug and the palliative care doctor had a long talk. He told her he was contemplating suicide and wanted the truth about what to expect in the upcoming weeks. She carefully outlined what to expect, describing how as his pain increased, his morphine would be increased and when the morphine caused constipation, they would add more laxatives. If breathlessness occurred, then they would introduce another drug for that. She never mentioned swelling, or the possibility of dementia. When she left, Doug seemed calm, as if the crisis had passed. "Well?" the three of them asked. "I am more convinced than ever that I want to do it now," Doug said. His reasoning was as follows: he was quite willing to endure pain, discomfort, degradation and indignity if there was a chance he would get better and return to normal life; he would go through such torment for two years or more if it meant he might have an extra ten years of good health. But he saw no point of going through one crisis after another, each one worse than the one before, when it was certain he was going to die. The palliative care team's work was to respond to symptoms *after* they happened, there was nothing that could be done in advance to avoid the symptoms. His death was assured in six weeks or less anyway. What was the point?

Peter, June and Louise couldn't argue against his logic and so they finally agreed. "How do you propose to do it?" asked Louise. To their surprise, Doug then pulled out a suicide kit he had fashioned based on recommendations in *Final Exit* and other self-deliverance literature. He had taped together two green garbage bags one inside the other just in case one leaked, and taken a long piece of sewing elastic from Louise's sewing kit with which he would secure the double bag around his neck. He would put the bag over his head and fall asleep, gradually asphyxiating himself in the process, he said. He also pulled out two suicide notes, one to police and ambulance personnel telling them not to resuscitate him, and one to Louise, saying he was sorry to have to "spring this surprise on you." "When did you do all this?" Louise asked. "About a week ago," he replied.

"This was not an impulsive gesture," recalls Louise. "This is not something one can do while in the throws of a panic attack. He had been thinking about it and preparing for a long time." The manuals recommended that sedatives be taken to help the person go to sleep while wearing the bag over the head, so the foursome began searching through Doug's existing medication for what might work. They settled on Ativan, a mild sedative Doug used to help him sleep and control his anxiety. Thirty of the sublingual tablets were on hand. Peter had read that pills should be crushed and mixed with applesauce. No, said Louise, these tablets are meant to melt under the tongue. Doug decided to eat them with applesauce. "There we were, four pathetic people who had never seen anyone die before and we were planning my husband's death because society would not provide the help to do so. This was a do-it-yourself job, just like an abortion with knitting needles."

The trio would have to leave the apartment because Doug was adamant he didn't want anyone else incriminated in his death. They were to go to a restaurant and wait while he took the sedatives. Then he'd put the bag over his head and according to the books, he'd be dead in twenty minutes. They would return at midnight. When the time came for the trio to leave, Louise said to Doug one last time: "Look, you can change your mind . . . There is no losing face here," "Oh, no," said Doug, "I'm ready. I've been thinking about this for a long time." Since the day they had received his terminal diagnosis, two months earlier, Doug and Louise had been saying their goodbyes, crying together, talking about their good times. "We had told each other how much we appreciated each other, how grateful we were to have had each other, and how maybe this horrible, horrible thing was the price for the wonderful time we'd had together." Now, in the final moment, the words were replaced with hugs and kisses. "One can never be truly ready to lose the person one loves the most in the world. But when the moment came for me to leave, I was as ready as I could possibly have been. What made it bearable was the knowledge that Doug would die when he was still himself and at a time of *his* choosing."

Leaving Doug alone for his death was not how Louise had envisioned their parting. "All I wanted was to be able to lie with him on the bed, to hold him, to stroke his head as he closed his eyes, to tell him how much he was loved while he went to sleep in my arms, that was my vision of his death," recounts Louise, tears of uncontrollable grief wracking her body. "Instead I had to turn my back on him, leave him there in the apartment knowing what he was going to do, leave him all alone at a time he needed me most." The threesome walked out into the night. By chance, it happened to be New Year's Eve, but in the blur of dealing with Doug's illness and suicide plans, the date had gone completely unnoticed by all of them. Louise wanted to go to the beach, to sit in the dark on the sand as the waves rolled in; Peter said it would be better to be seen in public. They walked downtown to an Italian restaurant. They were oblivious to others ringing in the New Year around them. At one point Louise said: "Doug is dead now." "Yes," Peter replied, "But it was going to happen anyway and he's done it on his own terms. It's better that way."

They walked back to the apartment, each person dealing with their own emotion and grief over Doug's expected death, and their fear and trepidation of the encounter with his corpse. Louise walked into Doug's room first and stood stock-still in horror at what she saw. Doug was lying in his hospital bed, the garbage bag flopped over so that it obscured the upper half of his body, but the bag was moving up and down. He was snoring. "Something had gone wrong. And I knew that I must finish what Doug had started. There was no question. He had gone through all this, and there was no way I was going to let him wake up." She said to Peter and June, "We have to finish it. Whatever went wrong, we have to fix it."

"Let's not act rashly. Let's go talk about it," Peter said, ushering them out of the room and across the hall to a neighbour's apartment where Peter and June were staying while the owners were on vacation. Peter and June sat motionless, almost in a daze, while Louise did most of the talking. "We must finish what he started," she said.

"Doug didn't want us to be involved, he didn't want us to be incriminated," said Peter.

"How can we let him down, how can we let him wake up again after he has said his goodbyes? He's gone through his death once. I don't want him to have to go through it a second time." Louise told them then, for the first time since she had known them, that twenty years earlier her younger brother at age seventeen had attempted suicide with carbon monoxide but was unsuccessful. He was left severely brain damaged, unable to function on his own. He died a year and a half after the attempt. She was afraid the same thing would happen to Doug, that his failed attempt would leave him brain damaged. Despite Louise's pleading, Peter and June sat as if paralysed by their own indecision. "If you can't do it, I'll do it," said Louise. "But I need you to come with me. Please come with me, don't let me do this alone," begged Louise, as tears streamed down her face.

Peter and June got up and accompanied her back into the apartment. Louise stood by the bed and looked down at her husband. With shaking hands, she gently lifted the bag up off his chest and could see, then, that the elastic was above his nose and mouth. She steeled herself, mustering her courage. With her hands shaking and her heart pounding in her ears she reached to grab the bag to pull it back down over his chin but just as her hands were about to touch the plastic, Peter reached past her and pulled the bag off Doug's head. "It is all right,

Louise," he said. When Doug awoke he was hallucinating and confused. For days he was incoherent and groggy. As his brain cleared, he kept apologizing: "I'm so sorry I botched it. I'm so sorry."

One quiet afternoon almost a week later, Doug described to Louise what had happened. He had finished the last of the applesauce mixture and lay down on the bed, waiting for the sedatives to take their calming effect. Afraid they might hit at once, he had placed the bag over his head, but its hot, dark, closeness sucking around his face had made him panicky, claustrophobic. He pulled it off his head. Why weren't the sedatives working? He tried again. Same panicky feeling. He pulled it off. He looked at the clock, time was passing too fast. "I've got to calm down," he told himself. He put the bag back on, trying to relax in its hot darkness. A minute later, when he could stand it no longer, he pulled it off again. "I need more drugs," he thought and went roaming around the apartment, rifling through drawers and the medicine cabinet, trying to find something — anything — to make him drowsy. There was nothing. "Eating the tablets must have delayed their effect; they are bound to kick in sometime," he thought. He went back to the bed, and placed the bag back on his head, leaving the seal above his nose and mouth, thinking that when he felt tired, he would just pull it down again. The Ativan must have hit all at once, because the next thing he knew he was waking up to a spinning room wondering where the hell he was.

Doug felt no resentment towards either Peter or Louise for what had occurred. Louise heard him tell his sister on the phone, "Peter was doing what he felt was right and Louise was just carrying it through to its logical conclusion." The doctors, however, weren't so understanding. Victoria Hospice informed the couple that while Doug had every right to make decisions regarding his own life, the philosophy of palliative care did not support suicide. If he was going to attempt again, he must first withdraw from the hospice program. They removed from the apartment an emergency kit of medication — a fishing tackle box filled with extra doses of pain killers, morphine, sedatives and other supplies usually left locked on the premises — and said because Doug was suicidal it was no longer safe to keep it there. His own doctor was concerned he might try again, so in January, when Doug experienced increasing trouble sleeping at night he was refused a prescription for more effective medication in case he had plans to stockpile it. "Couldn't a nurse just come by the apartment each day with one pill and watch him take it?" Louise asked, wanting to spare her husband his agonizing nights of wandering the apartment. The request was refused.

By mid-January, the tumour in his abdomen had grown so large that Doug's belly had distended to the size of a nine-month pregnancy. "Doug would lie in bed, almost frantic, with his hands holding his belly, moaning, 'How much bigger is it going to grow? How much bigger can it grow?'" With each passing day Louise felt she was losing her grip on her sanity. She had a recurring image of taking the hammer out of the desk drawer and smashing Doug over the head with it, to put an end to his suffering, and to hers. To her, that image gave expression to her utter desperation. When she told people about this horrifying vision, either they were appalled and shunned her, or they tried to reassure her that such thoughts, in a situation like this, were normal. "I was clearly a basket case. Yet everyone thought it was fine to leave a mad woman alone with a dying man."

Meanwhile, Doug was still intent on suicide and Louise was even more intensely looking for help. "December had been difficult but we had Peter and June's support, we had obtained the self-deliverance books, and we had thought we had some answers. But January was frantic and absolutely desperate," recalls Louise. "If we had been able to obtain a prescription for barbiturates from our doctor, Doug and I would have been able to set the whole issue aside. We would have known that he had

the means to die at the moment of his choosing. In the mean-
time, we would have been able to concentrate on other things
and have a relationship as husband and wife," says Louise. In her
search, Louise called Chris Considine, Sue Rodriguez's lawyer,
to see if he would give her the name of any doctor who'd come
forward to help Sue. Considine gave her no names, but told her
if she resorted to anything illegal and faced charges, he would
represent her. She even called Dr. Kevorkian in Michigan, and
Dr. Quill in New York. Kevorkian was under house arrest
and therefore could not receive any calls. But Quill came to the
phone and talked to her compassionately for twenty minutes. In
the end he said he couldn't help her as he only helped patients
under his care.

"In my desperation, I began pressuring Doug's doctor to
change his mind," Louise recalls. One day in their apartment,
the doctor accused her of being on a campaign to kill Doug. "Is
that what you think?" she raged. "Let's go ask Doug!" she said,
as she practically pulled him into Doug's room. "It's my idea. It
is not Louise. It is what I want," Doug assured him. "You mean
you would like to die right this minute?" the doctor asked.
"No, not today," said Doug. "But I would like to have the
means so I can die whenever I'm ready." "Give it up, for both
your sakes," the doctor urged. "You are not going to get it."

By then, both Doug and Louise were so emotionally exhausted
that the doctor convinced them help was not available. Doug
gave up his search. "It was not his choice, but the cost of finding
the means was just too high." Doug realized that the publicity
of the Sue Rodriguez case made more people aware of the ille-
gality of assisted suicide and therefore they were reluctant to
help. "I guess this is happening in the wrong year," he said.

The growth of tumours in his lymph system meant that he
had been experiencing swelling in his legs, called edema, caused
by the sluggish return of lymph fluid from the extremities. It
had started with his toes and ankles, then climbed to his calves,

then a few days later had climbed as high as his thighs. The skin was stretched so tight that blood seeped through cracks and fissures formed by the tension. Louise phoned the palliative care staff in concern. "Don't worry," they said. "It is a normal part of the tumour progression." One beautiful day in late January, about two weeks before he died, Doug wanted to go for a walk to enjoy the weather. When they returned from the walk, Doug's legs were swollen as thick as tree trunks, stretching out the seams of his pants. He couldn't bend his legs. He went to the washroom to urinate, but he couldn't pull out his penis through his fly. He called in distress to Louise, who came in and struggled to pull down his pants. When at last she succeeded, the two looked at Doug's genitals in horror — his penis and his testes had inflated into huge round orbs, filled with lymphatic fluid like balloons filled with water. Doug began to scream in hysteria.

"Over the course of the next two hours, Doug became demented. He just lost it, and he never again regained his clarity," recalls Louise. "I think that pushed him over the edge." Despite his dementia, Doug still had his mobility and his energy from the steroids. "It was a horrible combination — demented, with energy. I couldn't control him." Doug would wander naked around the apartment, aimlessly dragging himself along the wall. He had paranoid hallucinations. At times, he would try to go outside, naked. Louise once had to call a neighbour to help keep him in the apartment. He lost his ability to manage the care and cleaning of his colostomy and one day Louise came into the bathroom to find faecal material sprayed over the walls after the bag had slipped from his hands. Doug was crouched on the bathroom floor, like a two-year-old, saying "I'm sorry, I'm sorry."

In mid-January, her doctor and Victoria Hospice had referred Louise to Dr. Shabehram Lohrasbe, a psychiatrist who specializes in grief and bereavement. He became Louise's lifeline and it was he who convinced her that she must have a break from

Doug's twenty-four hour care. At the end of January Louise began to spend the night at a nearby bed and breakfast while a homecare worker stayed at the apartment. Doug had cried when she told him of the plan. Louise felt guilty as now she was at the apartment for just ten or twelve hours and some days for as little as four or five, but Lohrasbe told her that Doug in his dementia would not know the difference.

On February 3, 1994 according to homecare workers' nursing notes, Doug slipped into semi-consciousness, unresponsive to others yet moaning for hours on end. His moaning continued intermittently for five days and nights. On February 8, Doug began to run a fever. Later that evening his breathing became strained, accompanied by a mucous-like rattle. At 10:30 the next morning, while Louise was at Dr. Lohrasbe's office, Doug took his last breath and died in the presence of his brother, who had arrived a few days earlier, and a homecare worker. When Louise arrived home she looked at her husband and felt numb relief. "Well Doug," she said, "no more pain. I'm sorry I didn't have the guts to help you die." Doug's facial expression had been so pained for so long that Louise had forgotten what he looked like without the frown and tension lines creasing his face. Now his brow was smooth again and his features relaxed. "He looked wonderfully peaceful, a sight I treasured and which I wanted to be able to hold on to. I took his picture." Then she put on Beethoven's mournful choral masterpiece, *Missa Solemnis* and lay down on the bed beside Doug, wrapping her arms around his body and laying her head on his shoulder. She lay there for five hours.

Three days later, less than twenty kilometres away, Sue Rodriguez, in the presence of Svend Robinson, consumed an overdose of morphine and barbiturates provided by a sympathetic doctor. She then closed her eyes, lay in Robinson's arms, and had the peaceful death she had been seeking for almost two years. Doug, seeking the same warm embrace as he died, the same assistance from a physician, the same control over death, all in the same city as Sue, had been unable to get it.

When the ethics committee of the Canadian Medical Association in 1994 recommended the organization remain neutral on the issues of euthanasia and assisted suicide and let doctors follow their consciences, it was a definite step away from the hardline position that doctors must never be involved in these acts. Even though the recommendation was then defeated by the 200 doctors at the general assembly, the ethics committee's moderate position was indisputable proof of mainstream medical opposition to euthanasia and assisted suicide weakening. In the United States the American Medical Students Association, representing more than 3,000 students in U.S. medical schools, changed its position in 1994 from neutral to in favour of assisted suicide under specific circumstances — including a voluntary repeated request, unbearable suffering, no reasonable alternatives and an independent consultation. Evidence from other countries increasingly shows that many younger doctors are more accepting of euthanasia and assisted suicide becoming a legitimate medical act.

When a historic bill allowing physicians to prescribe fatal doses to dying patients squeaked by Oregon voters in November, 1994 it was the state medical profession that was credited with tipping the balance in favour. Unlike two previous public initiatives in Washington State and California where the local medical associations had opposed euthanasia bills, in Oregon the medical profession decided to remain neutral on assisted suicide, neither endorsing nor opposing the initiative. When asked about fears of the "slippery slope," the president of the Oregon Medical Association, Dr. Leigh Dolin, replied: "In the real world of modern medicine, it's all slippery slope." Although the newly proclaimed bill was immediately mired in court challenges launched by the opposition and may never come into force, yet another brick in the wall of mainstream medical opposition had been loosened.

Individual doctors, too, have been coming forward in greater numbers to acknowledge their role in assisted deaths. In an unprecedented move in March of 1995, seven doctors in Melbourne, Australia wrote to the state premier openly declaring that they had helped terminally ill patients to die, and challenging him to uphold the law and charge them with crimes. The letter ran on the front page of *The Melbourne Age* and the seven doctors — three GPs specializing in AIDS, one cancer specialist, one surgeon, one anaesthetist, and one retired GP — all signed their names. The text, in part, read:

> There are many who cry out for help and who are denied it by doctors who may sympathize with their plight but who are unwilling to break the law. There are some who attempt to end their lives unaided and who botch the attempt and survive with their misery redoubled. There are others who may be helped by a doctor but who, for fear of incriminating their friends and family, die alone without a chance to say farewell.
>
> It cannot be right to tolerate this totally unsatisfactory situation, where it is a matter of chance whether patients will receive the treatment which they so desperately seek ... For the sake of all those who may be unfortunate enough to be trapped in suffering and anguish, we ask you to put an end to the uneasy hypocrisy of our law and to allow us to work without fear of prosecution.

The doctors might have been writing about Doug Miller, but instead they were writing about hundreds of other Doug Millers half a world away facing the same obstacles and despair in death. Months after the public confession, and despite a police investigation, the seven doctors still had not been charged with crimes. The government seemed unwilling to risk a "show trial" on the issues and the uneasy hypocrisy remained. Yet in September of 1995, the parliament of Australia's Northern Territory passed the world's first law that permits medically assisted voluntary euthanasia. The "Kill Bill," as it was called by its opponents, allows the sick to end their lives provided that a physician and a psychiatrist determine the patient to be both terminally ill and sane. Other Australian states are expected to consider a similar law.

Three weeks to the day that Doug died, the federal government announced the formation of the Special Senate Committee on Euthanasia and Assisted Suicide. In newspapers across the country it advertised that it was seeking input from health professionals, ethicists, advocacy groups and individuals with personal stories who had views on the subject. Any witnesses wanting to testify before the seven-member committee were to contact the committee clerk at the Senate office in Ottawa. Louise wasn't sure if she should do it. It was too soon after Doug's death. She didn't want to probe that wound, expose it for all to see. She wondered if she could keep her composure. She felt it would not be worth the emotional cost, unless her presentation made a difference. Her psychiatrist, Dr. Lohrasbe, was the one who convinced her. "To be honest, until I followed Doug and Louise's case, as a physician, I was uncertain whether legalizing assisted suicide was a good idea. It was Doug and Louise's horrific experience that moved me to the side of choice," Lohrasbe told me. "No one should have to go through what they went through." The senate committee, he told Louise, for the most part would be hearing from people speaking in the abstract — health professionals, academics, spokespeople from various associations, ethicists — but it was people like her who the senators really needed to hear from; individuals who had lived through the agonizing death of a loved one who begged to die. Few of those people would have the emotional resources, stamina, and motivation to do it, they would be too overwhelmed and intimidated by the process. "I knew she could do it. She is a remarkable woman who is both extremely intelligent and extremely emotional. I felt she had the strength and the ability to articulate in a way that others did not."

On May 11, 1994, Louise Normandin-Miller appeared before the senate committee in Ottawa. Ironically it would have been Doug's forty-first birthday. She had worked for more than a month on her presentation, paring down the experience to its essentials. "I knew I couldn't change the world and I didn't want to be disappointed with the results of my efforts. So I told myself my goal should be to simply convince one person on the committee. If that was all I could do, it would be enough."

The one person Louise chose to direct her message to was Senator Wilbert Keon. As the only doctor on the committee, Keon represented the epitome of success and influence in the medical establishment. His medical credentials were impeccable. A respected cardiovascular surgeon who founded the Ottawa Heart Institute, Keon pioneered surgical techniques to rescue patients in acute heart attacks. He was the quintessential high-tech doctor, doing heart transplants and cardiac by-passes to stave off death. For fifteen years he was professor and chair of the department of surgery in the University of Ottawa's Faculty of Medicine. Leadership roles in the surgical, academic and scientific areas of medicine were prominent throughout his career. He had held elected offices in thirty-six different professional organizations. In 1990s' Canada one would be hard pressed to find a doctor with more respect, authority and influence among others in the medical profession. It was well known among his peers that, as a Catholic, he was opposed to assisted suicide. It was also clear from his questions early in the hearings that he shared the common medical belief that a request for assisted suicide might be a product of mental illness or depression that might be treated. "Do we know whether the chemistry of the

brain is dysfunctional in a dying person who wishes to be killed
and whether that chemistry could be reversed with appropriate intervention?" Keon had asked Dr. Paul Henteleff, of the
Canadian Palliative Care Association, who spoke directly before
Louise. It was a question Keon was to pose again in various
forms to numerous medical experts on dying.

Louise made sure to address the question from her own perspective, lifting her eyes to stare directly at Keon as she spoke.
"Doug was not psychiatrically, clinically depressed. I repeat,
Doug was not depressed." At the end of Louise's riveting, emotional testimony, as she was packing up her papers, Senator
Keon came up beside her. "He took both my hands in his, and
he looked me in the eyes and he said in the most kind, compassionate way, 'I am so sorry you had to go through what you
did.' I was incredibly touched by that," said Louise.

A year later, when the Senate finally released its report, four
of the seven senators recommended against changing the law to
allow assisted suicide or euthanasia. It would undermine the
universal value of respecting life; it would be too dangerous to
the weak and vulnerable in society; it would be too difficult
to regulate and control. Keon, however, was among the three
senators who came out in favour of allowing doctors to write
fatal prescriptions for competent, terminally ill patients. Unlike
the committee's chairperson, Joan Neiman, and Senator Sharon
Carstairs, however, Dr. Keon did not support euthanasia,
believing that it would be safer and a more prudent first step in
changing the laws if patients themselves were required to perform the final act to end their lives. When I reached him in
Ottawa Keon acknowledged that during his year on the committee his thinking had changed dramatically on the issue of
assisted suicide, in part as a result of the personal testimonies
of individuals like Louise Normandin-Miller. "The personal
stories had a great influence on me. Mrs. Miller, and a couple of
others that I particularly recall, took time out of their lives for

no other reason than to help someone else. They were very sincere and very moving. There is no question that they were part of the reason my thinking turned around."

Dr. Keon was troubled that as many as 5 per cent of all dying patients experience pain or emotional distress that cannot be relieved by even the most expert palliative care; that compassionate doctors who want to honour a patient's clear and well-defined request might face jail or lose their medical licences; and that unregulated acts of assisted suicide are now taking place in Canada completely underground. It troubled him that those who spoke against the option appeared to him to be "terribly rigid" and "didn't appear to be opposed for very good reasons." "People in favour simply seemed to me to be approaching it on a compassionate basis and had compassionate reasons for wanting to get on with the business of dying," he said. "In the end, for me, however, it came down to the fundamental issue of autonomy." Keon said his own personal beliefs meant that he would never commit suicide, nor as a doctor would he be able to help a patient to do so, just as he would not perform an abortion. But he believes other doctors should be allowed to follow their own conscience when they are faced with a patient who asks for help. He believes the acts must be regulated by a strict procedure that scrutinizes the decisions before and after the fact, but that there are indeed circumstances where it can be medically justified.

After the Special Senate Committee released its report, no one in the mainstream media reported on the overwhelming significance of one of Canada's leading medical figures putting his seal of approval on physician-assisted suicide, but it didn't escape doctors like Ted Boadway of the OMA. "It is a very dramatic change," Boadway said. "You could not find a doctor in Canada who is more highly regarded. That respect is well deserved — the guy is great. And his opposition to assisted suicide was very well known. He didn't campaign against it, but his position was known. The fact that Willy Keon could spend a year looking closely at the issues, hearing all sides, and change his position is highly significant." That doesn't mean, however, that after Dr. Keon's endorsement, the Canadian medical profession, *en masse*, will suddenly change to supporting assisted suicide. "Doctors are not sheep," says Boadway. But it does mean that in the wall of mainstream medical opinion yet another brick — this one a keystone — has loosened.

7

PALLIATIVE
CARE

IN MEDICINE, the phrase "to palliate" means to treat the symptoms, not to cure. It comes from the Latin, *palliatus*, meaning "dressed in a cloak," a *pallium*. To say that palliative care cloaks the symptoms of dying wouldn't be quite accurate, even though, at times, this is precisely what it does. At its best, palliative care does more than that; it is a comprehensive program aiming to help patients and families cope with the physical, emotional and spiritual distress of dying. During the course of an acute illness or injury, both the medical profession and the sick patient know that sometimes painful symptoms and troubling side-effects must be endured in the pursuit of effective treatment. The probing and prodding of diagnostic tests, the pain and discomfort of surgery, the nausea and sickness of chemotherapies, the invasive technology of intensive care are all seen as short term sacrifices in patient comfort for the long-term gain of a patient's return to relatively good health. If and when a disease reaches a stage where no treatments can slow or stop its inevitable course to death, however, the philosophy of palliative care maintains that invasive tests and arduous therapies should stop and the focus should turn to keeping the patient as comfortable as possible for the time he or she has left to live. It is a philosophy in which the patient is treated as a person, not a mere vessel for the disease. Many commentators have rightly pointed out that such a philosophy should be dispersed through *all* medical care.

In the debate over the right to die, however, palliative care and euthanasia are often pitted against each other, as though they were mutually exclusive. Time and time again governments and society have been urged to throw their support behind comprehensive palliative care rather than the legalization of euthanasia and assisted suicide. Part of the rationale for this recommendation lies in the observation that when terminally ill patients are comfortable and well cared for the need for euthanasia all but disappears. Few disagree with such an observation, even among those who support euthanasia and assisted suicide. Instead, the disagreement arises over what to do for the 5 to 10 per cent of dying patients who reject palliative care, or for whom it is not effective in removing their pain and suffering. According to Marilynne Seguin, executive director of Toronto's Dying with Dignity, "Even if we poured billions of dollars into palliative care, we would not remove the demand for physician-assisted dying. We must look at both options. It is not an either/or situation." Among those who promote palliative care as the alternative to euthanasia in *every* case, and those who see it as only a partial answer are differing predictions about what would happen to the compassionate care of the dying if euthanasia or assisted suicide were legalized. One side fears palliative care would be undermined, its support weakened, forcing all individuals to opt for euthanasia because they couldn't get good palliative care or even any palliative care at all. The other side envisions a flourishing of palliative care, bolstered by laws or guidelines that would make palliative care consultations a necessary step in all euthanasia decisions and by the fact that patients naturally want to live for as long as they can be comfortable, which in itself leads to a demand for good palliative care.

In a small white car in the drizzling rain, Rae Westcott, Coby Tschanz and I pull into the driveway of a ranch-style bungalow a few blocks away from the University of Victoria. It is 3:00 p.m. and this is the first call of the day for Victoria's Palliative Response Team. I have come along to observe the two trained caregivers as they resolve difficult situations with dying patients still in their homes. Opening the car's hatchback Westcott takes out a thick binder of information on palliative care while Tschanz grabs a large, metal fishing tackle box filled with medication. Within a few seconds of ringing the door bell, the concerned face of Mary Howard is behind the screen door. "Hi, we're the Palliative Response Team," says Tschanz. "We've come to help with your husband." Mary's face lightens as she ushers Tschanz, a nurse, Westcott, a social worker, and me into the warmth of the front hall. Mary says in her warm British accent, left over after more than forty years in Canada: "Thank you for coming, we've been having a bad few days." In the bedroom down the hall, Howard's husband, Gordon, sixty-seven, is dying of lung cancer. Their adult son, Scott, hovers nearby, concern etched on his face.

Although Gordon Howard's cancer was diagnosed almost four years earlier, in the previous month he has suddenly become much worse. Now, in the last two days he has stopped eating, become incontinent, immobile, and has been unable to sleep. He is emaciated. His breathing is strained. Although he doesn't complain, his wife can tell from his restlessness and agitation that he is in considerable pain. His sits in a reclining chair in the bedroom, his gaunt face stretched with the tension of fighting his constant discomfort, trying to smile as we enter his room. "What? All this attention for me?" he says in a weak voice, attempting some light conversation, but it is clear that it is hard for him to talk. Westcott and I, after introducing ourselves, withdraw to the kitchen leaving Tschanz alone to make him comfortable. "I promised him he wouldn't go back to hospital,"

Mary Howard says as we sit around the kitchen table. She is vis-
ibly stressed by having to deal with her husband's illness and her
own grief at losing her long-time partner.

Over the last day it had become clear to Mary Howard that
she would need help to keep her promise and care for her husband at home. That's why her doctor called the region's palliative care program run out of Victoria's Jubilee Hospital, which
supports some 150 dying individuals either at home or in the
hospital. Doctors, social workers, counsellors, nurses, pastors
and volunteers are available to come into the home or wards
to try to help address whatever physical, emotional or spiritual
needs a dying patient has. The Palliative Response Team, the
quick response branch of the service, is on call every afternoon
to deal with emerging crises before they get out of hand. If
patients and their families can get help quickly it often removes
the need to transfer patients to the seven-bed hospice or to the
acute-care wards of the hospital, and strengthens the home
care arrangement. Within a few hours of the doctor's call, the
nurse and social worker were at the door, offering medication, advice and support. Both Tschanz, a woman in her mid-
thirties and Westcott, a man in his late-forties, exude calm and
competence. Tschanz has been a hospice nurse for eleven years;
Westcott has counselled in palliative care, specializing in grief,
dying and bereavement for ten years.

In the bedroom with Gordon, Tschanz talked to him in
her quieting tones, making an assessment of his pain, mobility,
mental clarity and comfort. She gave him a series of medications
including morphine injections, steroids and a stool softener.
Unlike most nurses, Tschanz and other RNs on the palliative
care team carry no stethoscope or blood pressure cuff — there is
no point in taking vital signs any more, the focus is on comfort.
She transferred him from the chair to the bed so that when the
morphine began to relieve his pain he could comfortably fall
asleep. Meanwhile Westcott looked after Mary and Scott in the

kitchen, gently taking them through a binder of information about palliative care at home, answering their questions and talking about what to expect in the process of dying. "He's very reluctant to admit pain to me or anyone. He's very stoic," says Mary. Westcott shows her how to gauge pain by facial features and shows her a thermometer-like drawing with which she can get her husband to point out his pain on a scale. He shows her how to accurately measure out the oral morphine, getting her to try it a few times until she can draw up the correct amount without her hands shaking, how to prepare the 20 milligram doses to be taken every four hours and the half-sized 10 milligram "break-through" doses that can be taken in between regular doses. For each item of information, Westcott shows her the corresponding page in the binder, which she can keep on hand for her own reference.

"This is wonderful. This is so wonderful," Mary Howard kept repeating, while her son nodded his head in agreement. Westcott's open style of attentive listening seems to encourage them to talk. After about forty-five minutes, Tschanz comes out of the bedroom and joins the group at the kitchen table. Gordon is sleeping comfortably now, she tells them. The morphine has taken effect. "We have been so frightened of the morphine," says Mary. "We gave him some and it seemed to knock him right out." "In a day or so he will get acclimatized and then he will become more clear," explains Tschanz. "It is important you don't deny him pain relief. Remember he has been in considerable pain and unable to sleep. Sometimes it isn't the morphine knocking him out, but his body catching up on lost sleep now that the pain is removed."

They go through the various phone numbers she can call — the twenty-four-hour hospice number that will get her in touch with a nurse, the number of the outreach team, the number for homecare, who will now come for a few hours each day to help Mary tend to her husband's needs. They talk about what should be done during Gordon's last days. "It is important that if you don't want to go to hospital, you don't dial 911 when Gordon is dying. They will have to take him to hospital, something that you don't want, right?" explains Westcott. "Right," says Mary. "So call the hospice, not the ambulance, okay?" "Okay," says Mary.

After the two-hour visit the team left, with Gordon Howard comfortably asleep in bed and Mary Howard feeling able to keep her promise and look after her husband at home. Tschanz and Westcott got back in the car and drove across town to the next home on the "hot list" of patients needing a visit. It was a young man dying of AIDS. Originally from Ontario and living on his own, when he became seriously ill he had been taken in by a middle-aged couple who are part of Victoria AIDS Respite Care, a volunteer agency that looks after people dying of AIDS in their homes. The man, only thirty-two-years-old, lay semi-conscious in one of the bedrooms, only hours away from death. His mother, step-father, and sister, who had travelled across Canada to be at his side, were crying in the living room. He had left Ontario a few months earlier without telling them he was sick. Just as with the Howards, Tschanz looked after the patient's medical needs in the bedroom, while Westcott comforted the distraught family, talking to them about their feelings of loss and helplessness, their fear of the dying process, their shock of learning that not only did their loved one have AIDS but that he would soon be dead from it. Three hours later Tschanz and Westcott were on their way to a third home to visit another young man with AIDS named Franklyn who was hallucinating on the drugs being used to ease his pain.

The next day, the team checked on the three patients by phone. Mary Howard was coping well although her husband had spent most of the last twenty-four hours sleeping. The first young man with AIDS had died during the night. Franklyn was still having trouble with confusion. A week later, when Gordon became unable to swallow and slipped into a coma, a hospice nurse went to the house after midnight to help Mary give him his morphine, and prepare her for his impending death fifteen hours later. The day before Franklyn had slipped into a coma and died.

Thirty years ago palliative care medicine, or what the British and Americans more commonly refer to as hospice care, did not exist. (The term "palliative care," which is now used worldwide, in fact, had its origins in Canada to deal with the pejorative meaning of "alms house" that was imparted to "hospice" when it was translated into French.) The founding of the hospice philosophy is credited to Britain's Dame Cicely Saunders, a devote Christian who in 1967 founded the first modern hospice, St. Christopher's, on the outskirts of London. Trained as a nurse during the Second World War and then moving into social work, Dame Saunders was responsible for the care of a forty-year-old Polish man, David Tasma, dying from cancer in 1948. She began to feel that without relatives, without a home, this dying man needed something more than what the busy surgical ward could give him. "Visiting David in the ward I realized he not only needed better symptom control, even though his ward sister was extremely good and understanding, he also needed something to help him gather his life together, to deal with his feeling that he had made no difference to the world by being here. Dying at forty, with no family, no career, he needed some way to make sense of his life," Dame Saunders told an audience of about fifty international visitors, myself among them, who had made a pilgrimage to St. Christopher's in the spring of 1994.

After he died, Tasma left a £500 bequest to Dame Saunders, who used it to start her campaign to fight the alienation and isolation of dying, the uncontrolled pain, and the lack of attention given to the grief and spiritual needs of dying individuals and their families. She began to envision a comprehensive program of physical, emotional and spiritual support for dying patients. While there were a number of religious hospices which treated dying patients with tender-loving care, none of them incorporated medical science and pharmaceuticals to help comfort the patient. In the 1950s, Dame Saunders trained as a doctor, during which time numerous new drugs became available that could help ease the suffering of dying patients: antidepressants, tranquillizers, sedatives, steroids, better formulations of pain medication. "They were all introduced over a remarkable ten years, so that we had tools that we could use," she said. After finishing her medical training she joined the staff of London's St. Joseph's Hospital, and working with the nuns, she began to show that by giving drugs regularly to prevent pain from happening, rather than waiting until the pain appeared, as was the common medical practice, the patient's comfort was greatly improved. Their anxiety decreased and their outlook brightened. "If you can quiet the pain and the fear of pain, you can give them space to be with their families, space to find out what is the most valuable thing for them in their own scheme of things," Saunders said. In the early 1960s, she and a small group of like-minded individuals, many of them health professionals, began to plan and fundraise for an integrated medical hospice to be backed by a Christian Foundation. It was to have a strong research and educational arm in order to disseminate new techniques in comfort care and train individuals to spread the knowledge. In July of 1967, St. Christopher's opened. Its philosophy, as articulated by Dame Saunders, is that "you matter until the last moment of your life, and we will do all we can, not only to help you die peacefully, but to live until you die." Within a short time other free-standing hospices, usually supported by Christian charities, began to open across the United Kingdom.

In the United States, the hospice model was slightly different. Rather than build or renovate free-standing institutions as in-patient facilities, the Americans have tended to establish home care programs in the community, so dying patients could stay at home with doctors or staff on call. The first U.S. hospice home care team began in 1974 in New Haven, Connecticut, founded after Dame Saunders visited Yale University. It had no back-up beds in a local hospital for ten years. Today in the U.S. there are some 2,200 hospice programs. And in Canada, the model has tended more towards hospital-based palliative care with community outreach. The first palliative care units opened in 1975 in wards in the Royal Victoria Hospital in Montreal and St. Boniface Hospital in Winnipeg. In 1994, the Canadian Palliative Care Association listed 415 palliative care programs across the country. Despite the prominence of hospital-based programs there are free-standing hospices like Casey House in Toronto and Maison Michel Sarrazin in Quebec City. Community-based programs such as New Brunswick's Extra-Mural Hospital provide integrated care for dying patients at home. There are hospital-based palliative care units, with palliative care beds collected together on one ward of a hospital. There are palliative care teams that act as consultants for patients dispersed throughout a hospital, rather than locating the patients on a single ward. And there are programs which combine a hospital-based unit with home care outreach such as Victoria's program, or Montreal's extensive network of eight hospitals with home care programs run out of McGill University.

The medical tools of palliative care are not high-tech. Rarely are fancy machines or difficult procedures employed. Rather, symptom relief relies on the staff having knowledge of an arsenal of drugs, and how they can be combined to combat common distressing symptoms. "It's attention to detail," says Gabor Maté, medical co-ordinator of the Vancouver General Hospital's palliative care unit. "It's using combinations of drugs, at their lowest levels, to achieve the most comfort for the patient. It's listening to the patient, spending time with them." Medically, it is a "stepped care" approach — starting with over-the-counter analgesics like ASA or acetaminophen preparations, moving to products containing codeine, and then on to morphine in its various forms, or other synthetic narcotics to provide relief regularly around the clock so that pain does not break through. Palliative care physicians believe that as much pain-killer should be given as the patient requires, even if it may hasten the patient's death by depressing respiration. They even have a saying: "Douse the pain with the dose that does it."

Morphine, derived from opium, which in turn comes from the juice of the poppy seed, is the mainstay of palliative care because it is so highly effective. Giving morphine by mouth is the preferred route, either in a concentrated syrup or tablet every four hours, or in a sustained release capsule every twelve hours. Morphine can also be given "subcutaneously," either by regular injections or by putting a fine needle with attached tubing under the skin and leaving it in place. This allows morphine to be injected into the tubing without causing pain to the patient every four hours. Alternatively, a pump can be attached to the tubing, which the patient controls, allowing delivery of the morphine as needed. Or, if the pain is severe, morphine can be delivered directly into the patient's veins by an intravenous drip.

There are two common misconceptions about morphine, which palliative care specialists stress aren't true: morphine almost always causes the patient's brain to become cloudy and confused, and increasing the morphine to combat the pain invariably hastens the patient's death. "In the first two days of morphine use, it is common for patients to be dopey, but that resolves usually by the third day and then most patients are able to sit up in bed, converse, even read," said Dr. Derek Doyle, medical director of Scotland's St. Columba's Hospice and one of the world authorities on palliative care. "As for shortening life, I think it is more common for good palliative care to lengthen life. It is very common for us to get a patient who is hovering on the verge of death, but once we get his pain and symptoms under control he goes on to live three or four months longer than anyone had ever expected."

Morphine given to a patient for the first time, particularly in large doses, may suppress respiration enough to cause death, but in a patient who has been on morphine for a few days, a rapid increase in the dosing will likely only lead to increased sedation and barely affect the patient's breathing. Nevertheless, there are some patients who can't tolerate morphine at all. They may hallucinate on even the smallest dose. They may have an allergic-like reaction that causes them to itch or develop a rash. Some patients experience a side-effect of uncontrollable muscle twitching, called myoclonic jerks. In those cases, or when patients who have been previously kept comfortable on morphine have become tolerant to it, or if patients experience pain that's too severe, then doctors will use other narcotics that act like morphine but aren't derived from opium. The synthetic narcotic hyrdromorphone, more commonly known as Dilaudid and eight times as strong as regular morphine, is one such drug that may be given in those circumstances.

Severe pain in specific, localized areas, not responding to morphine or synthetic derivatives may be treated by nerve blocks or epidurals. In extreme and rare situations, where pain cannot be controlled, an operation called a cordotomy may be performed, in which nerves of the spinal cord are cut to stop the transmission of pain signals. In the most severe, uncontrolled cases, the decision may be made to render the patient unconscious with drugs — a technique called total sedation. Such a technique, which usually uses barbiturates to place the patient in a coma, has been highly controversial. In an important landmark, however, all seven members of the Special Senate Committee on Euthanasia and Assisted Suicide said total sedation was a legitimate practice where patient consent has been given, but national guidelines must be established to ensure its appropriate use.

Severe constipation is a side effect of narcotics' use and so palliative care patients are often put on a host of laxatives, stool softeners and bowel stimulants. To families and patients themselves, worrying about constipation often strikes them as a trivial concern when a patient is dying and yet severe constipation can contribute to incontinence, unrelieved nausea, pain, or even hasten death. Bedsores, too, are a common problem arising from long-term bedrest in palliative care. Special beds, laser treatment and attention to hygiene and regular turning are all used to stave off skin breakdown, but it remains a recurring problem and is often very distressing and painful for patients.

In some situations more aggressive therapy from the armamentarium of acute care medicine will be applied to palliative care patients. A man dying of lung cancer, for example, who suddenly develops numbness or pain in his arm might quickly be referred to radiation therapy to reduce any further growth of the tumour to prevent it pressing on the nerve to his arm. The radiation, while not prolonging his life or curing the cancer, may simply give the patient a number of weeks without pain in his arm and is therefore worth doing. "There is a debate in medicine about how aggressive palliative medicine should get — when does it cross the line away from comfort care back to being more like acute care," explains Maté as he takes me around VGH's seventeen-bed ward.

He introduces me to Mrs. Kathleen McCullough, a seventy-six-year-old woman with throat cancer, who has been on the ward more than two months. Aggressive palliative therapies have given her a better quality of life, while not changing her terminal prognosis. She sits upright in bed, giving the doctor and visitor a big smile. She is on daily morphine yet her mind is clear and her pain well controlled. No longer able to talk because surgery to remove the cancer in her throat also removed her voice box, she writes her comments on a pad she keeps by her bed. Maté explains that when the tumour in her throat grew very large, interfering with her breathing and preventing her from eating, more surgery was conducted to lessen its size. She has been tube fed to keep her well nourished. Blood transfusions have boosted her energy. After the surgery she fell and broke her hip and so ensued an operation to set it to reduce the pain and hopefully, get her walking again. She had a procedure called thoracentesis to drain fluid from around her lungs to help her breathing. "These are major procedures, but in terms of her quality of life, definitely worth doing," Maté says. "You still get a lot of enjoyment out of life, don't you Mrs. McCullough?" She nods in agreement, and writes on her pad: "4 children, 6 grandchildren."

Maté leaves to see another patient, and I remain with Mrs. McCullough. Despite her inability to talk, she responds to my questions by charade-like gestures, mouthing the words, or writing brief responses on her pad. She writes "very nice" when I ask her about the staff, and "okay now" when I ask her about her pain. I learn that she is comfortable but afraid to get out of bed after her fall. She is going to try later that day to get into a wheelchair with the help of a therapist. Her goal is to get strong enough to be able to go back home so that she can be in her own surroundings. "Good luck," I say, and she takes my hand, giving it a warm squeeze.

A few hours later as I am leaving the ward, I see her again. She has indeed overcome her fear, has been helped out of bed, and is sitting in a conference room in a wheelchair. An occupational therapist is showing her how to use an electrolarynx to speak. A palm-sized, battery-operated device that looks a bit like a small, cylindrical flashlight, it produces a vibrating tone. When Mrs. McCullough presses it into the flesh under her jaw, she can move her lips and teeth to form the tone into words. She waves to me, and then presses the electrolarynx under her chin.

"Hello!" she says and breaks into a huge smile. The therapist smiles with her. "This is the happiest day!" she says with her new mechanical voice. Her radiant smile is the last image I have as I leave the ward. It is to remain an enduring memory of how palliative care that meets the patient's needs can impart joy and meaning even in the face of terminal illness. Mrs. McCullough, I later learned, was to regain her strength and make it back home before moving on to a nursing home where she lived for more than a year.

Despite its considerable successes, palliative care techniques are far from perfect. For patients and their families, the process of controlling symptoms can seem like a constant struggle of trying one drug and then another, one dose and then a higher dose. Louise Miller described her husband's frustration with the process: "Doug would be comfortable for one or two days, and then a new symptom would arise, like nausea or more pain, and the palliative care team would scramble for a day or so to come up with the right combination of drugs. Then he'd be okay for a bit until the next symptom arrived. They couldn't prevent the symptoms from happening; it was always reacting, reacting, reacting. Maybe it took only a day or so to get things back under control, but to Doug it felt like a thousand days." In an esti-mated 5 per cent of dying patients the pain may be intractable, unresponsive to treatment. It is everyone's worst nightmare. Bone pain and nerve pain can be the most difficult to resolve. Nerve pain can be a burning, prickly sensation that is constant, like radio static, or a sharp, shooting jab of electrical sensation that recurs every few seconds or minutes. In some patients, good pain control is made more difficult by a high rate of what palliative care providers call "total pain." Along with the physi-cal pain of the disease process, total pain includes the emotional, psychological and intellectual pain of dying that can't be fixed with a pill or a shot. It is the pain of leaving the world.

Often the patients suffering total pain are those like Doug Miller, in their twenties, thirties, or forties when they face a terminal diagnosis. Or it may be older individuals who feel their lives have been unsuccessful, or patients who regret something in the past that they want to amend before they die. Sometimes palliative care staff, such as counsellors, help to relieve total pain by helping the patient to find meaning or resolution in whatever has existed in their lives, getting to underlying concerns. "If you can find out what is at the bottom of the total pain, sometimes you can resolve it," says Tyleen Katz, a nurse who is director of the May Guttridge Hospice in Vancouver. She described a patient in his late fifties whose unremitting pain would not respond to treatment. Bewildered staff tried everything until they found out he had been harbouring a secret from them. The truth came out during music therapy. He was not a widowed man with no family, as he had told them. He had a wife and two sons who years earlier had left him and moved back to England. He no longer had any idea where they were. It was only after he was encouraged to write some poems, putting them to music with the music therapist, and then putting the songs on a tape, that his pain came under control. The tape was his legacy for his sons, if they ever came looking for him, that told them of his undying love. He then died in peace.

Intractable pain is not the only difficult problem in palliative care. There is a huge need for better drugs and treatments with fewer side-effects (such as sedation and constipation), particularly better treatments for nausea, vomiting and itching; better laxatives; and better treatments for the terrifying sensations of choking or suffocation that some dying patients feel. "Shortness of breath is, in the palliative care field, often the paradigm of the difficult death," explains Montreal palliative care expert Marcel Boisvert. "The patient is struggling, running after each breath, forty to fifty times per minute. We can very often relieve 100 per cent of the pain, but rarely can we relieve 100 per cent of severe shortness of breath except by severe sedation." Right now, because of a lack of other ways to treat such distressing symptoms, one in six palliative care patients "require medication to control all symptoms," according to the Canadian Palliative Care Association, as stated in its brief to the Special Senate Committee. That means, according to Boisvert: "they were drugged to a degree which does not permit meaningful interaction with the family."

Australian palliative care physician Dr. Roger Hunt has conducted research that shows many of the common distressing symptoms of dying are only partially relieved by state-of-the-art palliative care. His study of the cancer deaths of 100 patients showed that while the vast majority of those with severe pain were helped by medication, less than half of patients suffering severe constipation, difficulty breathing, or nausea were helped. The record of success was even poorer for those suffering from severe confusion — very few achieved a return to mental clarity. While the majority of patients suffered moderate to severe weight loss, weakness and loss of appetite, palliative care could relieve those symptoms in practically none of them. Certainly that was the experience of Dr. Walter Dunn, a retired gynecologist from White Rock, British Columbia, who watched his seventy-one-year-old wife die of ovarian cancer in 1993, the last three weeks of which she spent in a palliative care unit. Dr. Dunn now heads the White Rock chapter of Choice in Dying after hearing his wife plead with him to end her life — a request that because of the law neither he nor anyone else was able to fulfil. "Palliative care in her case provided everything that could be expected of it, but it cannot cope with the patient who is getting weaker and weaker. In the end, she could no longer stand up. She finally became incontinent. All these things palliative care could do nothing about. And it distressed her greatly."

Dr. Boisvert, one of the few palliative care physicians in

Canada who openly supports the right to die, delivered moving testimony to the Special Senate Committee about the difficult clinical cases he faces in which there is nothing he can offer medically to relieve distress. One of the patients whose case he discussed was a sixty-six-year-old woman dying of bowel and rectal cancer. The tumour had invaded into her vagina and bladder. For months she endured stool and urine leaking out of her vagina, which caused a terrible odor. "You walk into the house and it catches you at the throat. She is well aware of it. She was an absolutely meticulous, clean lady. Pain is not her problem, it is well controlled. The problem for her is this total indignity. She has been asking me to send her to heaven for months . . . What do I do for her?"

Hampering the development of innovative techniques for symptom control is the fact that palliative care has never been an academic discipline with a strong research base, notes Dr. Neil MacDonald, an oncologist and palliative care expert who now leads the cancer ethics program of the Clinical Research Institute of Montreal. "Many people are attracted to palliative care, not as the result of intellectual interest, but because of strong emotional, religious and ethical drives to correct a striking imbalance in the existing system. Therefore, palliative care groups may contain superb humanists and clinicians but not individuals with research pedigrees." MacDonald has been leading a movement in Canada to enhance palliative care's research base and academic standing. MacDonald is unusual in that he both treats cancer and delivers palliative care — two fields with almost opposite philosophies as discussed at the beginning of this chapter. "I try to point out if you are looking after cancer patients, you can't say: 'Well I look after cancer patients but not when they start dying.' Oncologists are very incomplete if they don't regard palliative medicine as a major part of what they do."

The fact is that more than half of the people diagnosed with cancer will eventually die of their disease. MacDonald, along with many other palliative care physicians, believes it is high time for the traditional powerhouse centres of cancer research to begin to consider problems of pain and symptom management to be equally worthy of study as new anti-cancer drugs. Each year, for example, the National Cancer Institute of Canada (NCIC), through money raised by the Canadian Cancer Society, doles out some $30 million to cancer research projects, but less than 1 per cent of the budget has gone to find ways to keep patients comfortable during cancer treatment or after the treatment has failed. In 1993, when the NCIC began to recognize that improving quality of life for patients during and after cancer treatment should be an essential part of cancer research, only $66,000 went to an area of palliative care.

Medical schools, too, have been slow to integrate the principle of palliative care into the medical curriculum. Death denial is still rampant in the teaching of medicine. U.S. ethicist Daniel Callahan notes that "one can read entire textbooks on cancer and have a hard time figuring out that people actually die of the disease." A survey conducted in 1992 by MacDonald of Canada's sixteen medical schools showed that none of them offered a formal palliative care course. The schools varied with the number of lecture hours devoted to palliative care principles and techniques. The Special Senate Committee Report released in 1995 noted that McGill leads with twenty hours, Dalhousie and McMaster follow with about sixteen hours, Calgary with eleven, and Queens, Western and the University of B.C. were at the bottom with three or less hours in the entire medical curriculum. As a result, many graduating doctors do not know how to give adequate pain and symptom control to dying patients. They may have little knowledge of the various combinations of drugs, and they may harbour misconceptions about morphine. The same lack of training in palliative care techniques occurs in the United States, notes Dr. Timothy Quill, a former hospice director. "We would never graduate a person from a residency program who didn't know how to do CPR, yet we graduate thousands of residents every year who don't know how to use high-dose narcotics, or are afraid of using them, who don't know how to do continuous infusions or various methods of advanced pain relief."

Many of the limitations of palliative care were addressed by the Senate committee in their recommendations, which included a need for national standards or guidelines, and an alternative payment system such as salaries to doctors practising palliative care because the fee-for-service system is often inadequate to cover the intensive time needed to deliver care. Many programs that deliver palliative care in the home rely on the twenty-four-hour caregiving of a spouse or family member, who may become overwhelmed by the demands of constant care, and the physical and emotional toil of looking after a dying loved one. Respite beds — in which the patient can go for a few days to give the caregiver a break — are woefully lacking. A 1986 survey of palliative care programs, reported first in the Canadian Palliative Care Directory in 1987 estimated that only 5 per cent of Canadians had access to comprehensive palliative care. That figure of 5 per cent has been widely quoted since that time, but no one really knows whether the number is still true.

However, that figure doesn't mean that 95 per cent of terminally ill Canadians are dying in pain and discomfort. Many are looked after by caring family physicians who keep them pain-free and living at home without having to admit them into a designated palliative care program. In fact, in interviews with general practitioners across Canada, many expressed the concern that if they refer the patient to a program, they can be shut out of the patient's care in his or her last weeks or months even though they may be the doctor who knows them best. One Ontario doctor told me, despite having access to one of the province's best programs, she rarely refers patients to it: "I have good relationships with my patients. I usually treat them, as well as their spouses and their children. I know a lot about them. When they are dying, if I suddenly transfer their care to another doctor, I no longer look after them. It feels — to both them and to me — like I am abandoning them. I won't do that. If I get a case that is so difficult that I just can't handle it, then I would seek out the advice of the palliative care expert, but I always try to keep them as my patient." The Senate committee was told by numerous presenters that if practising doctors were updated on pain management techniques, 80 per cent of the country's palliative care needs could be successfully met by family doctors in patients' homes, in small community hospitals, and in small local hospices. The Senate committee subsequently recommended that the focus be on disseminating the techniques through family doctors and the community, backed up by palliative care consultants.

No matter how good palliative care becomes there will always be some people who do not want it; some individuals whose needs cannot be met. For some to accept palliative care means they must accept that they are dying. To them it feels like giving up and so they reject palliative care. Then there are those people who don't want to be patients at all, who recoil at being bed-bound and cared for by others, no matter how compassionate and skilled the care. Ray Stelter, Gayle's husband, feels he would be one of those individuals. "Now that Gayle is dead, if I became terminally ill, I wouldn't want strangers looking after me, doing all those personal things like bathing me and changing my bedpan. And I don't want my children to do that, either, even if they wanted to. I don't want them to see their father that way, because that is not who I am." Russel Ogden, in his study of AIDS assisted suicide, found that the overriding concern for those who chose to commit suicide was the loss of independence and the inability to make personal decisions. The timing of four of the thirty-four planned deaths coincided with the need to be hospitalized, the individuals feeling that hospitalization signalled the end of their independence and their quality of life.

Even if palliative care will never meet everyone's needs, its existing shortcomings call out for attention from medical educators, the medical profession, bio-medical researchers, drug manufacturers and various levels of government. Should euthanasia or assisted suicide be allowed before any of these inadequacies are addressed? Palliative care practitioners answer with a resounding NO! They believe allowing euthanasia would prevent any improvements in palliative care from taking place at all. "In my opinion, we shouldn't even talk about changing the law until all Canadians are ensured access to comprehensive palliative care," MacDonald said. "Anything short of that and it would be pushing people to the brink, saying you can't have good palliative care, but we'll help you die. That, to me, would be a highly unethical act."

But those who are lobbying for the right-to-die see the issue from the entirely opposite point of view. "It astounds me that people say that until palliative care is good enough, the choice to die should not be possible! It should be the other way around: that until palliative care is uniformly good, then everyone should be offered euthanasia!" Louise Miller says passionately, pointing out that if you take away the option of an easy death, those unable to access palliative care are left with a long, slow suffering and inadequate pain relief. "They think that is some-how superior? It's unbelievable!" Is it possible that rather than undermining the provision of palliative care, as its providers fear, the freedom to have assisted suicide or euthanasia might actually improve it? Might it prove to be the stimulus to give palliative care the recognition and funding it deserves to address some of its shortcomings?

As was shown in Chapter Five, the availability of euthanasia and assisted suicide has spurred an improvement in palliative care in the Netherlands. "While there is still room for more improvement, I believe the care for the dying is getting much better here, rather than worse," said Dr. Paul van der Maas, lead author of the Remmelink study, the findings of which are credited with causing the government to act.

If the federal government passed legislation to allow patients a choice for euthanasia or assisted suicide, it could at the same time make a mandatory financial commitment to palliative care research and services to ensure that any choice for death is made in the context of the available alternatives. The requirement of national standards and guidelines for palliative care could be established, as could the inclusion of palliative care in the medical curriculum across Canada. Likewise, doctors receiving requests for euthanasia or assisted suicide from patients would seek an obligatory consultation with an expert in palliative care before the request is fulfilled. If, as palliative care providers claim, good palliative care actually reduces the requests for euthanasia, then areas of the country showing disproportionately high numbers of requests for euthanasia could serve as the focus of investigation into, and augmentation of, those regions' palliative care services. Taken together, all these factors could give palliative care the clout that formerly it has lacked in the power centres of academies, research and government. In fact, care of the dying would improve if patients were given the freedom to make choices about what they wanted for their own deaths.

It is no secret that the values and moral beliefs of palliative care have been strongly rooted in the Christian faith. The palliative care movement in its beginnings was a Christian protest against insensitive hospital treatment of the dying. In Britain most of the hospices are named after saints and are supported by the local parish. Many doctors and nurses openly acknowledge that they have been drawn to the practice of palliative care because of a spiritual desire to make a difference to the lives of the dying. At the outset of palliative care in the 1960s and 1970s, there was no recognition of it as a discipline, no possibility of an academic posting, no career advancement in the traditional medical hierarchy, nor any real monetary gain. "It was often a great sacrifice to do this kind of medicine — we were met with tremendous suspicion by others who would say, 'Who are you to say I am not caring or compassionate?' We were ostracized. We tended not to be ambitious for ourselves. So, the motivation, perhaps, was based more in Christian compassion. At the heart of any religion is the idea of care and caring," said Dr. Doyle.

There is no doubt that dying itself has always raised profound philosophical and spiritual questions that are addressed by various religions. Why do people die? Why do some people suffer so? What is the meaning of life? Why me? Why now? What happens after I die? It is little wonder that people with deep spiritual beliefs should be drawn to an area of medical care, and an area of life itself, that cries out for spiritual understanding, especially when so much of our culture is deep into death denial. If a dying patient wants to talk about some of those frequently asked questions, there are pastors and counsellors available in palliative care programs, as well as the doctors and nurses themselves. Most palliative care programs are careful not to push religion. The programs are open to all denominations or those with no religious beliefs at all. Most palliative care providers do not attempt to proselytize.

Sometimes the religious penchant of some of those who are drawn to work with the dying slips through. Louise Miller says one of the first overnight homecare workers who came to help look after Doug was an evangelistic Christian. Louise woke up in the middle of the night on the woman's first shift to find that Doug had struggled out of bed and was shaking in rage, in the dark, beside her bed: "She just asked me if I have accepted Jesus into my heart!" Doug, an atheist Jew, sputtered to Louise. The woman, who was not an official part of the palliative care program, was released as Doug's caregiver the next day and a

similar intrusion never arose again, but the incident made a
strong impression on both Doug and Louise. "Before Doug got
sick we had joked that our worst nightmare would be to be
stuck somewhere with someone quoting scripture at you, being
unable to get away. And then here he was, sick in bed, dying,
with someone asking if he'd accepted Jesus. It was too much."

There is a saying that is common among palliative care
providers: "You die as you have lived." The phrase was used by
palliative care workers when addressing the Senate committee.
It was said to me dozens of times in my research among palliative care workers who often used it to explain the difficult death
of a patient in the program. To be fair, they often meant that
individuals don't change personalities when they die; if they
have been accepting and resolute in their life they tend to
remain so in death; if they have been angry and aggressive, they
will still be angry and aggressive. But the saying also has a quasi-
religious, judgemental tone to it, one that individuals who are
not religious can find deeply offensive. It seems to say that if
you have lived badly you will die badly, that a painful, difficult
death is retribution for some earlier transgressions. "I find it
very painful when I hear palliative care workers say, "People die
as they have lived," says Louise. "This was not true in Doug's
case. He had lived as an autonomous, self-directed individual.
However, he was forced to die on everybody else's terms but
his own."

It is understandable that those palliative care doctors or
nurses with deep religious beliefs would be unable to comply
with a request to help end a patient's life, no matter how rational the request may be. That right to refuse should always be
theirs to make; no one should ever be forced to act against their
own beliefs. But the question must be asked whether palliative
care providers, consciously or unconsciously, are letting their
personal beliefs intrude on the choices they make available
to their patients. There is evidence that they do. Just ask Tom

Sigurdson, a former member of the legislature in Edmonton, Alberta who was by the side of his wife, Cynthia Verbonac-Sigurdson, when she died of breast cancer at the age of thirty-four. According to Tom, some of the nursing staff's religious beliefs prevented Cynthia from having a choice that even the Senate recommended patients should be allowed: the option to be sedated and to have food withdrawn to allow the patient to die.

I met Tom Sigurdson about six months after Cynthia's death. He had moved from their Edmonton home to a condo in Surrey, B.C. They had bought the place while she was ill but had never been able to move into it together. Nevertheless, Cynthia's presence is felt in the stylish decorations, and the pictures of her that adorn the book cases and walls. In most of the shots, she still had her sandy-coloured, wavy hair. In one, however, she is touching her shiny, chemo-bald head up against the shiny bald head one of their close friends, two human billiard balls side by side smiling. It is one of Tom's favourite pictures, showing as it does, his wife's sense of humour and lively nature even in the adversity of cancer.

Tom is in his late thirties. Even as an ex-politician, experienced in speaking under all kinds of conditions, it is hard for him to talk about his wife's death. When he appeared before the Special Senate Committee, less than a month after she died, he wasn't sure whether he would be able to do it. He practised his speech four or five times at home with his sister but not without crying. On the day of his appearance before the Senate committee in Vancouver, he took along a small nail clipper. With his hands beneath the table, unbeknownst to the committee members or anyone around him, every time he felt himself becoming emotional, he jabbed the blunt end of the clipper in the palm of his other hand. "It hurt like hell," he said. But it worked — he didn't cry. Six months after her death he still speaks slowly and carefully with long pauses between words. Every so often he must excuse himself to regain his composure.

They first met back in 1982, when she was a reporter at a small Alberta paper and he was the campaign manager for a local politician. Tom knew within a half hour of their meeting that they would wed, which they did in 1985. A year later Tom ran for political office and won a seat for the opposition New Democratic Party. Cindy, after finishing her journalism degree, ended up managing the public relations department of the Alberta Blue Cross. In 1989, when they began to think about starting a family, Cindy went to the doctor for a full check-up. For some reason — perhaps because she had been a heavy smoker and on birth control pills — Cindy insisted on a mammogram despite being only twenty-nine and not having any palpable lump in her breast. Medical staff almost tried to talk her out of it, but Cindy's intuition was correct; the test revealed a suspicious spot. The biopsy proved it to be cancerous. "We were told that we were very lucky it was caught — it was an *in situ carcinoma* — it was contained and would not spread," Tom said. Cindy had a mastectomy early in 1990 but they were told there was no need for radiation or chemotherapy. "After that scare our life could return to normal. In a way it made us appreciate our lives together all the more."

Cindy, being the confident woman that she was, refused to wear a prosthesis to replace the missing breast, walking proudly with her lopsided bosom like it was a well-won battle scar. Until surgical breast reconstruction she let her figure speak the truth, even on the beach. If people gave her startled stares, well, that was their problem. To Tom and Cindy, they were survivors and despite check-ups every six months, to them, the worst was behind them. Then, two years later, the Sigurdsons returned home from a conference and vacation in Australia to a message on the answering machine that Cindy's annual PAP test had shown abnormal cells in her cervix — stage one cancer. She was told to report immediately to the Edmonton cancer agency for surgery.

"Again, after the surgery, we were told that all was well and life could return to normal," said Tom. But in the fall of 1992, Cindy began to develop an aching pain in her back, legs, hips, and shoulders. A bone scan showed nothing and she was told it was osteoarthritis. Over the next eight months the pain never really went away — she'd have good days when she could go to work and bad days when she couldn't get out of bed. By June of 1993, she had begun to complain about Tom's driving — he was accelerating too quickly, stopping too suddenly. She was dizzy and nauseated. More tests were run, and yet again, they came back negative. Since Tom had recently lost re-election after a difficult campaign and because she had had the earlier diagnosis of osteoarthritis, the doctors put her symptoms down to the stress and disappointment of the defeat. Perhaps she was suffering from depression, they said. Her symptoms persisted through the summer until finally on the Friday of the 1993 Labour Day long weekend Cindy had another bone scan. When the results came back, almost a week later, the news was devastating. The localized cancer that "they didn't need to worry about" had spread to eight locations: her left leg, her hips, her pelvis, her spine, her left shoulder and three spots on her skull. Her life expectancy was six months to a year. Tom put down the phone and numbly walked into the bedroom to tell Cindy the news. He lay down beside her and putting his arms around her, began to cry. She didn't need to be told, in a sense she had been suspecting it for months.

"We naively hoped that she'd have six good months and then quietly one night she'd simply die, but it wasn't like that." Over the next two months Cindy became increasingly ill, sleeping twenty to twenty-two hours a day. Her tumours grew rapidly. By mid-November, Tom was dressing her, assisting her to the toilet, and helping her to bathe. He would help her to the table where she would eat her meals. Unlike many cancer patient's Cindy's appetite never diminished — some of her greatest enjoyment in her final months came from food. That healthy appetite would eventually cause a problem when she was trying to die. For many weeks, with the help of their family doctor, they were able to control the pain by either increasing the dose of narcotics or changing the medication. The problem, however, became bowel care. "Codeine and morphine constipate so additional medications have to be given to find the equilibrium between pain and poison. We never found that equilibrium," said Tom. As a result, Cindy became incontinent. "The first time I had to change my wife after she soiled herself, we both cried."

As her thirty-fourth birthday approached in February of 1994, Tom asked her what he could get her. She told him the only thing she wanted was to die. He began to ask around about physician-assisted suicide, but like Louise Miller, all he met with were closed doors. "Maybe it was because I was doing the asking, maybe it was because of the publicity of Sue Rodriguez, but no one would help us." By the end of February Cindy's pain had become so bad that it could no longer be controlled at home. She was admitted to the Edmonton General's palliative care unit, recognized as one of the leading palliative care programs in the country. To the couple's relief, her pain and symptoms improved with the staff's expert handling of a variety of medications. Palliative radiation shrank the tumours in her spine, shoulder and skull, and enabled her to walk again. She had a course of tamoxifen chemotherapy to extend the quality of her life. After seven weeks she was well enough to return home. They had dinner parties with friends, entertained, enjoyed what was left of life. Tom got Cindy a cane so she could manoeuver around the house. It was still tricky walking, however, and one day she slipped and fell. As she lay on the floor as Tom rushed to her side, she laughingly yelled, "Help,

I've fallen and I can't get up," acting out a well-known commercial that was playing on television at the time. When he tells this story, proof of his wife's remarkable resiliency and humour as cancer whittled her away, Tom's voice becomes choked with emotion. A man who doesn't like to cry in front of others, he apologizes for his tears.

In retrospect, those good weeks in April and May were a treasure that Tom and Cindy were glad to have, but according to Tom those days didn't remove the rationality of allowing her the choice to die in February. "She would have been content to go in February. Sure, April and May were good, and we would have missed that, but both she and I would have rather given up April and May than have had to endure the horrendous suffering of early March, and of June and July. Some days were so horrendous and the pain so incredible that even 100 good days hardly make up for them." In late May bowel care once more became a problem and whenever she became constipated, which was often, she would vomit. Agonizing pain returned. "At times I couldn't even touch the bed without her crying out in pain." Less than six weeks after returning home, Cindy had to be hospitalized again, waiting first in a regular hospital ward until a bed opened up again in the palliative care unit.

The relentless progress of the cancer, and its wake of devastation continued. In early June her tumour-riddled left hip, which was as fragile as an egg shell, fractured during a simple transfer in an ambulance. "The pain was so excruciating for her that I cannot describe it to you. There was nothing they could do at the time except drug her into oblivion. The bone was so honeycombed with cancer it could not be set." From that time on she had to remain in traction, lying in a special, $40,000 air-baffled bed. She would cry out in pain when she was bathed. She could not be turned so her skin began to break down from bedsores. Numerous tumours were in her brain and her bones. Many times in June it appeared she would not live through the night. Tom would say his goodbyes thinking he would not see his wife alive in the morning, but somehow her body kept going. By the end of June she regained her mental clarity, but by that time Cindy was refusing most visitors because it was too heart-wrenching for her to say goodbye to friends, over and over again, each time they left.

By mid-July she was taking enough drugs to stock a small pharmacy. Tom pulls out a list: mycostatin mouthwash twice a day to fight fungal infections of the mouth; 10 mg of the steroid Decadron every eight hours to slow the growth of the brain tumors; the laxative Senekot three times a day; 30 mls of Chronulac, another laxative twice a day; a Dulcolax suppository to help bowel movements as needed; 10 mgs of Ritalin each morning to help with her mental awareness; 1000 units of vitamin C daily to help her amino acid balance; 250 mg of Dilantin once a day to control seizures; six 10 mg injections of Maxeran every day to help nausea and improve her G.I. tract motility; 220 mg of methadone every eight hours for pain, with 70 mg breakthrough doses every hour as needed; Ativan and Halidol each night for sleep; Buscopan injections as needed to stop bladder spasm to keep her catheter running smoothly. And then Tylenol, enemas and more Maxeran as required. "Often people will say, good palliative care can control most pain and symptoms and to that I say, well, here's her list of medications. She had the best that was available and yet she still had pain and discomfort," Tom said.

Although she repeatedly asked Tom and their medical friends to help her die, while she was in the hospital she knew she was not going to be able to get physician-assisted suicide. She and Tom began to think of other options. They could stop the medications, but that might cause her a great deal of pain — the object was to avoid pain — and even then to stop might not bring about her death. The problem, they realized, was that tremendous appetite of hers. Every morning she would eat a

bowl of hospital oatmeal with cream and fresh blueberries that
Tom would bring. She looked forward to lunches and dinners
and often would instruct Tom to either cook her a lobster or filet
mignon, or to bring food from their favourite Vietnamese,
Chinese or Thai restaurant so she wouldn't have to eat what the
hospital was serving. She could sit and eat an entire container of
fresh strawberries, one by one, slowly savouring each delectable
bite. Tom and Cindy decided that she needed to stop eating.
Cindy felt that the only way she could do so was if she was
sedated to an unconscious state. Tom and Cindy asked the palliative care staff at the end of July if they would help her stop eating by giving her the necessary sedatives. There are many names
used by the medical profession for what Cindy and Tom were
asking for: artificial sleep, total sedation, "snowing," pharmaco-
logical oblivion, "obtundation." Many palliative care physicians
say that in the most difficult cases it is the final arrow in their
quiver of techniques. It is controversial, as many see it as being
one step away from euthanasia; others like Dr. Quill have called
the practice of sedating a patient to allow them death by dehydration, "a cruel and absurd process," one that forces a patient to
die by "natural causes" when almost always the individual would
prefer to die more quickly by overdose or lethal injection.

The technique has received the seal of approval from Dame
Cicely Saunders and the staff of St. Christopher's. Using a combination of barbiturates, the patient is put into a deep sleep.
Occasionally the individual will be fed through tube feedings,
more often all feedings and hydration will stop. If the patient has
requested it, he or she may be roused periodically out of the
drug-induced coma to see if the symptoms are still causing discomfort; if they are, the patient is rendered comatose again.
During the Senate committee hearings, numerous palliative care
physicians said they considered total sedation, at the patient's
request, to be the choice of last resort. No one remarked on how
this choice affects the family, perhaps for days or even weeks

until their loved one dies, or for the individual who, like Cindy, would rather have euthanasia or assisted suicide to get it all over at once.

Tom will never forget the meeting that took place in Cindy's hospital room August 2, 1994. Cindy sat in her airbaffled bed, her hip in traction, slowly eating a container of fresh blueberries as a hospital psychiatrist asked her questions. In the room were her oncologist, a pain specialist, two pastoral care counsellors, a social worker and Tom. The psychiatrist asked her questions, "Do you know what you are asking?" "Why do you want to die?" "Are you aware what this means?" Cindy calmly ate the blueberries, taking her own sweet time to answer. The psychiatrist finally became exasperated because Cindy seemed more interested in the food than in his questions. "I knew what she was doing, she was making them wait on her terms. When the psychiatrist became flustered, Cindy had him exactly where she wanted him." Finally she looked up and held his gaze: "Yes, I know what I am asking," she said. "Yes, I know what this means." After the meeting and their own long private consultation, the psychiatrist, doctors, social workers and pastoral care counsellors all agreed that Cindy should be allowed to be sedated while food was withdrawn. The next day the couple celebrated their ninth wedding anniversary, believing that Cindy would soon be resting peacefully and would gradually die. But later that afternoon one of the doctors came to Tom and told him there was a problem: some of the nurses were refusing to administer the sedatives that would render her unconscious. Tom was livid. "It was religious beliefs. Some of the nurses involved felt such a death was too much like assisted suicide, they said they couldn't be involved. One of them gave me a prayer card and told me it might help. I told her I respected her beliefs, but that we had our own beliefs, too — I am not Churchy but I do believe in God — and my belief allowed this sort of dignified death. It wasn't like getting an injection in which the person died immediately. It wasn't suicide — no one could predict what day or what hour she would die. There was still room for a miracle if God wanted. But they wouldn't have it. It was the beliefs of some of her caregivers that interfered with her choice." When he told Cindy that some of the nurses were refusing the request, Cindy said wryly: "Well, if I'd known I'd have to win the nurses over, I would have done a better job of sucking up to them."

A few nurses, who were supportive of her request, quietly came to see her and offered suggestions about what they could do to speed her death: try stopping the steroids, and Maxeran and Ritalin; the sudden swelling of the tumours in her brain might place her into a natural coma. With all other options closed to them, that is what Cindy and Tom decided to do. For the first two days after those medications were stopped there was no noticeable difference, Cindy simply slept more. On the third day she woke up and told Tom she wanted to take the Ritalin in the morning because she needed to be alert; there were a few things she wanted to do. She made Tom and the staff put her in a special, bed-like wheelchair — one that enveloped her body in malleable cushions so that she would not be jarred during the ride. She had not been out of bed for more than six weeks. Her pain and discomfort were so intense that she vomited almost every fifty yards. Nevertheless she told Tom to first push her to the hospital's roof-top garden so she could smell the flowers. Hospital staff had also planted a small vegetable garden there and seeing the leafy green tops of the carrots, Cindy wondered whether they might be ready. Tom pulled out a small carrot and washed it off; Cindy held it in her hands and savoured its musky, fresh smell. Next she asked Tom to push her along the walkway by the North Saskatchewan River so she could see the trees and flowers along the river valley. Their last stop on the way back to the hospital was a specialty chocolate shop so she could get a box of chocolates for the nurses. In the card she thanked them for their months of care. It was her way of saying she forgave those of them who were unable to cede to her request.

Later that afternoon, when she was back in bed, she stopped the medications for good. Two days later she lapsed into a coma, but her eyes remained wide open. She moaned softly. She was not responsive when Tom asked her to squeeze his hand, but her eyes would follow his voice around the room. He sat by the bed and sang to her. Then, the next day her eyes became fixed, unmoving, like those of a plastic doll. "It was this horrible blank stare, I could hardly look at her." Tom would try to shut her eyes so they would not dry out, but they would pop back open again. When Tom arrived at the hospital the next morning, August 11, six days after she had stopped her medication, Cindy was still staring blankly; her mouth was open and her lips were dry. "I called her name and there was no response to my voice at all." Tom met again with the medical staff and demanded that sedation be reconsidered so that Cindy could close her eyes. "I told them that they could either sedate her or sedate me, but one of us needed sedation. They told me that she was not in any pain and she would die very soon. Their exact words to me were, "You can measure her remaining time in hours and days, but not weeks.""

The doctors' refusal to sedate Cindy made Tom angry. Friends who were visiting from Vancouver wanted to get him out of the hospital to calm him down. "I went back into Cindy's room and told her I had tried my best, but the doctors wouldn't budge. And then, with tears in my eyes, I whispered in her ear, 'if the pain is too great, go to God.'" Tom then closed the curtains and joined his friends in the parking lot. While he was out of the room, Cindy took her last breath and died. When he returned her eyes were finally closed and the look of pain had melted from her face. Tom told the seven senators, as he jabbed the nail clipper into his hand, "had Cynthia been given her choice, there could have been a time that I would have kissed her goodbye and held her until she exhausted her last breath. Instead I am left with a memory of horrible pain and a hollow, haunting stare."

An increasing number of individuals, some within the palliative care movement itself, believe an evolution will take place so that good palliative care will no longer be pitted against the choice of euthanasia or assisted suicide. Instead, it will be a continuum of care that focuses on the patient's needs and well-being throughout the entire journey of their terminal illness. Ideally such a continuum would start during the acute care treatment of the cancer or illness, with doctors and nurses taking into account ways to make the patient more comfortable during the aggressive battle against their disease. Then, as the hope for a cure of the illness receded, pure palliative care would come into full force, doing its best to keep the patient comfortable from physical symptoms while helping fulfil him or her and the family's psychological and spiritual needs. Then, when palliative care was no longer able to meet all the patient's needs and when no other options were available, then total sedation, euthanasia, or assisted suicide, would emerge as possible options. This evolution is what Australian hospice specialist Dr. Roger Hunt sees developing. Hunt says while the development of the palliative care philosophy was founded by Christian idealists, in recent years more and more secular scientists and humanists have been joining the movement. They are beginning to take leadership roles and they are less influenced by traditional religious teaching. He believes palliative care, over the next decade, will eventually grow to embrace euthanasia as a small sphere inside its larger orbit, just as it grew to accept total sedation as a last resort, and the right to withdraw treatment or refuse treatment before that.

There are caring, compassionate, spiritual individuals in Canada now delivering the best of palliative who support legal change to allow euthanasia and assisted suicide. They do not see it as being pitted in opposition to palliative care. They do not believe it will undermine care for the dying. They see it as simply being a final choice available to patients when no other choices will do. One of those individuals is Montreal's Marcel Boisvert; another is Tyleen Katz, the director of May Guttridge Hospice, a six-bed facility situated on the top floor of a subsidized housing apartment in Vancouver's downtown eastside — the city's equivalent of Skid Row. It is Vancouver's only free-standing hospice for terminally ill adults. Trained as a nurse in the early 1980s, Tyleen is the driving force behind the operation of the hospice, which opened in 1990, and in its first four years cared for 140 people. Along with Tyleen (the registered nurse co-ordinator) the hospice has an attending physician who bills visits as house calls on the medical plan, two full-time registered nurses, four part time RNs, two nurse's aids, a music therapist who works twelve hours a week, volunteers working for eight hours a week, and a part-time secretary. Despite its staff, the hospice has been able to keep costs down to $223 a day per patient compared to $960 a day in a hospital ward. Patients do not lack for comfort or amenities: the hospice has two lounges, a sunroom, six residents' rooms each with its own television, a communal dining room where everyone sits for their meals, a kitchen, nurses-station, a bathing room with a whirlpool, and a balcony that overlooks the water of Burrard Inlet and the mountains of the North Shore. Unfortunately, it also has a long waiting list. Only 25 per cent of those on the list eventually make it into the hospice — the others die before a space becomes free.

"This city desperately needs another free-standing hospice. It is a tragedy that we have to turn away the number of people we do," says Tyleen, who is attempting to fundraise $2 million to establish a second hospice in a renovated court-house in east Vancouver. It is Tyleen's philosophy and vision that infuses the May Guttridge home: philosophies of a home-like, non-judgemental atmosphere, of a place that respects individuals for who they are, not forcing them to fit into a pre-determined hospice way of dying. It is that philosophy that shines through as she describes some of the residents who have lived and died there. There was the story of Vera, a diabetic with cancer who craved chocolate cake. "It's her last few weeks of life and she's not had chocolate cake for years. If she wants to eat it until it is coming out her ears, that's fine. That is her choice." Or Barry, the AIDS-infected IV drug user who came to the hospice still addicted to cocaine. Each day he would go out to get his fix on the street and come back to the hospice high, an act that was known and accepted by the staff. One day, while shooting up in his $9,000 computerized bed, he had fallen asleep and the needle had slipped and punctured one of the air pockets, destroying it. When the damage and the needle were discovered, he was told that while they hoped he wouldn't use drugs on the premises, in future if he had to shoot up, to please put his needle in the sharp's box, a special garbage bin for needles. "Having needles around is a hazard to our health, as well as to our mattresses," said Tyleen, who adds, "but you know, these terminally ill people who are drug addicts, I am not going to cure their addictions in the last month of their life. If I could just give them cocaine or heroin, then I could really control their symptoms, but I am not allowed to do that, so I can't give them what they really need."

Through all the stories, of which there were more than a dozen, the underlying current is the hospice's respect for patients' needs and choices. Whether the choice is to drink wine at 9:00 a.m., do drugs, eat chocolate cake, or refuse food and fluids to die faster, all seem to be accepted. In the four and a half years of operation, only two residents have been evicted, one a young drug addict with AIDS whose irrational behaviour and thrashing fits put staff and other residents at risk, and an elderly alcoholic man with lung cancer, who became abusive when he drank and threatened the staff with knives from the kitchen.

As we talk, I am still under the assumption that like 95 per cent of all palliative care providers, Tyleen, too, is opposed to euthanasia, but this talk of needs and patient choices leads to the obvious question, what if the patient feels they need to die? Do you think that is something you could help them with? "Well, right now it's illegal, but I think it should be something that patients are able to ask for. They say that with good palliative care, we don't need euthanasia. But you never know what another person feels. I wouldn't even try to guess. If someone is adamant, then of course, we need to talk, find out the issues. But yes, in the end, I think it should be available." Does she know that most palliative care providers don't agree with her, that they think the options of deliberate death and compassionate care for the dying are incompatible? "Yes, I know."

How does she feel about that? She gives a long sigh. "I think it saddens me. It saddens me because I don't see that we are truly following through on what the preaching is — acceptance of the whole person, respecting autonomy, caring for the patient's individual needs. I know that my colleagues would argue back and say, well, I am also a person, too, and I have my own beliefs. That's true, but I think it is disappointing because our personal beliefs shouldn't affect what our patient's choices are. I don't know what the answer is. I think if you asked anybody who worked here, though, they support the choice. When you come to a little unit like this, which is totally geared to creating a home, it is so much different from a service which you offer in a hospital, or in an institution. I don't know if you really get to know people in a big institution. Here we do a lot of hands-on stuff, like massage, making them a special meal in the kitchen. It seems that when you are working more in a close situation like this you develop more of a kindred spirit with the patient. You feel that your emotional involvement is much deeper. Maybe when you start to share this level of relationship you can feel their needs better. And you understand what true autonomy is."

She describes to me a patient named Linda who was dying of ALS in the hospice at the same time Sue Rodriguez went public. Linda, too, wished for an assisted death and she had tried committing suicide in a hotel room with a friend, but the friend couldn't go through with it at the last moment. Linda then went to May Guttridge Hospice and as her disease made its insidious progress into the muscles of her chest and throat she began to struggle for breath. Instead of going on a respirator, Linda chose to be sedated into unconsciousness to let the disease continue its assault without her having to feel the terrifying sensation of suffocation. It was a choice the hospice respected and provided. She died sixteen hours later of respiratory failure as her muscles finally gave out. "Linda's death was peaceful. It was a good death, but it took sixteen hours and she really wanted the lethal injection. I think Linda should have been able to ask for it and get it when she wanted it."

Believing, philosophically, in such a choice is one matter, but could Tyleen, physically, be the person who gave the shot? "If all other avenues had been explored with the patient, the physician and myself, I don't believe I'd have a problem answering the cry of a human being whose needs palliative care had not met. I think it is quite pathetic, when you get the argument that doctors, if given this authority, will be killing vulnerable patients out of their own convenience or with pressure from the families. I think that says a lot about how doctors see their professional colleagues; they must have a rule forbidding it, otherwise they would kill indeterminately. To me that argument totally backfires and makes the medical profession look really, really bad. Doctors are dealing with patients in life-determining situations every day, for heaven's sakes."

Our euthanasia talk was brief — perhaps fifteen minutes out of a three-hour conversation, a tiny snippet in the total picture of what palliative care could grow to encompass if the action was made legal. It would be inaccurate to report it as the centre-piece of the conversation. Most of the time we talked about individuals, their stories, their particular needs and how, as best they could, the staff at the May Guttridge Home tried to meet those needs. Like the man, dying of cancer, whom Tyleen took for a drive around Stanley Park one afternoon because he felt glum. On the trip he let pass that what he really craved was a good, rich, meat-and-potato meal. So the next night, Tyleen made him rack of lamb, crème caramel for dessert, and bought a nice bottle of red wine. The man's son, along with the other residents and staff, joined in to share the special meal around the hospice's big dining-room table. There was lots of talk and laughter and second helpings. It was a grand evening. The next afternoon, the man felt tired and lay down for a nap. When one of the staff went to wake him to see if he wanted tea, she found he had died in his sleep. Perhaps one day all Canadians will have access to such compassionate, respectful care that meets their individual needs as they die, and maybe it will be delivered by people who truly listen to what each patient is saying, whatever it may be.

8

WITHHOLDING
AND
WITHDRAWING
TREATMENT

I T WAS SUNDAY, four days before Christmas, and
Dr. Brian Burkell was driving from the emergency room of one
Victoria hospital to that of another. He was seeing two patients
who were being admitted; little did he know that he would
soon be a patient there himself. The thirty-five-year-old general practitioner had been in Victoria just seven weeks, moving
from Kamloops to start a new practice. He and his wife, Pat, a
child psychologist, had been worried about their youngest son's
worsening asthma and decided a move to the coastal air might
improve it. When Burkell had seen the advertisement in a medical journal, placed by Dr. Scott Wallace, looking for a third
partner to join a busy medical office in the heart of the city, he
responded eagerly. The interview couldn't have gone better.
Not only did Burkell have an excellent reputation as a family
doctor in Kamloops, he was bright and personable, with the
sort of outgoing, caring and congenial personality that Wallace

and Dr. David Hosgood were looking for in a partner. Leaving Pat and the three children up in Kamloops to sell the home while he established the new practice in Victoria had been hard. He missed them, but the next day he would be driving back to the Interior to be with them for Christmas. That was one of the reasons he was on call this weekend — so he could take the next ten days off.

It was a rainy afternoon, about 4:00 p.m. and he was approaching a busy intersection, going about 20 kilometres an hour when the man driving in the truck behind him went into a sudden epileptic seizure. The man had blacked out before while behind the wheel, and his family had urged him not to drive, but for some reason he'd ignored them. This time when his extremities began to jerk and twitch uncontrollably, his foot locked on the gas pedal, sending his vehicle careering into the back of Brian's Volvo. The force of the collision on the wet road spun Brian's car out into the stream of perpendicular traffic. He was hit first on the passenger side by one car, spun around and was hit a second time on the driver's side by another car. Even though Brian was wearing his seatbelt, the impact sent Brian's head and shoulders flying sideways into the metal frame of the driver's window and then rebounding back to smash into the side of the passenger seat.

By the time the ambulance rushed him to the hospital he had just left, the bleeding inside his brain was plunging him into a deepening coma. The emergency room staff thought they recognized him, but rifling through his personal belongings trying to find the name of any friends or kin to phone, they found Wallace's name and address in his wallet — Brian had been heading there later that day for dinner. Wallace will never forget the call. He was in his kitchen as all his adult children, newly returned from university for the Christmas holidays, milled about talking and laughing. The atmosphere was happy and festive, until the emergency physician asked, "Do you know a Dr. Brian Burkell?"

When Wallace put down the phone he was in shock. He told the emergency physician that he would phone Brian's wife.

"It was ten minutes to five when the phone rang. The kids and I were just sitting down to dinner and I said to them, 'That must be your Dad now,'" recalls Pat. Instead it was the devastating phone call from Wallace that irrevocably changed their lives. "I remember Scott said to me how much he regretted what he had to tell me, but Brian was in a serious car accident, that he was going into surgery to try to reduce the pressure on his brain. He said I'd better get the first plane down to Victoria." She called her in-laws to come to watch the kids and took the 7:00 p.m. plane. "I kept thinking, 'It's going to be okay. This sort of stuff happens to other people, it doesn't happen to us. He's hurt, but he'll be back home.' Even when I got to the hospital, I didn't realize how serious it was."

Meanwhile, Wallace had rushed to the hospital. In his heart he felt a faint flicker of optimism, too. Maybe it wouldn't be so bad, maybe it would be just a mild head injury. One look at his young partner, however, and he knew it was as bad as it could get. His skin had a ghostly blue-grey pallor, meaning he was having trouble getting enough oxygen. Blood-tinged fluid was trickling out of his left ear and one nostril — a sign that his brain was leaking cerebral spinal fluid. His pupils were unresponsive to light, his body motionless, his reflexes gone. He was being placed on a respirator. Wallace knew almost immediately he was looking at what was probable brain death and that eventually the life support must be removed to let him die. Wallace and Hosgood met Pat at the airport later that evening and drove her into town, escorting her to the ICU where her husband lay hooked up to monitors, IV lines and the respirator. "The most shocking part of seeing him there in the ICU was that his eyes were wide open and glazed over, so glassy," she said. "He was such a pale colour and he lay very, very still. But part of me thought he is just going to wake up out of it."

The neurologist and ICU doctor told Pat "the night will tell" so she sent her husband's two partners home to get some sleep while she placed a chair by his bed to sit with him. She held his motionless hand and listened to the click and whoosh of the respirator, the beeps of the monitor and her own internal prayers. She kept imagining that she felt a twitch, or saw Brian move. "Did you see that?" she'd say to the ICU nurse. But Brian remained motionless and the nurse thought it would be better if Pat had someone sitting with her. She phoned Dr. Wallace at about 1:30 a.m. and he came back to hold vigil with her, watching Brian's chest move in and out with the force of the respirator, listening to the machines, watching for movement that never came. In the early hours of the morning, Brian began to bleed again into his brain. Pat went home with Wallace to sleep for a few hours while the doctors tried to stabilize her husband. When a brain scan was taken that Monday morning it showed what they all had feared — a flat line, no brain activity. "Everyone was very good, they didn't push me. I know they were probably thinking that it was time to remove the respirator, but I wasn't ready. For my own peace of mind I needed to have a second scan later that day, just to see if there was any change. I knew the decision was in my hands and, fortunately, they didn't rush me."

It wasn't until the next morning that the results of the second brain scan were analysed by the neurologist. For Pat the results made it clear that she must give permission to turn off the respirator sustaining the life of her husband, her best friend, the father of her children, the wonderful, caring man who had been the foundation of her life since they began dating sixteen years earlier. She must allow him to die. "It helped that Brian and I had talked a lot before about what we'd want in a case like this. I knew that this is what Brian would want me to do," she said. "And I was thinking about the kids and Christmas. If we kept him on the respirator he might live three or four more days, they told me, but that would mean he could die on Christmas Day, and I didn't want that. It seemed better, now that we knew it was hopeless, to just let him go."

Pat was in the ICU by Brian's bed when, at 11:00 a.m., December 23, thirty-six hours after the accident, the respiratory technician turned down the settings on the machine. The nozzle of the plastic tube that plugged into the tracheostomy in Brian's throat was unfastened; the machine was wheeled away from the bed. "Scott had warned me that when they take people off respirators, they can move. Sometimes it is not peaceful. He had tried to prepare me, but I guess I hadn't processed it," said Pat. As Brian's body became starved of oxygen, all the muscles in his body seemed to react in protest. His back arched as if he was rising from the bed, his arms and legs jerked. "It was quite startling. His whole body was contorting. There was a significant amount of movement. I thought, He's coming back! He's waking up! It was just the loss of oxygen, but it wasn't easy to see." With no brain activity left to tell the lungs when to breathe, no machine to do it for him, and no oxygen getting to the muscles, Brian's heart went into cardiac arrest and ceased beating less than five minutes after the respirator was removed. The ICU nurse gently took Pat by the elbow and ushered her out of the room. "I guess it's time to go now, dear," she said.

Each year in Canada tens of thousands of individuals die after treatment with the potential to sustain life is stopped, or in some cases never started. For some, like Brian Burkell, the decision to stop treatment or remove a respirator, in medical terms, is fairly straightforward no matter how wrenching and tragic the particular case. It is clear to both the medical staff and the family that further medical treatment is pointless and life-support is only prolonging inevitable death. Other decisions to stop treatment may be much more difficult or complicated; the proper course of action less certain. Perhaps it's a decision to not give antibiotics to an elderly demented person with pneumonia, thereby setting the stage for death from "the old man's friend." Or maybe after a discussion with the patient or the family, a "Do Not Resuscitate" order is placed on the patient's hospital chart in the event of a cardiac arrest. Or perhaps it is the patient him or herself who refuses life-saving treatment no matter how helpful it may be, such as a Jehovah's Witness who refuses a blood transfusion, or a person with chronic kidney failure who decides to stop dialysis.

The exact number of times each year such non-treatment decisions are made in Canada is not known — no one has ever compiled the statistics and, furthermore, death due to the termination of treatment is usually recorded under the disease being treated. But everyone agrees that such decisions are increasingly common. As medical technologies have become ever more able to hold death at bay, the conscious decision to stop treatment to allow death has become ever more necessary. Medical studies indicate that half of all deaths in intensive care units in North American hospitals arise from the decision to either withhold or withdraw treatment. In Canada it is estimated that more than 35,000 individuals each year — one fifth of all deaths — may die after a non-treatment decision is made; in the United States that figure is more than 400,000.

With such decisions now a familiar part of modern medicine, it seems hard to believe that fifteen years ago the whole area was as controversial and as rife with disagreement as assisted suicide and euthanasia are today. In fact, non-treatment decisions were in the past called "passive euthanasia" and opponents predicted a whole host of dire events if such acts became common: treatment would be withheld from vulnerable individuals against their will; individuals who might survive if given enough time would have their life support prematurely halted; families, tired of looking after a chronically ill parent, might coerce them to stop treatment; individuals themselves, fearful of being a burden, might ask for treatment to stop; doctors could be brutalized by the process; cash-strapped hospitals might resort to withholding and withdrawing treatment as a way to save money. Sounds familiar, doesn't it?

Now, however, the cessation of treatment is called good medical care. Indeed, all but a handful of the more than 150 individuals appearing before the Special Senate Committee on Euthanasia and Assisted Suicide endorsed the withdrawal or withholding of life saving treatment under two situations: when the disease or injury is so severe that any further treatment would be futile, or when a competent individual, either in person or in an advance directive, has made an explicit, well-informed request that the treatment stop. "There is virtually universal consensus on withholding and withdrawing treatment," says Arthur Schafer, the director of the Centre for Professional and Applied Ethics at the University of Manitoba. "No one says that a competent individual should be forcibly kept alive on a respirator or a kidney dialysis machine against his or her will, that life is a supreme value and that physicians should always protect life. What was controversial fifteen years ago is now understood as a fundamental human right."

Over the last decade what has occurred in the area of withholding and withdrawing treatment is nothing short of revolutionary, says Schafer. "Our society, even if we are reluctant to admit it, has accepted another category of justifiable homicide in the death of an individual, besides that of self-defence and war. When a physician allows a patient to die, either by withholding an antibiotic that permits pneumonia to kill the patient, or by taking them off a respirator, as a society we have recognized that under certain conditions it can be justified to be an agent in bringing about the death of another person, even if it is in an indirect way." B.C. ethicist Eike Kluge agrees: "The medical profession's acceptance of passive euthanasia, and its endorsement by religious groups such as the Catholic church, indicate a consensus on the proposition that sometimes it is ethically appropriate that death occur." Once society accepts that under certain circumstances the act of helping someone to die can be legitimated, as it has done in withdrawing treatment, then Kluge notes, it follows that active euthanasia and assisted suicide must be ethically defensible as well.

For many ethicists, philosophers, and health care professionals, however, there is a firm distinction between deliberately giving a fatal dose as in euthanasia and assisted suicide, and removing life support or not giving a drug to allow nature to take its course. Even though both acts result in the patient's death, one is killing and the other is letting die. One is an act, the other is an omission. One is an unnatural death; the other a natural death. This moral and philosophical distinction has been exhaustively debated in hundreds of articles in the academic literature over the past twenty years. In a now famous article, "Active and Passive Euthanasia," examining the distinctions in 1975, philosopher James Rachels presented the analogy of two men: one who sneaks into the bathroom and pushes a child's head under the water to drown him; the other who watches as a child hits his head on the tub and slips under the water, doing nothing to save him as he drowns. One killed the child, the other merely let him die. Rachels contends that there may be a physical difference between the acts, but there is no moral difference.

Rachels' classic piece concluded that because what the two men did is morally the same, then killing and letting die are morally the same, and therefore active and passive euthanasia are morally the same. Therefore, it doesn't make sense to make one illegal and consider the other appropriate medicine. That conclusion, however, set off a fierce philosophical debate that twenty years later still hasn't stopped. Health professionals in particular state that while both actions may result in the ultimate death of the patient, the actions of giving a fatal dose compared to stopping treatment *feels* different to those doctors and nurses involved in the act. By withholding or withdrawing treatment they are not the direct agents of death, rather it is the underlying disease process that kills the patient. For health professionals such a difference is easier for them to live with.

Others argue that the difference hinges not on the act itself, but in the intention of an act. If, like Rachels' two men, the intention is to bring about the death, then there is no difference between killing and letting die. But when the medical profession withholds or withdraws treatment, either on patient request or when it is medically futile to continue, the intention is not to cause the patient's death but to either respect the right of the individual to refuse treatment, or to remove burdensome medical technology that is no longer helping. The death may be foreseen, but it is not wanted. The precise moment of death is not known and no one assumes God-like power over the life of another person. In the same way, when high doses of morphine are given in palliative care, the intention is not to bring about death, even though the drug may cause it to occur, but to relieve pain and discomfort.

Justice John Sopinka, in writing for the majority of the Supreme Court in the Sue Rodriguez decision, reaffirmed that distinctions based on intent are important and, indeed, form the basis of criminal law. "While factually the distinction may be difficult to draw, legally it is clear." That legal distinction, however, leads to some philosophical hair-splitting bordering on the absurd, as was seen in the reasoning of the Nancy B. case. Nancy B. was a twenty-four-year-old woman from Montreal, paralysed from the neck down because of the effects of Guillain-Barré syndrome. As her disease was not terminal she might have lived for years in her condition had she not asked the hospital staff to remove her respirator. The hospital was afraid that if her request was granted, they would be seen as having killed her and be open to prosecution under the Criminal Code. Justice Jacques Dufour ruled that turning off her respirator would not in any manner constitute the crimes of manslaughter, murder or assisted suicide, because it would not cause her death, her illness would. Yet everyone involved in the case, including Nancy, her doctors and the judge himself knew full well that she could not live without it and therefore turning off the respirator would indeed bring about her death.

"As an empirical claim — that death ensues because of underlying pathological conditions and the doctor doesn't intend that death — is in my view, worse than implausible; it is almost certainly false," says B.C. philosopher Earle Winkler. "It is a case in which the doctor understands the patient's desire for release from life is authentic and reasonable. And so the intentional state of the doctor is to allow the patient her release." The natural/unnatural distinction so commonly made by those who defend removing life support but who reject euthanasia is also dubious, critics claim. If "natural" is inherently superior to that which is "unnatural" then the argument can be made that we should not treat sickness at all, or give pain relief, or intervene in any medical way during illness and death, even if this means a much more painful, arduous form of dying. Taken to its extreme, an adherence to what is natural would mean that as human beings we wouldn't wear clothing, build skyscrapers, drive cars, or fly in airplanes. "It is patently unacceptable to suggest that doing what is natural is somehow more desirable," says Glen Owens, a professor of psychology at the University of Auckland, who is active in international debates over euthanasia. "One could suggest that the whole point of civilization is to transcend what is natural."

Schafer views the present-day debate over euthanasia with a sense of *déjà vu* — he has heard it all before during the debate about withholding treatment. He believes that contemporary ethicists who list the severe ramifications of allowing active euthanasia or assisted suicide are suffering from "historical amnesia" when they fail to see how similar the concerns were for passive euthanasia. "Every argument advanced against the liberalization of euthanasia or assisted suicide was used fifteen years ago against stopping treatment. The same concerns apply." Take, for example, the difficult problem of determining whether an individual's request to turn off a respirator is truly voluntary. "How do we know it is not the illness speaking? How do we know that they are genuinely competent? How do we know they have not been coerced by family or doctors? These are perfectly sensible questions, but they apply with equal weight to whether a dying patient is competent to request euthanasia as they do to the decision to withhold or withdraw medical care, acts which happen thousands of times every month in Canadian hospitals," Schafer notes.

The decision to stop kidney dialysis is a case in point. In North America, each year some 80,000 individuals are sustained by the process of dialysis, which assumes the role of their failed kidneys in cleansing the body of waste compounds. At least three times a week or more they must either hook themselves up to a machine to filter their blood (hemodialysis) or infuse and flush fluid into and out of their abdominal cavity (peritoneal dialysis). If this is not done they will die, usually within two to three weeks as the waste compounds build to toxic levels in their blood. Dialysis is a physically and emotionally demanding routine, one that requires adherence to a rigid schedule and a special diet. The psychosocial demands of chronic dialysis are so well known in medical circles that dialysis programs almost always involve a team comprised of specially trained doctors, nurses, a psychiatrist, social worker, nutritionist and others, such as pastoral care workers, to help patients deal with all potential issues. Some chronic dialysis patients may be freed from their bondage to the machine through a kidney transplant — usually after a wait of two years or more. But each year a small percentage of patients may decide to give up on the process, a decision that brings about certain death. The statistics for how often this occurs vary depending on the study or region — most programs report less than 1 per cent of the dialysis population dropping out each year, more often among those who are old, or who have other complicating diseases. Some long term studies in the United States, however, estimate that one in ten people on longterm dialysis eventually decide to stop, and die. "What are they choosing when they choose to do this?" asks Dr. Timothy Quill. "They are saying life as I have to live it with dialysis and with disease is no longer worth living — it's too hard and I would rather be dead than live the way I have to live. As doctors we say that's okay — we challenge them to make sure they are sure, we are conservative and cautious, but in the end we say okay." Dr. Angus Rae, a Vancouver nephrologist who has specialized in dialysis for thirty years, says the decision to stop is relatively rare; "more often our patients are clinging to life." But if a patient really wants to stop, the team will bring the family together, talk about the decision, what it means, bring in a social worker or psychiatrist to find out if there are any matters that can be addressed to change the desire. "If they are certain and unwavering, then we will stop treatment. We will usually admit them to hospital to keep them comfortable with morphine, anti-nausea medication, and other drugs, as necessary, until they die." Rae says that the patient's motivation to stop treatment is rarely pain or unacceptable physical symptoms, but rather boredom and fatigue with the constant routine — they've simply had enough.

Sometimes, however, the desire to stop is mitigated by other factors that can be resolved by the dialysis team. Patricia Rodney, a Canadian nurse doing a doctorate in nursing ethics addressed the Senate committee about one seventy-six-year-old patient with diabetes who had been coping well with dialysis for a number of years. One day Mr. C. announced that he was going to stop treatment. The team was perplexed because he had never discussed this desire before and his physical health had not suddenly deteriorated. For two or three days the team talked with him to try and understand why. "With some reluctance he disclosed that he wished to stop dialysis because he felt he was becoming an increasing burden on his wife and was stressing her own resources. After finding that out the team . . . had a much better understanding of how to proceed. They negotiated a new plan of care for him. They arranged to get more homecare support . . . He and his wife were able to cope much better. He withdrew his request to have the treatment stopped and lived what he described as a good quality of life for another four years."

The process of determining the rationale for the request that Rodney describes is exactly what should happen when a patient or a doctor is about to make a decision that will end a life. As Quill notes, "Before making such a vital decision to stop treatment, it is important that all alternatives have been explored in depth and are understood by the patient. Such a decision should never be distorted by inadequate treatment of potentially reversible problems, nor should it be coloured by depression that may be treatable." Just as there is a potential for a euthanasia or assisted suicide decision to be made hastily without careful deliberation between the patient and physician, there is just as much danger that a decision to stop treatment could be made poorly. If the communication and relationship between the patient and the health care team is bad, Rodney points out, then exploration of the deeper issues might not occur. There is as much risk in both passive and active euthanasia that a decision can be wrong, or arbitrary, or taken too lightly, or tragically irreversible. Yet we now call one good medical practice and the other a dangerous precedent that must be kept illegal.

John Griffiths, a Dutch professor of the sociology of law, contends that by making an ethical distinction between stopping or not starting treatment on the one hand, and euthanasia on the other, we obscure what is most important about all these decisions: they all lead to death and therefore they are decisions that all need to be made carefully. Those who fear the "slippery slope" of abuse if euthanasia is allowed, but embrace the stopping of treatment as good medical care risk being blinded to the dangers of the latter, which are already around us. "It is like guarding the front of your house so euthanasia won't get in, but leaving the back door wide open for abuses to occur with stopping treatment." Winkler agrees. Those who argue that euthanasia and assisted suicide will harm the ethos of the medical profession, for example, have to explain why turning off a respirator, or stopping tube feeding with the knowledge death will result, pose no threat to the medical profession or society and is instead good medical care. What is most important is not the difference between passive and active euthanasia, but their similarities.

The widespread consensus that exists about stopping treatment does not mean that the acts occur without controversy. Are food and fluid given intravenously (or through a gastric tube) forms of medical treatment that can be withdrawn? Can the medical profession stop treatment and allow a patient to die against the patient's or family's objections? Can the medical profession continue with treatment the patient or the family has requested be stopped? When is medical treatment futile and who should have the right to define such a value-laden term? What should the medical staff do if life-support is withdrawn but the patient doesn't die quickly and instead suffers a lingering, painful demise?

Stopping food and fluid has been one of the more controversial areas of treatment withdrawal. Food has strong emotional resonance, a normalcy to it that seems to set it apart from other medical treatments, even if it is delivered by a tube to the stomach. Some groups, such at the World Federation of Doctors Who Respect Human Life, maintain nutrition and hydration are a "basic life-maintaining need" and reject any suggestion that they can be stopped, even if they are delivered through surgically implanted feeding tubes. The Canadian courts have been divided about whether food and fluid are medical treatments that can be stopped. In one case in British Columbia, in which a Doukhobor woman had gone on a hunger strike while in prison, the court ruled that food could not be forced on her by doctors against her will. In a case in Quebec, however, the judge ruled that a hospital could feed and even operate surgically on a competent man who had refused all medical treatment. The U.S. Federal Court leaves it to the discretion of individual states whether feeding tubes can be withdrawn and many states make it difficult to do so.

The Special Senate Committee on Euthanasia and Assisted Suicide, in what may turn out to be one of its most immediately influential recommendations, stated that it considers artificial nutrition and hydration to be medical treatments that can be refused or withdrawn like all other medical treatments. The Senate committee cautioned, however, that such actions must always be done under strict guidelines. Even before the Senate committee's recommendation, however, a growing number of Canadian health care professionals had begun to accept the option of stopping artificial nutrition. Such acceptance doesn't mean those deaths are easy ones to be involved with. Montreal palliative care physician Dr. Marcel Boisvert tells the story of a forty-six-year-old patient, a once-athletic, successful individual who suffered from what the medical profession calls "locked-in syndrome." A series of bleeding episodes at the base of his skull had damaged the lower portion of his brain. He was completely paralysed except for the tiny movement in the finger of one hand and the ability to blink his eyes. He communicated with his wife, his children, and caregivers in coded blinks; one blink no, two blinks yes. His intelligence was unaffected. He decided at Christmas of 1994, after more than four years of being locked in, that he wanted his tube feeding stopped so that he could die. "He had a loving wife who had been at his bedside all along as well as two kids. He was stable. He was seen by two neurologists and psychiatrists at the Montreal Neurological Clinic; he was seen by myself, another physician, all the nurses on the floor and we all agreed that this man understood . . . Always the answer came back yes, I want to finish this."

After four months of deliberation, the team decided to grant his request and the feeding tube was pulled out. It took twelve days for him to die. "For at least five or six of those days, he was fully aware of what was going on," said Boisvert. "Ethicists talk about intent. Well, let's not play on words here. The intent was to grant him his wish to die. We can rationalize and say, 'Well, we pulled the tube out and we let the disease kill him.' But unless we pulled the tube out he would have lived for another ten years until the next major bleed. The intent of removing the tube was to bring his death about. Yet we let it go on for twelve days. Can we argue from the medical point of view that this was in the patient's best interest?" The distinction between killing and letting die, as Boisvert and other health professionals have realized, can sometimes be reduced to a diminishing point. And what makes that distinction harder to rationalize is when the process of stopping treatment to allow a "natural" death becomes a medical nightmare. Just ask Scott Mataya.

For two years, up until December, 1991, Scott Mataya was a nurse at Toronto's Wellesley Hospital. He thought of himself as a good nurse — caring, professional, even though he was new to the job. He had worked first for fifteen months on the general surgical wards after graduating from Ryerson in 1989 at age twenty-four. Looking for a greater challenge, he and a friend decided in January of 1991 that they would take the critical care nursing course to train as intensive care nurses. It was a good deal, the hospital paid them while they went back to school for two months and it was interesting, high-tech stuff. When he finished in March of 1991 he joined the staff of the hospital's twelve-bed intensive care unit (ICU). He loved working there. He got along with the other staff and they seemed to like him. He was known for his biting wit and dark sense of humour, which in the stressful life-and-death atmosphere of the ICU removed tension and kept people sane. Mataya's story of what happened in the last week of November 1991, illustrates just how blurry the lines can become between the legal acts of withdrawing futile treatment and giving morphine to control symptoms, and the illegal act of deliberately ending a life. Says Quill: "This story gets to the core of our ambiguity on this issue and it shows how we — the medical profession and the health care system — need to set up protocols to establish the proper procedure when we are withdrawing treatment to anticipate everything that might go wrong."

Mataya had been working in the ICU for just ten months when an elderly man named Joseph Sauder was transferred to the Wellesley Hospital's ICU from Queensway Hospital. Otherwise healthy and active, Sauder had undergone an operation on his arthritic knee three days earlier, but inexplicably the day after surgery a massive infection set in, which compromised all his organ systems. The infection put him into a coma, requiring life support on a respirator, dialysis and cardiac monitor in the Wellesley ICU. Mataya was assigned to his one-on-one nursing care. "He was a big man and nothing was working. His liver didn't work. His kidneys didn't work. His gut didn't work. His skin was covered in blisters and where it wasn't blistered it was bright red. He was on every ICU life-support equipment known to man," says Mataya. After ten days in the ICU Sauder showed continuing organ failure, no gag reflexes nor pupil response. With no hope of improvement, his wife and doctor decided it was best to unhook him from life support to let him die. According to court transcripts, the doctor wrote an order for 40 mgs of morphine and 30 mgs of valium, which Mataya drew up. The doctor injected the drugs into Sauder's intravenous line. As ordered by the doctor, the respiratory therapist turned down the settings on the machine. The doctor wrote an order for a second infusion of the same amounts of morphine and valium, which could be given in half an hour, if needed. The respirator was removed from Sauder's tracheostomy and the doctor left the room.

Mataya told the respiratory therapist: "I hate it when they take a long time to die," as she was leaving the room to clean the respirator for another patient. Mataya was then alone with Sauder. "I dimmed the lights. And I waited. And he keeps breathing and breathing. It wasn't like I could leave the room. He was my sole patient. I couldn't leave a patient to die." Half an hour passed and Sauder was still breathing laboriously. Mataya called the resident to come and give the second dose of morphine and valium, which the resident did. "And he still goes on breathing with 80 mg of morphine and 60 mg of valium — a massive dose. And then he started to twitch. He started to produce tons of mucus which was frothing out of his tracheostomy. I was trying to suction this stuff up. He was coughing and hacking. The twitching was getting more and more severe. It was going against all the drugs we had given him. I didn't want his wife to come back and see him like this. I didn't want her to learn that he had choked and suffocated to death." Mataya said he looked at the heart monitor and could see the heart's strong, steady beat. "It was a healthy, bloody heart and I thought this guy's heart has got to stop. I knew there was a drug right on my tray that would stop it. I drew up some potassium chloride — we use it all the time to balance electrolytes. I diluted it in an IV chamber, because I didn't want it to burn going in. And I gave it to him." Four minutes later Sauder's heart stopped.

Did Mataya not realize he was crossing a boundary? Did he not know it was considered murder and that he would put his career in jeopardy, face jail, or receive a criminal sentence? Did he not even understand that, in the medical hierarchy, for a nurse to act on his own without a doctor's orders is strictly forbidden? "None of that crossed my mind. I just thought a man shouldn't have to choke and suffocate to death. It wasn't as if he was going to recover. His fate was decided when the respirator was turned off. I thought he shouldn't suffer." Mataya said all he felt was relief, not remorse, when Sauder finally died. Mataya left the room, told the nursing supervisor that Sauder's death had been "a bad one" and that he was going on his break.

When he came back Sauder was being readied for the autopsy his wife and doctor had requested to find the source of the infection. "And the nurse says to me,' So are you worried about the extra morphine you gave him?' And I said, no I didn't give him any morphine, I gave him potassium chloride," Mataya said. According to Scott Rowand, president of Wellesley Hospital, the nurse Mataya told originally thought it was "Scott's notorious black humour, but over the next few hours he realized Scott wasn't joking." The nurse gathered up the garbage from Sauder's room in a sealed bag for evidence, and then told Mataya he was calling the senior staff and hospital administrators. "So they all start marching in . . . the vice president of this, the supervisor of that. Everyone in the whole hospital," Mataya said. "I'm sitting in the conference room, crying my eyes out. I told each one of them what I did — I had nothing to hide. The coroner comes and looks at the charts and keeps telling me, 'Don't worry it will be okay,' but I knew for certain it was all over." Says Rowand: "It is absolutely clear, he killed the patient. He administered a drug which he knew would stop the heart and which had no other therapeutic value."

They sent him home around midnight with a union representative to make sure he was not suicidal, or about to flee the country. The union arranged a lawyer who came by the apartment the next morning. "The first thing he says to me is, 'Did you tell anybody what you did?' And I said, 'I told no less than twelve people, I didn't have anything to hide.' And he says, 'Oh my God.' At noon the next day, after the lawyer told him to dress in warm clothes, the union rep and lawyer walked him back to the hospital, where Mataya was charged with first degree murder by two detectives in the hospital boardroom. His eyes were so red from crying all night that he hadn't been able to put in his contact lenses. When he arrived at the police lock-up they took away his glasses so that he wouldn't smash them on the floor and fashion them into a weapon — a notion that never would have entered into the mild-mannered nurse's head. "I'm blind without my glasses," he says. So standing in the court room when he was remanded into custody, he was unable to see anything but a blur of faces around him. He was transferred from the police station to the Don Jail in a line of other suspected criminals, handcuffed by one wrist to a man charged with armed robbery and on the other wrist to a drug trafficker who was high on crack cocaine. Mataya was fearful about what might happen to him behind bars, but to his surprise he was placed in a cell away from other prisoners, ate his meals on his own, and exercised in an empty yard. "I guess they figured that they didn't want anything weird to happen to the nice nurse who helped the suffering man die. It might inflame the political situation." He spent a week there until his parents could post the $100,000 bail and his trial date for murder was set.

Joseph Sauder's widow, Isabel, has declined to comment on the specific circumstances of her husband's death, but she has never criticized Mataya and his motives for what happened in that hospital room. Both the hospital and the police have acknowledged that her reluctance to press charges resulted in a reduced charge against Mataya. In May of 1992 Mataya pleaded to the lesser charge of administering a noxious substance. He was put on three years probation and lost his nursing licence for life. He was forbidden for three years from seeking work in any area of health care. "I can't even get a job in a drug store," said Mataya who was unemployed for more than three years after his arrest. Mataya knows that when he gave the lethal injection he crossed over a line between what is acceptable in the care of dying patients and what is considered murder. But he is not apologetic. "For months I would ask myself, 'Oh my God, did I really murder this guy?' Maybe I deprived him of a half-hour of life but it was probably only five minutes. But to this day, in my heart, I do not feel that I did anything wrong."

"I think the line shows the hypocrisy of how we treat the dying. If I had used a bit more morphine, it would have been okay. But because I used potassium chloride, and I was naive enough to be upfront about it, I am branded for life," Mataya said. What is most painful for Mataya is that after Sauder's death he came under suspicion for every unexplained death that had occurred at the hospital in the previous two years. The RCMP and the hospital spent months researching old files of unexplained deaths, trying to link them to Mataya's shift times to see if they could connect him to any deaths. Everything he said and did for the two years he worked at the hospital was probed. During one shift an elderly patient on the general surgical ward he worked on was found dead in her bed with sheets stuffed down her throat. At the time, the investigation ruled it was a suicide, but after Mataya's arrest, the daughter became convinced that Mataya was responsible. The RCMP could not find any evidence against Mataya and no charges were laid. To this day the daughter still believes Mataya murdered her mother. "That is what really hurts, my credibility and honesty have been permanently called into question." Mataya said. "Everyone who talks to me, in the back of their mind they're wondering, 'Did he kill anybody else?'"

According to Quill, while Mataya's actions were clearly illegal and wrong under present laws, the case aptly illustrates how hospitals and the medical profession need to adopt standard procedures for the withdrawal of life support. When turning off respirators, for example, doctors should be obliged to stay in the room to provide adequate levels of morphine to control symptoms. Nurses, particularly inexperienced ones, should not be left alone with the patient. All possible complications of removing life support, such as a patient who doesn't die should be anticipated and the proper procedure for dealing with that agreed upon throughout the institution. "We can't have a situation where people are acting on their own, even with the best of motives. But nor can we have a situation where a patient is struggling and drowning in their own secretions," Quill said.

Wellesley's Rowand says that he, too, wants to see some changes. Particularly he wants to see the Criminal Code amended so that doctors and hospitals are protected from prosecution when the decision to remove life support has been reached carefully and with consent of the patient or family. "Often patients in ICUs are on very high-dose, long-term infusions of narcotics. In order to keep the patient comfortable at the time of discontinuation of ventilation, the doctor may be required to give additional doses of narcotics. This leaves them open to investigation and second-guessing by law enforcement. There should be legal protection so that the doctor is not afraid to give an adequate dose of morphine to keep the patient symptom free." But Rowand also adds that Canadian society also has to debate the ethics of letting a patient die "naturally" once the decision has been made to turn the respirator off. "When the outcome, death, has already been decided by removing the respirator, I think we have to start talking about whose interest we are serving by not, in fact, bringing about the end more quickly."

Mataya is not the first health professional in Canada to come under scrutiny for giving a dying patient a helping hand as they are being removed from life support. Some doctors and experts estimate it occurs all the time in hospitals but only a handful of cases have come to the attention of the authorities and the media. While Canadian case law has firmly established the right of patients to refuse treatment or ask that respirators be removed, there exists among health care professionals some uneasiness about the legality of the actions because the existing Criminal Code can be interpreted to specifically forbid the acts. In 1983 the Law Reform Commission of Canada recommended that the criminal code be amended to protect doctors who turn off respirators at a patient's request, or when the therapy is useless, but no amendment has been made. Over the last twelve years there have been numerous cases that show there is no consistent policy, only continuing medical and legal confusion about what is appropriate when removing life support. In 1990 in North Vancouver, the B.C. coroner's office, the RCMP and the B.C. College of Physicians and Surgeons investigated the deaths of two men under the care of Dr. Peter Graff in the Lions Gate Hospital intensive care. Both men — an eighty-five-year-old with colon cancer and a sixty-five-year-old with amyotrophic lateral sclerosis — had asked to be disconnected from their respirators. Graff gave both men repeated doses of morphine and valium over a number of hours until their deaths. Both the college and the coroner's office concluded that Graff's doses greatly exceeded what was necessary to relieve the patients' pain and discomfort. The college "found cause for serious criticism" of Graff's actions but did not discipline him. The RCMP investigated but decided against laying charges, primarily because both families praised Graff for his compassionate care.

In October, 1991, seventy-year-old Mary Graham, who had throat cancer, asked to be withdrawn from a respirator keeping her alive in a Timmins hospital. With her family sitting around the hospital bed, Dr. Alberto de la Rocha administered morphine into Graham's intravenous line and then removed the respirator. Graham, breathing with minor difficulty on her own with an oxygen mask, said goodbye to her family around the bed. Dr. de la Rocha asked a nurse to get potassium chloride and when the nurse refused, de la Rocha got it himself. Standing behind the bed curtain, out of sight of the family and without their knowledge, he administered the dose into Graham's IV, which caused her heart to stop a few minuteslater. In April, 1993, Dr. de la Rocha was found guilty of administering a noxious substance and received a suspended sentence and three years' probation. On the witness stand, Graham's son George refused to criticize Dr. de la Rocha, calling his act one of "kindness and care," which had enabled their mother to have a "humane and peaceful death." In a disciplinary hearing before the Ontario College of Physicians and Surgeons in April 1995, the committee determined de la Rocha had crossed the line when he gave the potassium chloride even though the patient was only minutes from death. They ordered that he write guidelines for community hospitals about the proper procedure for withdrawing life support.

And in yet another case, in April of 1993 in Winnipeg's King George Hospital, a forty-eight-year-old man with ALS was removed from his respirator, at his request, and given multiple doses of morphine by his doctor until he died. The death, which was kept quiet by the staff, was leaked to the media six months later, prompting a six-month investigation by crown prosecutors and an inquest by the provincial medical examiner. Both concluded that no wrong-doing had occurred, but not before putting the family and medical staff through more than eighteen months of legal uncertainty.

In its recommendations about withholding and withdrawing treatment, the Special Senate Committee stated that "it is unacceptable that life-sustaining treatment is being withheld and withdrawn without adequate guidelines in place governing such practices." The committee recommended that the Criminal Code be amended and legislation be enacted in order to explicitly recognize and clarify the circumstances in which stopping treatment is acceptable. They also recommended that Health and Welfare Canada, in conjunction with professional organizations and the provinces, establish guidelines governing the withdrawal or withholding of treatment.

Usually, when the decision is made to withhold or withdraw treatment, the family and the doctors both agree it is the best course of action. The family doesn't want Mother subjected to CPR if there is no hope that she will ever recover; the doctors agree that further treatment is hopeless. A "Do Not Resuscitate" order is placed on the chart. Sometimes, however, the family and the doctor do not agree. Either the family wants to stop treatment, but the doctors feel aggressive therapy should continue, or the doctors want to stop treatment, and the family is pushing for everything to be done.

In January of 1994 one such case hit the Canadian headlines when Toronto's Hospital for Sick Children wanted to disconnect four-month-old Kandice Knowles from the respirator sustaining her life. When Kandice had been born, she appeared to be a healthy child, but when she was three months of age, her mother, Tami, noticed that she seemed to be having trouble focusing her eyes. Within days she was comatose and on life support in the hospital where doctors diagnosed a fatal degenerative brain disease. When Kandice had been on life support for six weeks, the doctors believed that any further treatment would be futile and would not prevent the infant's inevitable death. They gave her mother a week's notice that the ventilator was going to be turned off. Tami objected, got a lawyer, and went public that the doctors were going to shut the ventilator off against her will and kill her baby. The hospital capitulated and said the ventilator would never be turned off without her consent. They loaned Tami a ventilator and the mother took her daughter home. At the child's first birthday, eight months after the respirator would have been withdrawn, Tami told the media her daughter "was doing really well." The infant was still deeply unconscious, unresponsive, with no hope of ever waking, yet her mother cared for her, giving her apple juice and formula through a feeding tube. Kandice died in late December of 1995.

Similar cases are becoming increasingly common throughout North America. An anecephalic baby in Boston, born missing most of its brain, was kept alive for more than two years, despite the hospital making two trips to court to try to obtain permission to turn off the respirator against the mother's wishes. Also in Boston, the daughter of a seventy-one-year-old woman in chronic ill health has sued a hospital for failing to do CPR when her mother had a heart attack and died. The patient, Catherine Gilgunn, had entered hospital for a hip fracture. She suffered from diabetes, heart disease and Parkinson's disease. She had had a stroke the year earlier, and prior to that a mastectomy for breast cancer, and three previous hip replacements. While in hospital, she began to suffer repeated seizures that left her with irreversible brain damage and rendered her comatose. She was in a coma for more than six weeks yet the daughter refused to allow a "Do Not Resuscitate" order to be placed on her mother's chart because her mother had always wanted everything to be done for her. The hospital ethics committee overrode her wishes and allowed a DNR to be written on the chart. When she eventually had a heart attack and the crash cart wasn't called, the daughter sued.

The question at the heart of these issues is what is medical futility and who defines it? Should it be left to doctors to determine when it is inappropriate for medical technology to prolong an inevitable death? Should families legally be able to demand that treatment continue indefinitely, even if it appears an inability to accept death lies at the root of the request? As many observers have noted, it comes down to individual value judgements about whether a specified treatment will have the desired end or create an acceptable outcome.

"The problem of futility is one the most difficult ones in medical practice today," Canadian Medical Association ethicist Dr. John Williams told the Special Senate Committee. "For instance, is a resuscitation which should perhaps keep a patient alive for another two weeks futile or not? The answer may be yes and no. It would not be futile in the sense that it would achieve the goal of keeping someone alive for two more weeks, but whether that goal is worthwhile or acceptable is really a decision that is based on the values of patients, caregivers or whoever." Many doctors have told me how upsetting and frustrating — sometimes even sickening — it is for them to be doing repeated resuscitations on hopelessly ill patients or sustaining a dying person on life support simply because the family won't say no to treatment. The medical profession feels its role is not simply to acquiesce to the demands of patients or families giving them whatever treatment they want. Doctors have the right to exercise professional judgement. Many academic articles studying the issue of futility conclude that doctors should be under no obligation to offer, nor even discuss, medical treatments with a patient or the family that will not result in a measurable improvement in the patient's health, such as allowing a release from the intensive care unit, or a discharge from hospital. John J. Paris, a Jesuit priest and ethicist who is an expert witness for the Boston hospital in the suit over Mrs. Gilgunn, said while the right to refuse treatment has been established, there are some who think that means they have the right to demand any treatment, whether it will work or not. "This is madness, this is not what medicine is about," he was quoted as saying in *The New York Times*.

Recommendations to give physicians discretion in what they do makes a great deal of sense on the surface, yet when given as *carte blanche* authority for doctors to unilaterally make decisions about what is or is not futile treatment, without having any obligation to convince the patient, the result can be very undesirable. Notes Eike Kluge: "The claim that an action is useless is not an absolute matter. It depends on the context in which the claim of uselessness is advanced. . . . Given that the values involved are the values of the medical profession, that means that only medical judgement is accepted as competent in this regard. This is unacceptable."

Some observers of the Boston case note that unlike Mrs. Gilgunn and her daughter, most reasonable people with such chronic health problems would not want to be sustained on life support or subjected to repeated resuscitation. The wish to "do everything" can be a symptom of death denial and emotional problems that call out for counselling. If doctors are allowed to unilaterally decide what is appropriate treatment, then the need to communicate effectively with the patient is removed and the underlying problem is never addressed. Studies show that in most cases, if the physician takes the time to compassionately explain to the patient or family, for example that CPR in the elderly has a dismal success rate, most patients decide a DNR order or non-treatment is the right decision. It is worth enduring the few extreme cases like Mrs. Gilgunn to ensure others open, effective communication that allows them to make real choices. Winnipeg's Schafer is concerned that often it is the way that doctors phrase the questions that lead to families asking for continued treatment when the clinical outlook is dim. "Doctors will say, 'Do you want us to withdraw treatment from your mother?' placing the emphasis on what the family wants. They should be asking, 'What would your mother want in this situation? She is going to be comatose, she will never regain consciousness, she will never be released from the hospital, would she want us to continue treating her?' Framing the question in the latter way removes the burden of guilt from the family so they don't feel they are deciding that their mother dies, but instead that they are following what she would have wanted."

When doctors and families don't agree, however, it is most often doctors who wield the authority and override families' wishes. In 1995, a study by University of Pennsylvania researchers shocked both the medical profession and the public when it was found that one third of intensive care doctors in the U.S. had ended life support without obtaining formal consent from the patient or the family. In 3 per cent of the cases, doctors reported ending life support over the objections of the family. A large proportion of the doctors also reported that they had carried on with life support against the will of families, either feeling the families wishes were not well informed or not representing the patient's best interests. In some instances, however, there is simply not enough information to know what the patient would have wanted. The patient never talked about death and dying with her family, never discussed with her doctor what she would want for her treatment if she ever became seriously ill, or never drafted an advance directive, what is often called a living will.

"A crisis will arise — it is almost always in the middle of the night — and there is nothing on the chart to help the resident know what to do," says Schafer. In fact, without any patient or family input to guide them, doctors presented with the same scenario with a critically ill patient can make enormously different decisions. That was the conclusion of a widely publicized Canadian study that was published in the *Journal of the American Medical Association* in the spring of 1995. The study presented a questionnaire detailing twelve typical patient scenarios to more than 1,300 doctors and nurses working in the intensive care units across Canada. In only one scenario — an elderly woman on a ventilator with metastasized breast cancer, Alzheimer's Disease and acute renal failure — did more than half the respondents choose the same decision to withdraw treatment. In eight of the twelve scenarios, 10 per cent of the respondents chose the opposite extremes.

"The same patient may thus receive full aggressive intensive care from one health care provider and only comfort measures from another," said the study, led by Dr. Deborah Cook, an assistant professor of medicine and clinical epidemiology at McMaster University. The study found that the more experienced the doctor or nurse, the less likely they were to give aggressive intensive care. Even when the clinicians make decisions based on the best evidence available, their own ethical, social, moral and religious values influenced their decision-making, the authors stated. "We believe that most patients would find the situation in which the care they receive is highly dependent on the attitudes of the health care provider unsatisfactory," the authors stated. In a separate part of the study, however, the authors found that the intensive care staff would consider the contents of an advance directive in coming to a decision about limiting or withdrawing care. The authors concluded that patients should discuss their wishes with their physician and family members and put it in writing.

If Maria Perelli had written out an advance directive seven years ago before Alzheimer's disease robbed her of her mind, she might have saved her family a painful rift and herself a lingering demise in a Sarnia nursing home. Instead, when the seventy-two-year-old woman developed pneumonia in 1993, her husband and her adult children couldn't agree as to whether doctors should treat her with antibiotics. "My sister and I pleaded with my father and our other sister to allow the doctors to withhold the antibiotics and to let her die, but they thought she should get everything," said Paul Perelli, who asked that his family's real name not be used "because this issue has divided us enough already." Twice in 1994 Perelli was treated with antibiotics that saved her life. She lives on, unable to recognize those around her or remember her own name, while her family is barely speaking to each other. "They think we are cold and callous to want to let her die. And we think they are extending her life beyond anything that she would have wanted," her son recounted sadly.

Contrast that with what happened to Donald McGregor. The eighty-year-old Victoria man also suffered from Alzheimer's disease and lived in a nursing home, but he had specifically told his wife, Connie, that he never wanted any treatments to prolong his life. When he came down with pneumonia after falling and breaking his hip in May of 1994, Connie told the doctors not to give him antibiotics. Donald died five days later. "I had absolutely no hesitation. I felt so fortunate because Don and I had talked about it, he had given me specific instructions, so I knew that is what he would have wanted. I know many other people for whom that decision is agonizing because they never discussed it and they simply don't know," she said.

There is one issue in the debate over euthanasia and assisted suicide that both sides agree on: more people should write out an advance directive to detail what they would want for their medical care, if ever they are unable to make the decision themselves. It would help remove many dilemmas at the end of life. While most people use advance directives to refuse life-sustaining treatment, the documents are equally valuable to help ensure that people get the life-sustaining treatment they want. "It is a way for people to have their health care wishes respected, regardless of what is chosen," says Dr. Peter Singer, an assistant professor of medicine and associate director of the Centre for Bioethics at the University of Toronto. Advance directives have been receiving a higher profile in the last few years. When news reports revealed that both Jackie Kennedy Onassis and Richard Nixon had one, calls to organizations providing forms increased five-fold, *The New York Times* reported. Few Canadians, however, have bothered to write one, and doctors, too, seem reluctant to initiate discussions with patients about the benefits of drawing one up, perhaps because it means talking about future incompetence, serious illness, and death. "The healthier you are, the more the onus is on the individual to fill one out. But as people become sicker, or where there is a predictable pathway of decline, such as in AIDS or Alzheimer's disease, the more I think the onus should be on the medical profession to raise the issue with patients and to actively seek their input about what choices they want," Singer said.

Advance directives can have their pitfalls, particularly if they are vague, therefore they should be as specific as possible. When a patient writes "no extraordinary treatment" or "no heroic measures," family and medical staff don't know what that means. Blanket statements, like "No respirator" are also not helpful because they don't take into account that sometimes short term use of a respirator can return the patient to normal health. Doctors are often unsure what to do if a situation arises that is unforeseen and not covered by the living will. For example, a man infected with the AIDS virus develops a sudden severe allergic reaction to a drug. His advance directive states "no respirator" but doctors know that if they put him on a respirator he will overcome this short-term emergency, and probably have months or years left to live. Did the patient want it to apply in this situation? Will the doctors be sued by the patient if they ignore the will and put him on a respirator?

Advance directives, too, can sometimes predispose patients to more distressing symptoms when they thought they were asking for a more peaceful death. A patient, for example, may state that she refuses surgery or radiation if her cancer is hopeless and death inevitable. But surgery and radiation can be used to reduce the size of a tumour that is perhaps blocking a bowel or obstructing a windpipe, making the patient much more comfortable in her final days. Similarly, a patient may write that if an illness is reversible he wants life-saving treatment, but no treatment if his condition is irreversible. But what do doctors and family do if there is a 20 to 40 per cent chance of recovery? Furthermore, people's health care choices can change over time. In a study that Singer conducted among people infected with the AIDS virus, 78 per cent changed their mind over at least one treatment choice within a six-month period. And six months later, 78 per cent had changed their mind again. Advance directives must be regularly reviewed and updated to insure they reflect the patient's current wishes. To avoid some of these problems, Singer recommends that individuals discuss their advance directives with their doctors to help them be specific in their wording, to go over possible health care scenarios, and to clarify the wishes of the patient and the contents of the will. It is also recommended that people designate a health care proxy — a person they trust and who knows their values and wishes for medical treatment — who can interpret the advance directive, override it, or make decisions in unforeseen circumstances.

A number of designs of advance directives exist. Singer has created one that combines the advance directive with the appointment of a proxy, and a written section where patients can express their values. It is available through the Centre for Bioethics. The main portion of the directive is a table-like grid with choices under various health scenarios that the individual answers yes or no. Health care professionals find this advance directive easiest to use because it sets out the patient's wishes in clear and straightforward terms for them. Patients, however, sometimes find its medical terms difficult to understand and may need help from their doctor. The Centre's advance directive is the one I personally prefer and I have reproduced the chart portion here, with the choices that I have selected if I were ever to become incompetent during a health crisis.

There are other models. Dr. William Molloy, a Hamilton geriatrician, along with Virginia Mepham, a Hamilton nurse, have designed a proxy/advance directive combination that appears in

	CPR	VENTILATOR	DIALYSIS	LIFE-SAVING SURGERY	BLOOD TRANSFUSION	LIFE-SAVING ANTIBIOTICS	TUBE FEEDING
CURRENT HEALTH	Yes	Yes	Yes	Yes	Yes	Yes	Yes
MILD STROKE	Yes	Yes	Yes	Yes	Yes	Yes	Yes
MODERATE STROKE	Yes	Treatment Trial*	Treatment Trial*	Yes	Yes	Yes	Treatment Trial*
SEVERE STROKE	No	No	No	No	No	No	No
MILD DEMENTIA	Yes	Treatment Trial*	Treatment Trial*	Yes	Yes	Yes	Treatment Trial*
MODERATE DEMENTIA	No	No	No	No	No	No	No
SEVERE DEMENTIA	No	No	No	No	No	No	No
PERMANENT COMA	No	No	No	No	No	No	No
TERMINAL ILLNESS	No	No	No	Comfort Surgery Only	Undecided	No	No

* Treatment may be attempted to overcome an acute health crisis only; not to be used to sustain life where there is little chance of being weaned from the machines.

their book, *Let Me Decide*. Dying With Dignity, the Toronto-based right-to-die organization, also has its own advance directive forms, as does Goodbye, a choice-in-dying organization in Vancouver.

While pre-set forms make it easier for individuals to fill in the blanks, even writing down your wishes on a piece of blank paper and carrying it in your wallet is better than doing nothing at all. Because of the problems of advance directives, some jurisdictions, such as those in Britain, have declined to give them the force of law, preferring instead to have them simply act as guidelines rather than binding documents for patients' care. Slowly, however, Canadian provinces are going the route of legal recognition. Quebec and Nova Scotia have legislation allowing the appointment of a health care proxy. Manitoba was the first province to put into force a statute that enables the appointment of a health care proxy and recognizes a legally binding advance directive. Ontario and British Columbia have both passed complex packages of legislation that recognize the legality of advance directives and health care proxies. The Alberta legislature is expected to introduce advance directive legislation in the near future. Saskatchewan's Law Reform Commission has recommended similar legislation. Even without supporting legislation, however, advance directives have been recognized by Canadian courts as valid documents, most notably in the case "Malette versus Shulman," where the judge ruled the card saying "no blood" that Mrs. Malette carried in her wallet should have been honoured by the physician.

Despite the remaining problems about withholding and withdrawing treatment, the need for better guidelines, the disagreements that can occur and the low use of advance directives, the last fifteen years of debate and struggle regarding withholding and withdrawing treatment have taught us a great deal. Manitoba's Schafer feels that "respect for the patient has increased. The humanity of our hospitals has increased. They are more sensitive, not less sensitive, to the wishes of the patient. Patients feel more secure, and more in control, not less secure and less in control." Perhaps the same will be said of assisted suicide and euthanasia twenty years from now, if, as is the case with termination of treatment, these acts are subjected to open discussion and scrutiny, and if those involved are willing to examine and address emerging problems. Perhaps those practices, too, will move from being unacceptable to being "good medical care" when used at the wishes of the patient in medically justified situations.

9

THE
QUANDARY OF
INCOMPETENCY

Donna Wilson walks into the four-bed room of a Victoria extended care hospital where her son lives, and starts into her regular, high-volume patter. "Hi ya little brat! How's my Paul? Gettin' into trouble?" She strokes the arms and kisses the face of the eighteen-year-old boy who lies curled in the hospital bed, weighing only seventy-eight pounds. She whispers in his ear, "I love you" and then sweeps her fingers around his eyes to clear away their crusty discharge, nodding towards a balding staff member over by a cupboard. "Has chrome-dome over there been lookin' after you? Did *he* choose that ugly T-shirt? I oughta knock his lights out. Whatta ya say? Should I knock his lights out?"

As Paul feels his mother's touch and hears her familiar, brassy voice hurling good-natured insults at the staff, a lopsided grin begins to spread across his face. As she keeps up the mocking patter, tousling his hair with her hands, his grin grows wider across his face and he starts a grunting laugh. His laugh sets the two staff members in the room and Donna chuckling with him.

After pulling the curtain and changing his diaper and pants, carefully washing and sterilizing her hands, Donna hangs a bag filled with hypoallergenic baby formula mixed with puréed meat on an IV pole, hooks it up to some plastic tubing that plugs into a Foley catheter into Paul's stomach and flips the switch on the machine. It is Paul's lunch and over the next ninety minutes it will be run directly into his stomach through a hole called a gastrostomy. She tidies up around his bed, putting out a fresh terry cloth pad by his head and changing his bib that have both become soaked with his drool.

Paul is blind, incontinent and paralysed except for a slight movement in the index finger of his left hand. He has severe food allergies and asthma, seizures that are controlled by medication, severe curvatures of his spine and severe brain damage. He has lost the ability to swallow and therefore must be tube fed. How much of the world around him he is able to perceive and comprehend no one knows; he is unable to communicate. They know, however, that there is something there. Over the past ten years engineers and therapists have tried dozens of methods to see if they can break through Paul's silence and connect with whatever intellect remains. Engineers from the University of Victoria have now designed a device that fits across Paul's left hand that shines a light beam into an electronic receiver. It is hoped that Paul can use his index finger to break the beam of light to turn on a tape machine or the television, perhaps some day even signal yes or no. Although he can't communicate, he does show emotion. He cries when he is uncomfortable or in pain, becomes agitated when he is stressed or anxious or when he hears other children cry, and he smiles and laughs when his mother playfully insults and threatens to beat up the staff. So, Donna, in her pseudo-brazen way, insults and threatens often. Somewhere in his mind, Donna thinks he must have retained his six-year-old self's fancy for slapstick.

Donna is just 5'1" tall. She has a bold, no-guff manner and a spirited intelligence. "I have had to learn to deal with a lot of shit in my life," she tells me, "but I am strong, and I'm a survivor." Paul is Donna's only son, and yet the forty-seven-year-old mother feels as if she has two sons: the rambunctious Paul she gave birth to and raised until he was six years old; and the Paul after the accident twelve years ago who now lies here in the hospital bed. For five years or more after the accident she couldn't look at the photos of the younger Paul, his happy, lively face so full of promise. Now, however, the pictures are hung on the wall of her small apartment alongside the framed photos of the latter Paul grinning as he sits strapped in his specially designed wheelchair. "I still grieve for that child I lost, but I buried him a long time ago. I now have another son — one I love just as much but whom I don't hold out any expectations for. My goal is to simply keep him smiling and comfortable as best I can."

That goal is not always easy. With Paul's chronic asthma and lung problems he is prone to recurrent pneumonia and respiratory infections. In the previous week, an infection had him on constant antibiotics, steroids and Ventolin, a drug to keep his bronchial tubes open. That week he was sick and unresponsive. With his lack of muscle movement, the tendons of his body have a tendency to shorten, pulling bones and joints out of alignment, even causing possible dislocations. Paul has had operations to cut and lengthen the tendons of his fingers, toes, ankles, knees, wrists, elbows, and hips. The painful operations required that Paul remain immobilized in casts for weeks on end.

When Saskatchewan farmer Robert Latimer was tried for taking his severely disabled, twelve-year-old daughter, Tracy, out into the family truck and venting carbon monoxide into the cab to kill her, there were some people in Canada who strongly condemned his arbitrary act. Donna Wilson was not one of them. While she loves her son with a fierce and protective love, and she does not want him to die, she understands why Latimer did what he did. "I don't think people should judge unless they know what it is like to have a child in constant pain, to know that you can't help, that you can't make it better. I don't think you can truly understand unless you are in it." In the years that Donna has been in and around hospitals and institutions that look after severely disabled children she has seen a number of children who were in constant pain, whose existence seemed tortured and without any meaning. One child who roomed with Paul was on constant morphine to control his pain yet still cried in agony with no relief for months on end. "If I had been that child's parent I don't think I could have let it go on for as long as it did," she said.

Donna has come to have this insider's view because of events that occurred in September 1983 after six-year-old Paul and her four-year-old stepson went out into the back yard to play before dinner. She was married then. She and her husband had just moved to a rural house with some acreage in Courtenay, on Vancouver Island. To the back and side were two deep irrigation ponds. At one time, the ponds had been stocked with trout, but now they were empty basins of murky black water. "We've got to fence those ponds," Donna had said when they first moved in. It was their second weekend in the house when the accident happened. Donna and her husband were in the kitchen making dinner. The boys went outside to play and about ten minutes later, the younger child came running back into the house. "Paul's underwater!" the four-year-old cried in panic. It took a few seconds for them to even understand what he was saying, and when they ran out into the yard, the child was too upset to tell them which of the two ponds Paul had fallen in.

For Donna, her recollection of the sequence of events that occurred that day so long ago, the who-did-what-whens, is blurry. "I was so hysterical; it was all so horrific — it's a bit fuzzy now." As she recalls, her husband dove into the nearest pond and kept diving down to the bottom trying to feel for an arm or a leg — anything — of Paul's to pull to the surface. Donna ran back into the house and called the operator who summoned police, fire and ambulance, and also called Donna's brother-in-law who lived only a few minutes away. The brother-in-law was the first to arrive, a few minutes later, with his girlfriend and another friend. While Donna's husband collapsed in exhaustion beside the pond, the two men took over the search, one in each pond, methodically diving in a grid back and forth in sweeps across the bottom. Meanwhile the girlfriend was trying to calm Donna and keep her inside the house. It was the brother-in-law who finally brushed against Paul's arm underwater and as he was pulling him to the surface, the police, firemen and ambulance were just pulling into the yard. Paul had been underwater somewhere between thirty and forty-five minutes.

He was blue, lifeless and had no pulse. The emergency crew worked feverishly to try to bring him back, shocking his heart, manually bagging his lungs to try to get oxygen to his brain. At one point they got a faint pulse, lost it, then got it back again. Bagging him continuously, they loaded him into the ambulance and sped away to the Comox Hospital, while Donna and her husband followed in the police car. The doctors and emergency staff were still working to revive and stabilize Paul when Donna and her husband arrived at the hospital. At one point Donna remembers a doctor coming out to tell them they had better come and see him because they kept losing him. That afternoon and evening, Paul was resuscitated five or six times. By 10:00 p.m. that evening, he was loaded into an air ambulance to be sent to Children's Hospital in Vancouver. With a doctor, nurse and two pilots, there wasn't enough room in the plane for anyone else. The ferries to the mainland had already stopped, so she and her husband had to watch their son fly off and then wait in unrelieved torment to catch the first ferry in the morning. Donna remembers it as a night of sheer hell. When they finally arrived at Children's Hospital the next morning, Paul was in a

coma in the intensive care unit, on a respirator and hooked up
to monitors. His body temperature had been lowered to slow
down his metabolism and prevent body movements. All the
doctors could say was, "we'll just have to wait and see."

"What you are going through as a parent is so much more
than grief. Your emotions are so raw. You are existing on pure
survival instinct; you can't think or eat — I didn't eat anything
for five days, I existed on pop and coffee. I'd never been a heavy
smoker and I started to chain smoke. I was so stunned, shocked;
it was a nightmare." On the tenth day after the accident the
doctors told Donna and her husband that Paul's brain damage
was so profound, his lungs so scarred from being filled with the
pond water, that further treatment would be hopeless, and they
believed the life support should be removed to allow Paul to
die. They sadly agreed. He was weaned off life support over
a twenty-four hour period, but to everyone's astonishment,
Paul didn't die. Although still in a deep coma he was breathing
on his own. "I can't tell you what it is like to reach the acceptance that your child is going to die, to agree that it is better for
him that way. And then to turn off the machines and have him
live. The medical profession's reaction seems to be 'Oh, well...
I guess we were wrong.' To them it's over. But it wasn't over
for Paul, it was just beginning."

Paul remained motionless and in a coma for six months and
he was moved to an extended care unit at Vancouver's Sunny
Hill Hospital for Children. Donna had asked a doctor, "Tell me
honestly what you think his outcome will be," and he had
replied, "Don't hope for the big things, look for the small
things." Donna began to pray that if only one part of Paul could
return, let it be Paul's smile. One day, as Donna was arriving
late, a nurse came running down the hall to meet her. She was
crying. She had been at Paul's bedside and when she said, "Your
Mommy's coming," Paul had smiled. Donna ran to her son's
bedside, "Mommy's here," she said. For the first time since the

accident, a tiny grimace pulled back the corners of Paul's mouth and Donna burst into tears.

In the twelve years since his accident, Paul's smile has showed his mother that he likes to listen to Robert Munsch and Dick Tracy stories, he likes the sound of sitcom chatter on the television set, and he likes his mother's voice. Donna is thankful that, at least for now, Paul is pain free and seemingly comfortable. She never knows, however, what may be around the corner, whether his twisted body or damaged lungs may put him in a situation where he is sick or in severe pain and neither she nor experts can do anything to keep him smiling. "If there comes a time where he has no quality of life, no enjoyment, if he is in constant pain, and there is absolutely nothing that we can do, then I would want the ability to have it end for him."

In the debate over euthanasia and assisted suicide, no aspect is more profoundly difficult, more worrisome and more insoluble than that of the suffering of incompetent individuals. Allowing competent, rational individuals a choice is one matter: Sue Rodriguez, Bill Davies and Doug Miller could tell us what they wanted in their own clear voices. Even a person who descends into incompetency through a disease like Alzheimer's may have had the foresight to explain to family and doctors their intended refusal of future life-saving treatment, or to leave an advance directive clearly setting out what they want for their care. Individuals like Paul Wilson or Tracy Latimer, however, are unable to tell us what they feel, what they want, or whether if given the choice they would rather die than continue to live their life as they know it. Before November, 1994, when Robert Latimer was found guilty of second degree murder in the death of Tracy, few people in the contemporary euthanasia debate in Canada ever lobbied openly for the need to allow suffering, mentally incompetent individuals to be compassionately killed. Such a suggestion has been unthinkable.

Those who wanted to see a change in the law reserved the acts of euthanasia or assisted suicide specifically to competent, suffering individuals who were able to weigh the options before them and rationally choose a timed death. Sue Rodriguez was the epitome of such a person. Intelligent, eloquent, dignified and dying of an incurable, terminal illness, Sue presented to the nation the face of a woman who knew her mind. One might argue, as the majority of judges at the Supreme Court did, that granting her wish might set too dangerous a precedent for the rest of society, but no one could argue Sue didn't know what she wanted, and that her wish was not enduring and voluntary. The essence of her argument was individual choice and personal autonomy. To expand the concept of assistance in death to those who may be suffering severely but who are mentally unable to request death, who never have and never will be able to communicate their thoughts or wishes about the value of their own lives, is fundamentally different. That sort of "mercy killing" was usually rejected by most right-to-die advocates because these were precisely the deaths (of such vulnerable individuals) that people wanted to prevent in any liberalization of the law. Yet when the trial of Latimer, the farmer from the small prairie town of Wilkie, Saskatchewan, began in early November of 1994, a number of commentators began saying the case was adding fuel to demands for legislation for euthanasia and assisted suicide. Suddenly, in the minds of the general public the scope of what constituted justified assistance with death had grown. It was a development that frightened and appalled people who have disabilities.

The details of Tracy's life that were revealed in court and through the media told of a difficult existence for both her and her family. Deprived of oxygen either in utero or during birth, Tracy was resuscitated when she was born and went on to develop severe cerebral palsy. She experienced repeated brain seizures that had to be controlled with medication. She experienced constant muscle spasms and had no control over any muscle movement. In her first few years of life she could move her hand to her mouth, but later on, that ability disappeared. She was unable to sit, walk, talk, or eat on her own. Yet pictures with her family and videos shown via television often showed a smiling Tracy, sitting on her father's lap, posed with her brother and sister. Teachers relayed that Tracy loved animals, responded to music and smiled to the feel of sunshine and the sight of familiar faces. Like Paul, the lack of muscle movement and continuous muscle spasms had caused her tendons to shorten, curling her arms, legs and spine. She had operations to cut and lengthen the tendons of her toes, knees and hips, which then required a six week period in casts. Tendons and muscles were released around her pelvis to help ease the muscle imbalance and prevent her right hip from being dislocated. Then in August of 1992, when Tracy's back had bent to a 72 degree angle, she underwent eight hours of surgery to implant two steel rods alongside her spine, wrapping wire around each vertebrae to hold them in place between the two bars.

Despite the medical success of the operation, Tracy was never the same after it, her parents said. She rarely smiled any more. She seemed to be in constant pain, a condition aggravated by the fact her right hip had indeed become permanently dislocated. At the trial, Laura Latimer testified that Tracy's seizure medication prevented her from having effective pain control because morphine or other narcotics would have amplified the seizure medication's effect, rendering her comatose. After the trial, however, advocates for the disabled and experts in pain control stated that Tracy's pain should have been controllable by medication. Was Tracy unable to access adequate services or medical expertise? Did Tracy's rural home make her and her family miss out on some of the more sophisticated techniques and services available to some people with disabilities in more populous centres? In the summer before her death Tracy entered a group home while her mother was pregnant with the couple's fourth child — Laura had already miscarried twice before and they thought the strain of lifting and carrying Tracy might precipitate a third. But Tracy did not fair well at the home, her weight began to plummet and her health deteriorated. The family brought her home.

Tracy's orthopaedic surgeon, Anne Dzus, testified at the trial that when she last saw Tracy on October 12, 1993, two weeks before her death, the young girl was in intense pain. Dzus felt then that the hip required immediate surgery. She booked an operation for November 4. Dzus testified that while it might have been possible to simply reconnect Tracy's hip if she had enough cartilage, it would most likely have been a "salvage procedure." In that case the top quarter of the femur would have been cut off and the exposed end of bone wrapped in muscle to prevent it rubbing against the socket. Dzus testified that it could take Tracy a year or more to recover from the surgery, that it might be necessary for the first weeks after it to freeze Tracy's lower body to prevent her from feeling excruciating pain, but the operation had the potential to eventually reduce Tracy's pain overall, as it did in the majority of children on whom it was performed. Laura Latimer testified how she burst into tears in the doctor's office when the operation was described. In his confession to the police Bob Latimer said that it was that night, after his wife returned home from the doctor's appointment with Tracy, that he began to think about killing his daughter. To people with disabilities this admission was even more chilling — not only was her death deliberately planned, but it took place less than two weeks away from an operation that might have solved her pain problem.

On Sunday October 24, 1993, while his wife and three young children were at church, Latimer wrapped Tracy in a sleeping bag and two coats, leaving her head free, propped her up with rags beside the steering wheel in his truck, and fed exhaust through the sliding window at the rear of the cab. He sat on a tire in the truck bed and watched through the window as it began to fog with exhaust. Tracy coughed three or four times and "jerked a bit," but she didn't cry. "If she had cried, I would have taken her out," Latimer told police in his confession. After thirty minutes he then drove back to the house and put Tracy in her bed as if she had been asleep. His wife Laura found her about ninety minutes later when she went to wake her for lunch. It was during a subsequent blood test that Tracy's blood was found saturated with carbon monoxide and the police immediately suspected Latimer. At 8:30 a.m. on November 4, the day Tracy would have undergone her hip surgery were she alive, two RCMP officers from North Battleford, Saskatchewan, went out to the farm and asked Latimer to come with them for questioning in the death of his daughter and that he had the right to have a lawyer with him. He declined to call a lawyer and voluntarily went with them.

When they arrived at the North Battleford RCMP headquarters that morning, the two officers took Latimer into a small office, where Latimer and one officer, Corporal Kenneth Lyons, sat in chairs at one side of the desk and the other officer sat behind it, taking notes. Here, from his trial testimony, is Corporal Lyons' description of what occurred in that room:

"I started talking by saying that we weren't here to judge him. I said we deal with situations like this frequently where people find themselves in difficulty and things that wouldn't ordinarily happen, do. I understand the situation you are in and we empathize with you . . . We have spoken to several people. Everyone said the same thing; that you were a very caring person, a good person. At the same time we know that this is not a natural death. Your daughter was in a great deal of pain. Bob, after considering all that is known, I have no doubt you caused your daughter's death. There was no response from him at that point. I noted that his eyes were heavy, glassy with tears, and I went on. This is not something you wanted or planned to do. You loved your daughter very much. At this point . . . he started nodding his head yes. This is something that you felt you had to do out of love for your daughter, isn't it Bob? There was no reply. I said, I imagine this is very difficult for you and I feel bad. I repeated the loving, caring, father aspect to him, and I said, You only did what you felt was best for her out of love for your daughter. Again there was no reply, and I repeated it, Isn't that right, Bob? There was no response. I noted that he was close to crying. I said again, That's what happened, isn't it Bob? Isn't that right? He replied, 'My priority was to put her out of her pain.'"

At that point, Latimer gave the officers a detailed confession. Nearing the end of the confession, Latimer began to cry and Corporal Lyons said, "You're getting tired are you, Bob?" Latimer responded, "No, it doesn't matter. I'm okay." Then the officer asked, "Now that you have told us what happened, how do you feel?" Said Latimer, "Oh, it, uh, doesn't really matter. This is not the hard part." Later that afternoon, he took them back to the farm where he explained what he had done and pointed out various items while one of the officers recorded it on videotape. Latimer was charged with first degree murder for the planned and deliberate manner in which he set about his daughter's death, yet the jury brought back a verdict of second degree murder. The conviction carried with it a mandatory life sentence with no possibility of parole for ten years. It was a verdict that shocked many Canadians.

In numerous articles and media reports, the trial's outcome was depicted as renewing the call for euthanasia and assisted suicide legislation. Tracy Latimer's and Sue Rodriguez's names were spoken in the same breath, as if their cases were essentially the same. Public support for Latimer flooded phone lines to radio shows and letters by the thousands poured in to newspapers and to the Latimers themselves. The support seemed to indicate that many felt it should be legitimate for a father or doctor to end the life of a severely disabled individual who was suffering but could not request euthanasia. A petition of 17,000 names was sent to Federal Justice Minister Allan Rock.

The public outpouring of support, however, appalled those who have disabilities across Canada who saw in Latimer's actions proof that many in the general public feel that people with disabilities have a lesser quality of life and so it is justifiable to help them out of their misery. In commentary in magazines like *Abilities,* and in panel discussions in the media, people with disabilities often compared Latimer's actions in killing Tracy to the actions of U.S. mother Susan Smith, who deliberately drowned her two boys by driving her car into a lake — that is how outraged they were by his act. "Not to send him to prison would send a horrible message to people with disabilities that their lives are of no value," said Priti Shah, a lawyer for the Canadian Disability Rights Council. "People with disabilities are murdered in the name of kindness more often than in hatred," wrote Jim Derksen, one of the founding members of the Council of Canadians with Disabilities, in the magazine *Abilities.* "Instances of so-called 'mercy-killing' arise . . . from the general misconception that life with a disability is an unending, unredeemed tragedy. The commonly mistaken notion that our quality of life is so poor that it is not worth living results in a social environment in which people with disabilities are vulnerable, in which they risk ultimate harm from apparently well-intentioned, caring people."

"I think the public support for Latimer reveals society's continuing, unconscious revulsion for disabilities. We think we have come far in the last twenty years in gaining understanding, but we really haven't come far enough," says Catherine Frazee, who started the group, Friends of Tracy Latimer, which held candle-light vigils and raised money to publicize the perspective of people with disabilities. People with disabilities felt threatened and disturbed that Latimer made the decision to take his daughter's life on his own, without consulting his wife, or a doctor, or experts in pain control, or others who knew Tracy and might have been able to help her. It was his decision, not Tracy's, that her life was so full of pain that she would be better off dead. Crown prosecutor Randy Kirkham, in his summation to the jury in the Latimer case said, "It is not for you or me or Robert Latimer to play God. It is not open season on the disabled."

Much of the general public's outrage, however, was not that Latimer was tried for his actions. The common sentiment was that he did, indeed, do something wrong in taking her life. But the feeling was that he did the wrong thing for the right reason and therefore he shouldn't be punished so severely. Karla Homolka, found guilty of manslaughter for her role in the brutal sex-slayings of Kristen French and Leslie Mahaffy, will be eligible for parole after serving just four of her twelve years. A few days after the Latimer conviction, in a story that received less than an inch in the local papers, a Toronto man who stabbed his wife to death in front of their children during an argument received six years for manslaughter. In comparison to cases like these, Latimer's ten year sentence seemed excessive, encouraging the public's dismay. Not only was he being punished, but his wife and young family were being punished by being deprived of a father and a breadwinner. (In the fall of 1995, Latimer's lawyer sought leave to appeal the conviction and the sentence to the Supreme Court of Canada and, when it was revealed the RCMP interviewed jurors before the trial, the Saskatchewan attorney general conceded Latimer deserves a new trial.)

Two of the three Saskatchewan Court of Appeal justices said that Latimer's sentence was appropriate, particularly because it was the premeditated killing of a vulnerable, disabled person. Chief Justice Edward Bayda disagreed, and said while the guilty conviction should stand, the ten-year prison sentence was grossly disproportionate and amounted to cruel and un-usual punishment. Bayda didn't compare Latimer's actions to Homolka's; he referred instead to four recent cases in Canada where individuals (without the patient's knowledge) ended the lives of adults who were suffering, and were not sentenced to prison. The cases were those of Toronto nurse Scott Mataya who injected potassium chloride into a patient taken off a respirator; Dr. Alberto de la Rocha, a Timmins surgeon who gave an injection of potassium chloride to a female patient with throat cancer taken off a respirator; Jean Brush, the Hamilton woman who stabbed herself and her husband who was suffering from Alzheimer's disease; and Halifax couple Cheryl Myers and William Power, who suffocated Cheryl's father, Layton Myers, with a pillow when he was unconscious, in pain, and a few hours away from death from terminal lung cancer. Bayda pointed out that in each of these cases the individuals, like Latimer, had reacted out of compassion and a desire to mini-mize suffering. The courts had recognized these extenuating factors by accepting charges of "administering a noxious sub-stance" and passing minimal sentences. For Latimer to receive such a harsh charge and sentence "exposes a stark inequality in the administration of justice in Canada," Bayda concluded. "The fact of the matter is — and the Crown in argument be-fore us so conceded — that the appellant does not need any rehabilitation or deterrence," Bayda continued. "Nor does the public need protection from him."

The two majority judges, Justice Calvin Tallis and Justice Nicholas Sherstobitoff, concluded, however, that if Tracy had been in constant pain but not disabled, Latimer would not have considered killing her. "This difference in approach between handicapped and non-handicapped children directly reflects a sense that the life of a handicapped child is of significantly less value than the life of the non-handicapped child in extreme pain . . . One would not be so inspired by love and compassion

to take the life of the non-handicapped child." Yet numerous parents — including those of non-disabled and disabled
children alike — took exception to that remark. Two of those
parents were Donna Wilson and Laura Latimer. "This isn't
about disability, it is about untreatable pain and suffering," said
Donna Wilson, echoing the comments that Laura Latimer had
made to reporters outside their farm when Robert Latimer was
first convicted.

Is that assertion true? What if Tracy had been a non-
handicapped child in extreme, unending pain with little hope
of improvement? If Robert Latimer had taken it upon himself
to kill that child because he could not bear to see her suffer,
would he have been treated the same by the criminal justice
system? Would public sympathy be less forthcoming, or would
those who have been troubled by his actions be less perturbed?
As Bayda points out we have four cases of incompetent adults
whose lives were ended by others, without their explicit
request, who went on to receive minimal sentences. Yet we
have no 1990s case of a suffering child to examine for help in
determining what our reaction might be. There is a Canadian
case, however, from more than fifty years ago in which loving
parents killed their two-and-a-half-year-old child who was in
severe pain from metastasized cancer.

The child's name was Victor Christopher Ramberg and the
year was 1941. He lived with his parents, Dorothy and Victor
Sr., in Keoma, Alberta, a small prairie town fifty kilometres
northeast of Calgary. His father was an agent for the Alberta
Wheat Pool; his mother a young housewife. By the time Victor's
doctor had discovered a tumour growing in his eye, its cells had
already spread in the blood stream to the other eye. It was a
retinoblastoma, a rare malignant tumour caused by a genetic
mutation, sometimes passed through families, but more often
appearing in children with no family history. The cancer cells
are usually discovered around the time of the child's second

birthday, sometimes through the strange "cat's eye" appearance of the child's pupil. There was nothing that could be done by the time the young Victor's cancer was discovered; the doctor told his parents he had six months to live. Perhaps it was the era, perhaps it was the prevalent feeling that children shouldn't be given narcotics, but the toddler had no effective pain relief. In court, the jury heard how Victor would scream in agony night and day and how his parents' inability to ease his pain drove them into their own unbearable torment. So, on October 3, 1941 the parents decided to end his suffering. The father backed the car up to the toddler's room, attached a hose to the exhaust pipe and ran the other end through the window. As the room filled with exhaust, the child started to cry; his mother came in to comfort him before placing him back in his crib. He died a short while later. It was Canada's first mercy-killing case and the couple were tried for first degree murder, a charge that, at the time, carried with it the death penalty by hanging. The jury, moved to tears by an impassioned summation from the defense counsel, deliberated for just ten minutes. The verdict: not guilty. After what the Rambergs had been through, however, the verdict could hardly be seen as a victory. The couple never had any more children, and media interviews with a family friend said Dorothy never got over her grief or feelings of guilt. Twenty years after her son's death, Dorothy Ramberg committed suicide by asphyxiating herself in the car.

Parents everywhere know the particular torment of having a child who is ill or in pain. As a parent, it is the prospect of the child's recovery — even if that prospect is as slim a chance as an experimental cancer therapy — that makes a child's pain endurable. It hurts to see them suffer, yet we believe that it is temporary, we hug them and tell them that soon it will be over and the pain will be a fleeting memory. But what if, as a parent, you believed that it would never get better, that the pain would never go away, that the chemotherapy or the operation you were putting your child through wouldn't, in the end, make a difference? Then what would you do? If Tracy Latimer had been a non-disabled child in seemingly endless pain, Robert Latimer's punishment for killing her most certainly would have been less severe or even non-existent. Given his family life and character, no one would have doubted the purity of his motives. In such a case it would seem ludicrous for a judge to declare that a harsh sentence must be passed because without one other non-disabled children would be put at risk of being killed by their parents; all would understand the exceptional circumstances of the case. But because Tracy was disabled Robert Latimer is being held to a different standard; there is a lingering suspicion, rightly or wrongly, that his motives were tinged with self-interest.

Crown prosecutor Randy Kirkham blatantly suggested this in his summation when he described Latimer as "cold, calculating and not motivated by anything other than making his own life easier." While everyone — even the trial and Court of Appeal judges — condemned that remark as glaringly false the comment hit upon a lingering suspicion in society and the law that most parents who raise children with disabilities must secretly wish to be rid of them. Love can't be the underlying factor, such a suspicion says. That feeling exists because of continued stigmatization of people with disabilities. Despite twenty years of consciousness-raising, people with disabilities are still treated as less-valued members of our society. Even if they are fully competent, sentient individuals their opportunities are less; they face unemployment at ten times the rate of the non-disabled; they still endure the curious stares, the sidelong glances and the discomfort of others in their presence. Parents of disabled children and those children themselves have heard for years patronizing comments from others — from friends, from relatives, even from the medical profession: "What a shame. What a terrible cross for you to bear . . .

I don't know how you can possibly cope . . . I know I couldn't do it." The assumption that parents want to be free of the responsibilities and hassles of caring for a disabled child is fed by the public's guilty realization that as a society we offer far too little financial, medical and community support to help them be equal participants in our communities. It is recognition that coping with disability in this country, despite gains made in the last twenty years, is still extremely difficult.

Less than two weeks after the Latimer verdict, more than twenty parents of children with severe disabilities met with Ontario Ministry of Health officials to demand provincial financial support. They were fed up with a system that seems to provide more incentives to parents to give up their child to foster care than to raise them at home. They wanted more money for lifts, beds and for special equipment to make their homes more accessible, to gain access to more education and recreation services, and to get respite care to give them a break. Mary Proctor, Ontario's then-deputy minister of Community Services, said she sympathized with their plight but no more money was available. "I am sorry for their pain and their difficulties, but we are working as hard as we can." To the parents' astonishment, however, ministry officials told them that if anyone was contemplating death or suicide, "to please give us a call." The statement seemed particularly callous and inappropriate considering that just two days earlier, in the wee hours of a December morning, Cathie Wilkieson of Hamilton, Ontario had taken her sixteen-year-old son Ryan, who was blind and deaf from cerebral palsy, in the car over to her parents' garage while they were on vacation. After she closed the garage door and left the car running, the forty-three-year-old mother cradled her son in the back seat and they both succumbed to the carbon monoxide. Her suicide note said that she was too tired to go on, "I just want to go to sleep and never wake up," she wrote. "I am at peace. Ryan is safe with me. I could never leave him behind."

In the aftermath of the death, media reports revealed that Mrs. Wilkieson had recently applied to the government to have additional home care, up from twelve to twenty-five hours a week, but the request had been denied. A support group for families with disabled children, Family Alliance, said the murder–suicide occurred because Mrs. Wilkieson had been driven to despair over the funding rejection, and that other families would be forced to such acts if the government didn't offer more support. At the inquest, the family angrily denied that assertion and charged the organization with capitalizing on Cathie Wilkieson's death. The family stated that she had been going through a personal crisis that had nothing to do with funding problems. Her brother did acknowledge, however, that Cathie Wilkieson was a perfectionist who worked herself to the bone looking after her son. "Ryan was a twenty-four-hour-a-day job. He demanded attention all the time. She always had to be there. She always had a string tied to him somewhere," Matthew Kras told the inquest.

Dr. Peter Rosenbaum, a developmental pediatrician at Hamilton's Chedoke McMaster Hospital and a professor of pediatrics, says some 30,000 families in Canada are raising a child with a severe disability and they do so at a tremendous personal cost — of money, physical and emotional energy, lost opportunities, and fatigue and stress. In a letter to *The Globe and Mail* he said, "What they desperately need from the community at large is the support that comes from well-organized medical, social and educational services. They need and want respite services that provide opportunities for them to recharge their batteries, to be freed temporarily from the daily routines of their disabled child, to have time with the rest of the family or perhaps alone. These services are vitally important to these families." Financial disincentives abound for families who try to care for their child at home. Although governments want to encourage home care — because it is so much cheaper for the system and better for the child — they do little to encourage it by way of grants or funding. The greatest proportion of money still goes to institutions and group homes. In Ontario, for example, the government spends $868 million each year on institutions and service agencies for the disabled, but only $26 million on its special services at home. In the minds of parents of disabled children, one of the great injustices across the country is that the system seems set up to encourage families to put their child into a foster home or institution. If the family raises their child at home, they are not given any compensation, even though they are saving the health care system tens of thousands of dollars each year. Yet if the family gives the child to a foster home, the foster family will receive a payment of $80 to $100 a day to care for the same child. That means that a single mother, unable to work because of the twenty-four-hour needs of her child, would have to live below the poverty line on welfare if she wants to keep her child at home. If she puts the child into foster care, however, another single mother might make a comfortable living of more than $30,000 a year.

"Governments feel that they can't set a precedent to pay families to look after their own children. If they did it for children with disabilities, they might have to do it for all children. But there must be recognition that families need help to get the things they need like catheters and hoists and vans in order to be able to look after the child," said Jane Holland, of Family Support International, a B.C. group acting as a collective advocate and resource for families raising children with disabilities. These parents stress that the experience is not all trouble and woe, it is filled with joy, love, meaning and personal growth. Says Donna Wilson, "Paul has made me a better person. It is almost as if he is here to teach me a life lesson about tolerance and love and being strong."

That said, no one pretends that it is easy. Donna knows only too well the financial and emotional stress that caring for a child with disabilities places on individuals and the family. Within eighteen months of Paul's accident, she and her husband had separated. "We probably would have split at some point anyway, but if there are any flaws in your relationship, this kind of thing blows it to pieces." At the end of eight months during which Donna looked after Paul at home by herself and never got more than two hours sleep at one stretch and rarely had time to eat, she was hospitalized with exhaustion and Paul was placed in an extended care unit. As Paul is in school four days a week, she usually spends most of Friday, Saturday and Sunday visiting Paul and calls every night at 10:00 p.m. to check in with the staff. If his health and hers permit it, she may bring him home on weekends, where she has an attractive room equipped with a hospital bed, TV and tape recorder and decorated with Robert Munsch posters, stuffed animals and a collection of baseball caps. Lately, however, because of recurring back problems and surgery on her wrists, she has been unable to manage the heavy lifting and turning Paul requires for his care. She hopes to eventually bring him back home permanently, but this will depend if she can get some kind of home support. She knows as she gets older, and Paul gets bigger, it will become harder for her to manage his care on her own. One of the hardest and most frustrating jobs has been advocating Paul's medical needs, getting doctors and staff to take her concerns about Paul's health seriously. Sometimes when Paul is sick, doctors can take a day or two to call Donna or to get out to see him, giving Donna the distinct impression that her son was seen as being less important than other children. The need to stand up for him has changed her as a person. "I used to be really passive, so nice to everyone, I would never say boo to a goose. Now I am much more aggressive and assertive. I don't take any crap any more. I have had to fight for myself and for my son."

In the slew of columns, radio shows and television panels that followed the Latimer trial, one theme kept re-emerging: medical technology, and a medical system that doesn't know how to pull back, must bear some responsibility for the predicament that Tracy Latimer was in. By resuscitating her, by giving her repeated operations and medical treatments, it was like pushing the family farther and farther out on a precipice but then leaving them to find their own way down. No one in the medical profession seemed to ask, "should we be doing this?" Up until the 1970s, it was common for individual doctors to exercise their own discretion about whether a child born with a severe handicap or one who had sustained severe, disabling injuries should live or die. There are stories about doctors quietly drowning babies with deformities in the wash basin soon after they were born and telling the parents it was a stillbirth. Before the advent of the rescue technologies in the 1950s and 1960s, many of the dilemmas about whether to resuscitate or not simply didn't exist — it wasn't technologically possible so it wasn't done. Most children with severe disabilities who survived were placed in institutions by the time they were nine or ten if not earlier. Institutionalization in both Canada and the United States peaked in the mid-1960s, with thousands upon thousands of children with anywhere from mild to extremely severe disabilities living in warehouse-like wards with minimal attention and appalling conditions. Statistics for the U.S. show that some 200,000 mentally and physically disabled individuals were living in state institutions at that time.

In the late 1960s and early 1970s the attitude towards institutionalization began to change slowly as parents and people with disabilities lobbied for more support and understanding, for educational services and opportunities. The disabled rights movement was the last of the string of civil rights movements that began in the 1960s. During the 1980s the real push came to move people with disabilities out into the community, integrating the children in the regular school system and adults into the work world, making buildings accessible; the goal was to have people with disabilities living as similar a life to those without disabilities in the same community. Disabled rights groups blossomed and raised public awareness about discriminatory practices and policies.

With the emerging recognition of disabled rights came increasing debate about the medical treatment, or non-treatment, of infants born with disabilities. The controversy dates back to an incident that occurred around 1970 at Johns Hopkins University Medical Center in Baltimore. A baby was born with Down's Syndrome as well as a congenital defect called duodenal atresia that often coexists with the disability. The defect, caused by an incomplete formation of the intestinal tract, results in a blockage that must be corrected by surgery or the infant will die. The parents of the baby, however, refused to give consent for the surgery. The doctor in charge agreed with the family's decision and wrote the order "Nothing by mouth" on the baby's chart. The infant was wheeled to a quiet corner of the hospital nursery, changed and occasionally held by the nursing staff, and fifteen days later died of starvation and dehydration. The relative ease of the decision — no ethics committee applications, no lengthy deliberations among staff, no court dispute, compliance of the nursing staff — seems to indicate that such decisions had previously been rather routine. The case might have never come to light except for the fact that after the event a few staff members remained troubled by it and discussed it with ethicists from the Kennedy Center for Ethics in Washington, D.C. The Center made a film dramatization of the incident in 1972 to use as a tool in ethical discussions. As Dr. Howard Brody notes in his book *The Healer's Power*, at the time the majority of medical literature supported the right for parents to make such a decision, which should not be overridden by the medical team. "Many defended the position that if parents did not wish to rear a child with Down's Syndrome, it was acceptable to take advantage of a coexisting life-threatening (if easily correctable) defect and allow the child to die." That attitude was common with both U.S. and Canadian doctors. Eike-Henner Kluge, in his 1980 paper, "The Euthanasia of Radically Defective Newborns" describes the case of a male infant born with multiple disabilities in an unnamed Canadian city in the 1970s who died of starvation and dehydration seventeen days after the medical team decided not to intervene. After an intense investigation, no charges were laid.

That attitude began to change in the 1980s, in part because of the reaction to what is called the "Baby Doe" case. In 1982, parents in Bloomington, Indiana, refused surgery for their infant boy with Down's Syndrome, who was born with an esophegeal atresia, meaning his esophagus ended in a blind pouch and did not join to his stomach. The hospital lawyer was concerned about any legal ramifications arising from the parent's refusal and contacted a circuit court judge for an emergency hearing. The judge upheld the parents' decision (and sealed the records so their identities and details would not become public), and the Indiana Supreme Court refused to hear an emergency appeal launched by pro-life groups. The baby died six days after his birth. Media coverage of the case was extensive. Almost immediately the Reagan administration issued what became known as "the Baby Doe Directive" prohibiting "the discriminatory failure to feed or care for handicapped infants." Mandatory posters were placed in all U.S. hospitals advertising a toll-free hotline which parents, nurses, doctors, housekeeping staff, or anyone else could call if they had information that a disabled individual was not receiving adequate medical care. A call to the hotline would trigger into action what came to be known as "the Baby Doe Squads" — officials from the U.S. Department of Health and Human Services and pediatric consultants who would investigate the allegations. While pro-life groups and citizen's groups for the disabled welcomed the directive, doctors and advocates for parents' rights saw it as being far too narrow and over-simplified. It didn't take into account the vastly different array of disabilities and their severity; whereas one child might be helped by a medical intervention, another child with different disabilities undergoing the same procedure might be relegated to a life of suffering.

During the 1970s a number of key court decisions were made, starting with the Quinlan decision, attempting to determine the best interests of the incompetent patient, or what that incompetent person would choose if she were not incompetent. These two legal standards of decision-making, called respectively "best-interests judgments" and "substituted judgments" have become the backbone of any medico-legal decision-making regarding the care of incompetent individuals. An important landmark was the 1977 case of Joseph Saikewicz in Massachusetts, a sixty-seven-year-old man with the mental age of three, who had lived all his life in an institution. When he was diagnosed with acute myelogenous leukemia the court ruled he need not be subjected to chemotherapy, which had a less than 50 per cent chance of extending his life two years. They stated that not only would he not understand why he was being put through the pain and discomfort of the treatment, or moved to new surroundings, but any benefits of the therapy, if it worked at all, were beyond his ability to comprehend. The Saikewicz case established that, at times, it could be in an incompetent patient's best interests not to intervene.

Yet many subsequent cases were highly controversial and the rulings reflected an individual judge's thinking, not widespread consensus. In Canada the year after "Baby Doe," the fate of another child with severe disabilities came into national prominence when the parents refused surgery. The child lived in British Columbia and his name was Stephen Dawson. As a newborn, he had contracted meningitis, which had resulted in severe brain damage and a condition called "hydrocephalus" or water-on-the-brain, requiring a shunt to drain the excess fluid. By the time he was seven years old he was blind, paralysed, and had no reflexes except a response to pain. He had cerebral palsy, seizures despite medication, and could not communicate. His shunt (a surgically implanted tube) had blocked, and an operation was necessary to replace it. The parents, acting on advice from their family doctor and a neurologist who told them that without the operation Stephen would die a peaceful death, refused permission. They took him home from Sunny Hill Hospital, where he had lived, because doctors there wanted the operation performed. The second night at home, police and social workers arrived at their house and apprehended Stephen under the province's Child Protection Act. A week-long custody battle ensued in court with the parents wanting the right to allow their son to die and the province wanting to issue an order for the surgery. The lower court judge ruled in favour of the parents, saying the issue was how best to determine Stephen's rights by proxy. Since competent individuals had a right to refuse treatment, then incompetent individuals should have the same right, she ruled. Stephen's parents therefore had the right and duty to make that decision on his behalf. The judge's ruling was immediately appealed by lawyers representing disabled rights groups and within four days it was reversed by the B.C. Supreme Court, which stated that no parent or court can judge the quality of someone's life as being "so low as not to be deserving of continuance." The court awarded temporary custody of Stephen to the Superintendent of Child Services and within a few hours of the court's decision he underwent the operation. His parents, who divorced soon after the court battle, refused any further discussion about Stephen or his health in the intervening years. However, it is known that Stephen still lives, with little change in his condition, in an extended care room at Vancouver's Sunny Hill Hospital. He turned twenty in March of 1996.

In the years after the "Baby Doe" and Dawson cases, the selective non-treatment of children with disabilities has remained highly controversial. In the U.S., court challenges and a change in administration eventually removed "the Baby Doe Directive"; the posters came down from the walls and the hotline was disconnected. Once again doctors and parents make the life and death decisions. In the 1980s Canadian and American pediatric societies issued position statements about the treatment of infants and children in order to help doctors and parents be clear about when it was appropriate to stop treatment for a child. The Canadian society deemed that usually the best interests of the child will require life-saving or life-prolonging treatment, but an exception could be made in four scenarios:

1) the child has an irreversible progression to imminent death;
2) treatment is clearly ineffective or harmful;
3) the child's life will be severely shortened regardless of treatment, and non-treatment allows for better care and comfort before the child's death;
4) the child's life after the treatment would be filled with intolerable pain and suffering.

The society stated that all children have intrinsic value, whether or not they are handicapped or have the potential to be handicapped and therefore all children have a justified claim to life. Doctors must simply weigh the balance of potential benefit of a treatment against the potential harm. "No other interest can override those of the child, whether they be family stability or well-being, or the well-being of other caretakers." If treatment is in the child's best interest, then the doctor has the responsibility to ensure that the parents "understand and agree," the paper states. If the parents refuse the treatment, then court intervention must be sought.

Since that document's release it has become much more common for some doctors in Canadian hospitals to stop treatment for dying or severely disabled children. Premature infants with extremely low birth weight and early gestational age of twenty-two to twenty-four weeks are more frequently removed from a respirator when it is believed that their future outcome will be bleak. It is more common for children with severe disabilities who have a medical crisis not to receive life saving treatment or resuscitation. In fact, most hospital and institutions that look after children with disabilities have put in place a "level of intervention" protocol; parents and the doctor fill out a form stating what medical treatment will be given in the event of an acute medical crisis such as whether to treat pneumonia with antibiotics, or revive the patient if the heart stops. Some advocates for people with disabilities, however, feel the tendency has gone too far. Richard Sobsey, director of the Developmental Disability Centre at the University of Alberta, told the Special Senate Committee on Euthanasia and Assisted Suicide that people with disabilities are greatly concerned that non-treatment — what he called "passive euthanasia" — is causing people with disabilities to die who should not die. For example, "Do Not Resuscitate" orders are frequently placed on the charts of incompetent disabled individuals who have no underlying health problems, simply because they are disabled; decisions are made not to treat routine infections that in any other child would be treated. In Ontario, for example, twenty children with severe disabilities living at an institute called Christopher Robin died over a two-year-period when staff decided not to treat curable problems and instead provided palliative care with little or no discussion with the family. An inquest found that the staff had done so out of a sense of caring but they had been too zealous and arbitrary in their acts. No criminal charges were laid (and indeed, only two parents were unhappy with what the staff had done).

Dr. Robert Armstrong, the medical director of the Sunny Hill Hospital shares Sobsey's concern that the Christopher Robin incident, or the initial refusal in Alberta in 1995 to place a teenager with Down's Syndrome on a waiting list for an organ transplant, show that physicians can be too quick to stop treatment or deny treatment to a disabled individual they wouldn't hesitate to give a non-disabled person. "I think we have to be very careful," said Dr. Armstrong. "We run the risk of becoming less and less tolerant of people with disabilities. With parents aborting disabled fetuses, with decisions not to resuscitate or treat children with disabilities, we run the risk of becoming a society that will not accept any disabilities in our children. All the gains we have made in the last twenty years towards disabled rights will be lost. If we need to draw the line, it should be more towards life than towards death."

Some, however, don't agree. They feel it hasn't gone far enough. They see a medical profession still rescuing babies for a life of disability and pain. They see a medical system spending hundreds of thousands of dollars on a single child, not to mention the cost of raising the child over his or her life-time, and wonder whether the money and effort might better be spent on the countless children in poverty or suffering malnutrition. They see doctors routinely usurping the power of parents to make decisions about their children's lives and then walking away leaving families to pick up the pieces. As U.S. author Helen Harrison, the mother of a premature baby, has noted: "families are at the mercy of an accelerating life-support technology and of their physicians' personal philosophies." While she sympathizes with physicians who are concerned and disturbed when parents ask for no treatment for their disabled child, "I sympathize infinitely more with families forced to live with the consequences of decisions made by others. Above all, I sympathize with infants 'saved' for a lifetime of suffering."

It was during the last month of Lillian Bayne's pregnancy that she began to feel that something might be wrong with her baby. The pregnancy felt so different from the first with her son, Eliot. Lillian, thirty-seven, worked with the Greater Vancouver Regional Hospital District — an "insider" in the health care system. Her husband, Mike Hayes, two years older than she, was a relative insider too. As a professor of geography at Simon Fraser University, his research focused on population health and health care issues. As highly educated professionals, Lillian and Mike felt like empowered individuals who were savvy about the medical system — until the birth of Oliver. Oliver looks like a large eight-month-old baby (though when I met him he was then twenty months old), a bit floppy and uncoordinated, with a tendency to topple to one side if left sitting on his own. It is his crossed-eyes and lolling head that hint at his profound brain damage. He also has epilepsy and partial paralysis. It is believed he will never walk and may never be able to speak. Despite his disabilities, Oliver punctuates the conversation with contented gurgles and whoops. "His central processing unit is all scrambled," says Mike. "He is strong and healthy, but the messages coming and going to his brain get all mixed up."

Lillian and Mike had decided early in the pregnancy that because of her age and an incidence of mental handicap in the family history Lillian would have an amniocentesis; the results were normal. By the end of pregnancy, however, Lillian had begun to feel that something wasn't right. The baby's movements were odd. She could feel the fetus go rigid, pressing into her side in a long, hard jab that would make her groan in discomfort. She felt as if her uterus was too thin, or as if there wasn't enough amniotic fluid and the baby was getting stuck. Routine tests, however, suggested such fears were ungrounded. Her labour in early October of 1993 was relatively smooth and problem free, but when Oliver was born, Lillian's concerns were heightened. "He was so flaccid and flat. I had this visceral attachment and I could just feel that there was something very, very wrong." No one else, however, seemed that concerned. The baby's Apgar scores (which rates the infant's appearance, heart rate, muscle tone, breathing and reflexes at birth) were low-normal — nothing to worry about, the doctor reassured her. Still, the baby wouldn't feed and seemed uninterested in the breast. It was decided that, just to be sure, they would place Oliver in observation over night. Mike was sent home to get some sleep and Lillian was moved on to the ward.

At about 4:00 a.m. Lillian awoke to find a pediatrician standing at the foot of her bed. "I have some bad news," he said. "Your son is having seizures and we need to move him to the special care nursery right away." Lillian remembers going into "professional mode," forcing her mind to become logical and clear-thinking despite the hour, her lack of sleep and the fact she was only a few hours post-partum. Suddenly Oliver's odd movements in the womb made sense, he must have been having seizures. She asked to be taken to see her son and walked down with the pediatrician to the observation nursery. She only had a glimpse of Oliver before they whisked him away. His eyes were opening and closing in rhythmic contractions, called doll's eye seizures. What is his prognosis? she asked. "It doesn't look good," the pediatrician said. When the baby was wheeled away, says Lillian, it was as if she and Mike lost any control over what was to happen to their child. "Suddenly, you are caught up in this machine of the medical system. It starts going and there is no way to stop it," said Mike. "There is no pause button, there is no time for reflection. It just goes and goes."

At 6:00 a.m., Lillian was allowed down to the special care nursery to see her son. She remembers sitting anxiously in the lounge outside the nursery, wearing the yellow cotton hospital gown with housecoat, slippers on her feet and identification bracelets on her arm, waiting for permission to enter the sterile ward. Behind the doors, only a few metres away, a medical team was making life-and-death decisions over Ollie's care, none of which were even discussed with his mother sitting in the waiting room outside. After scrubbing up, donning a sterile gown, shoe coverings and head covering, Lillian was allowed to enter. Oliver was in an isolette, with tubes coming out of his head and his arms. He was hooked up to a host of monitors and a doctor was in the process of putting a tube down his throat to hook him to a respirator. He was on massive doses of drugs to control the seizures. Medical staff were buzzing around him. "He was the patient now and I was the ex-person who was interfering and in the way — not the mother who had just given birth to him. It was horrible. He looked like he was in extreme pain. I was not allowed to touch him, even through the tiny portholes of the isolette, as the stimulation of my touch might be too much for him. I had this overwhelming urge to stuff him back into the yawning cavity in my womb, to protect him from his pain forever."

Oliver convulsed for three days. An early CT scan suggested severe brain damage. To Lillian and Mike, it seemed that the medical team expected Oliver would die and they were just prolonging his misery. The couple helplessly watched their son, who was black and blue and swollen, with numerous tubes, some the size of a garden hose, coming out of his body. His convulsions would send him into rigid spasm, as if he were being subjected to an electric shock. He appeared to them to be in extreme pain. Meanwhile a full-scale medical effort was being spent on saving his life. They began to feel that maybe it would be better if treatment stopped to allow Ollie to die. "We felt so conflicted," says Lillian. "On the one hand we had a fear that perhaps the medical profession had some superior knowledge about Ollie's prognosis and potential, which they weren't communicating to us, and if we asked for treatment to stop we would be wrong. And, on the other hand, we feared that, in actual fact, they knew very little but were insistent on preventing him from dying against what would be his best interests and we weren't stopping them! We began to feel they shouldn't intervene. All I could see, as the mother of this baby, was that he was suffering and desperately trying to say to us, let me go."

On the third day, Lillian and Mike asked that the respirator be removed. "To the medical team, that was just so strange to hear," says Mike. "They are used to parents saying 'Do everything. I don't care. Just save our child,' and here we were saying let our baby die. It was so atypical to what they were used to." Lillian and Mike felt, that in the medical staff's eyes, they were suddenly perceived as selfish yuppies who were unprepared to make sacrifices for a child with disabilities. "We felt it was a very judgemental atmosphere; we felt we were seen as being somehow less good people for asking to have treatment stop. We were trying to get across our belief that there are other values than salvaging a life at all costs and that those values have to be considered, too." The medical staff called a meeting to decide the proper course of action in the care of Oliver. The meeting was attended by almost a dozen people — two or three neonatologists, two pediatricians, the nursing staff and the social workers. Lillian and Mike's general practitioner was allowed to attend, to represent the parents' point of view, but they themselves were not allowed into the meeting. "They were deciding the fate of our child, and yet we were not party to the discussion," says Mike, still shaking his head in disbelief. "Even as his parents, we were not seen as being equal parts of the decision-making team. We had no part to play in determining our baby's best interests."

At the meeting it was decided that the respirator could not be removed until after a second CT scan and after the drugs in Oliver's system had been cleared — otherwise he might die from the drugs and not his condition. The couple were told that they could call an emergency meeting of the ethics committee, but it would be unable to convene until just after the CT scan anyway. "We decided to wait for the scan and the drugs to clear," says Lillian. The CT scan showed profound brain damage, but not brain death. Oliver's medication was adjusted to the lowest dose possible, and he was weaned from the respirator. After three weeks in the hospital, the couple took Oliver home. He was still heavily medicated to prevent seizures and he was feeding through a nasogastric tube. "Once we had accepted that Ollie was alive and disabled, our relationship with him became very simple. It was a matter of doing the best for him. It became a process of creating space for Oliver to declare himself," said Mike.

A month after Oliver's birth, the hospital's ethics committee held its regular meeting. For Mike, the need to talk about their case and experience was in the past. "Oliver was at home. We were adjusting." But Lillian felt the couple must appear to relate their concerns. "We had to speak up, we are articulate, we know the system. We had to speak for all those who might be unable to articulate it." The message Lillian felt the committee should hear was that parents must be active participants in medical decision-making about their child. "We are not saying that the parents have the paramount say, that their choice is the final choice. But their voice, and their values, must be heard. The decision must be holistic. When you are making decisions about someone's life or death, you must take into account more than short-term, clinical and technical factors. You must think about the rest of the child's life, the impact on the family, on other siblings. Those are the people whom those medical decisions affect, and those are the people who are not being heard."

As we talk about whether Oliver should have been allowed to die in those first few days in the special care nursery, Mike is cuddling Oliver on his lap, moving his hands in a pat-a-cake fashion, father and son both enjoying the rhythmic movement.

I am a bit confused. Doesn't it seem at odds to be saying that Oliver should have been allowed to die when as parents they obviously love and enjoy their child now? "It is not the same as saying that we want him dead now," says Mike. "Now we have a relationship, we know him and love him. Back then, there was no real relationship; if he had died there would never be that relationship. We would have had the chance to grieve — and our grief would have been very profound — but it would have been for a child we had never had a chance to know. It is all a continuum. It was an appropriate choice back then, weighing all factors. That doesn't mean it would be an appropriate choice for us right now. The equation has changed. It is a tough set of issues and there are no right answers. The crux of the matter is that we didn't have a choice once they intervened. All choices were removed from us."

In Michigan in February of 1994, another couple shortly after the birth of their child felt their concerns were being ignored by the medical team; their solution was to take matters into their own hands. When Traci Messenger went into labour fifteen weeks prematurely, she and her husband, Gregory, a dermatologist, told the doctors not to resuscitate their baby. The boy, who weighed 750 grams, was placed on a respirator against their wishes. Less than an hour later, Dr. Messenger removed the respirator himself and let the child die. He was charged with manslaughter, but a year later the jury acquitted him of all charges. "This is not a victory for anyone," said Messenger's lawyer.

In proposals that have been put forward about possible euthanasia and assisted suicide legislation, most limit the option only to those suffering, competent individuals who voluntarily request assistance for death. Only one proposal goes so far as to extend the process to allow a health proxy to apply to a court for permission for euthanasia on behalf of incompetent individuals like

Tracy Latimer or Paul Wilson. That proposal was put forward by University of Victoria philosopher and ethicist Eike-Henner Kluge. Kluge's position is that if society believes that deliberate death is ethically acceptable at all, then it must be ethically acceptable for competent and incompetent people alike. "We cannot have a situation where the choices of incompetent persons are less simply because they are incompetent," he says. Kluge contends that if legislation were passed that limited euthanasia or assisted suicide only to competent adults, it wouldn't be long — perhaps as little as ten or fifteen years — before someone brought a petition before the Supreme Court of Canada on behalf of an incompetent individual. The basis of the petition would be that the legislation offends the Canadian Charter of Rights and Freedoms because it discriminates against individuals with mental disabilities.

While many participants in the debate believe that Kluge's reasoning is correct, practically it is not only impossible, it is risky. A large part of the problem is that if proxy decision-makers were to look to the values of society in attempting to decide the fate of incompetent individuals, the continuing existence of discrimination against people of all disabilities would slant the choice towards death — and this is what most worries advocates for the disabled. Two presenters to the Special Senate Committee stressed that any legislation for euthanasia must be based solely on individual choice, not on factors such as the presence of terminal illness or disability. Richard Sobsey stated that if a law allows assisted suicide or euthanasia, it must be available to every competent citizen regardless of the reason behind it. "The safeguards should be based on somebody going to court to show that it is a voluntary decision and they are competent to make the decision — let them choose the reasons that are appropriate. To say that it is an autonomous decision but only disability or illness is a good reason, not poverty, not discrimination, nothing else is a good reason, displays a fundamental bias . . .

There can be no suggestion that suicide is rational for disabled people and not rational for someone else."

For Mary Williams, vice-president of the B.C. Coalition of People with Disabilities, individual choice is the reason she and the board of her organization support legislation that would allow assistance in death for those who request it — whether disabled or not. The group even intervened in favour of Sue Rodriguez's petition in her court challenges because they saw it as an issue of discrimination against people who do not have the physical ability to commit suicide themselves. Living as a quadriplegic since an accident twenty years ago, Mary Williams, too, would be unable to take her life if she wanted to; she would have to ask for help. To be forbidden from asking is a violation of her rights. Yet she knows too well, through her years of living with her disability — eight of those years in an extended care ward until she was allowed to move out into the community — that the lives of people with disabilities are often controlled by others who try to make decisions for them. In fact, the B.C. organization was founded in 1977 precisely to fight against medical professionals taking control from people with disabilities, denying them the range of choices and options that others were given. Those people with disabilities who support euthanasia and assisted suicide do so under one, and only one, condition: the rational choice of a competent individual.

Where does that leave individuals like Tracy Latimer or Paul Wilson? Where does it leave other children or adults who may be in pain, or who may be leading torturous, tormented lives but who are incompetent and unable to request help? Unfortunately, we cannot resolve this quandary of incompetency at this time. We do not have an objective way to determine an incompetent individual's experience of pain and suffering, nor do we have a way of knowing whether someone who is deemed incompetent is simply someone with whom we have not yet found a way to communicate. Maybe someday those problems will be solved. But that day is not now. For now, parents who feel their child's suffering is such that death is the only release will have to use the avenues of withdrawing treatment or palliative care, or if they decide they must end the child's life, face the consequences of their actions, whatever those consequences may be.

10

ARS
MORIENDI —
THE ART
OF DYING

W HEN RODNEY MITCHELL's aging father died
in his arms as he was helping the elderly man to the bathroom,
Rodney knew what to do. Ever since 1984, when Rodney had
learned that he was infected with the human immunodefi-
ciency virus (HIV), the Saanich horticulturalist had set out to
become comfortable with death. He had volunteered with
AIDS groups. He got a job doing homecare for dying individuals. He was at the bedsides of more than seven people when
they took their final breaths. Indeed, he became as comfortable
with death as is possible. So when his seventy-seven-year-old
father was dying of chronic lung disease, Rodney convinced
his mother that instead of putting him in hospital, they could
care for him at home. And in February, 1990, when his father
gasped, let loose his bowels, and collapsed dead on the bathroom floor, Rodney cleaned up the mess, sponge-bathed his
father, put him in a fresh pair of pyjamas and carried him back
to the bed, where he laid his body out.

"Shouldn't we call an ambulance?" his anxious mother said.

"There's no need for that now," Rodney reassured her.

"Shouldn't we call the doctor or the coroner?"

"Not yet," he replied. "They'll just take the body away." He opened the windows wide so the February air would keep the room cool. And then he called the family across British Columbia and told them to come.

He encouraged his mother to move normally about the bedroom and to touch the body, to say her goodbyes. "Talk to him, he's not that far away," he told her. At first she was ill-at-ease, but when he awoke in the early hours of the morning, Rodney heard his mother's voice in the bedroom next door, carrying on a conversation with her deceased husband. "Good," he thought to himself. At mid-morning family members started to arrive by ferry. Throughout the rest of the day Rodney encouraged each of them to spend some time alone with the deceased. By early evening all the family had paid their last respects. "Now we'll make the phone calls," Rodney said. When the police officer and the coroner walked into the house, they surveyed the unusual scene: long-dead body in the bedroom, entire family gathered in the living-room reminiscing. "When did he die?" they asked suspiciously. "Yesterday," replied Rodney. When the police officer and the coroner finally closed their notebooks and the body was taken away, the coroner turned to Rodney and said, "You know, I wish more people would handle death like this."

At the end of the twentieth century, death in our society is the big taboo. We have pushed it behind hospital curtains, where more than 70 per cent of Canadians die, often alone, alienated, or hooked up to machines. Many of us are frightened to have loved ones die in our homes, or to have bodies laid out on the beds in which we sleep. We have removed most of the rituals of grieving and funeral rites that gave our ancestors comfort, helped them to say goodbye and come to terms with their loss. Instead, we have worshipped at the altar of medical science, believing if we just spent enough money on this technique or that research we could beat death and make it go away. We cling to false hope, and urge one more treatment, one more test. U.S. ethicist Daniel Callahan notes that we seem to believe if we live right, or if we try enough treatments, death itself is avoidable. "There is faith that just over the next hill there will be a cure, a miraculous saving of life at the last moment."

In the last fifty years, death in Western society has been changed, not defeated. Now, instead of dying in birth, in childhood, or of an acute infectious disease, most people in North America die of long, drawn-out, chronic degenerative diseases such as cancer, cardiovascular disease, AIDS, or neuromuscular diseases. And that has given rise to a complex set of problems. "Technological progress has made the line between living and dying more difficult to discern. We do not know how to allow people to die peacefully," Callahan says.

The resulting "technological brinkmanship," as Callahan terms it, is seen time and time again in hospitals in Canada and other western nations. Over the last two years, nurses and doctors recounted to me, almost with shame, numerous stories of such brinkmanship. Here is just one. An elderly male patient, with pervasive cancer and extreme weight loss from the advanced disease, was transferred into the intensive care unit. Soon after arriving he suffered a heart attack. Because the patient hadn't written a living will or authorized a "Do Not Resuscitate" order on the chart or even talked to his doctor about his wishes, the crash team was called. A Toronto ICU nurse recalled the attempt to revive him. "I put the defibrillators on the patient's chest, but he was so emaciated from cancer — all bones — that I couldn't get a good contact. The paddles weren't flush against his body so they weren't grounded. So we zap him anyway and we can smell burning flesh. We work on him for three or four minutes, trying to get him back, zapping away. But it was no use. And when I removed the paddles, there were these massive burns on his chest. I felt sick to my stomach. Why the hell did we do that? He was dying, why couldn't we just let him die?" Observes Dr. Timothy Quill: "Sometimes what we do in medicine to the dying patient seems an awful lot like torture." Callahan and Quill are on opposite sides of the euthanasia debate — Callahan strongly opposed, Quill cautiously in favour. But no matter where one stands on the divisive issues of euthanasia and assisted suicide, there is one area on which most people agree: we need to become better at letting people die and that means we need to become more comfortable with death.

The first time I met Rodney Mitchell — not counting the time I talked about perennials with him when he was selling plants at a local market — was in the spring of 1994 when his friend, Franklyn, was dying of AIDS. Rodney was forty-five. I had been to Franklyn's house, about a week before he died, with Victoria's Palliative Response Team. Rodney and his partner, Ron Pal, were looking after Franklyn for the evening so Franklyn's partner could take a few hours' respite to see a play. When the palliative nurse, social worker and I arrived at the house, Ron, never much for crowds, quickly excused himself and withdrew to the solitude of a hot tub on the back patio. Rodney, however, stayed to explain Franklyn's problems and chat to the team. He was outgoing and sociable, funny and lively, and I was immediately struck by the fact he seemed at ease with himself and the situation. "How's he doing?" Coby Tschanz, the nurse, asked Rodney about the emaciated Franklyn who sat in a daze on the couch. "The nausea and vomiting are better, aren't they Franklyn? And the pain's gone, too, but now he's having problems with hallucinations. You're seeing some pretty interesting things, aren't you Franklyn?" said Rodney. "Hmmmmm" replied

Franklyn, his eyes roaming around the room as if he was following cartoon characters being projected on the walls. "Well, you
just relax and enjoy it. We're going to see if these people can
help bring you back to earth," said Rodney, placing his hand
on Franklyn's arm. Then, with what seemed like a lighthearted
sigh, Rodney began to show Coby and Rae the collection of
eight or nine pill bottles on the coffee table. Coby began to sort
through the labels, looking for combinations of medications
that might be at the root of Franklyn's hallucinations.

There was something calm and calming about Rodney in
the way he dealt with Franklyn and with the palliative response
team. He seemed natural and unstressed around a friend who
was sick and dying. I hadn't seen that too often. More commonly, friends or relatives would be in a state of anxious worry,
hovering awkwardly. Rodney talked directly to Franklyn, not
over his head about him to the team. In the time that I had been
around dying people, I was more accustomed to an air of
solemn seriousness, a hush pervading the room in which a dying
person lay. It felt good to be able to be normal, comfortable. It
was the sort of atmosphere that I would want around me if I
were dying.

Something in Rodney's ease told me he had been around
death a lot and that he had come to some sort of peace with it.
So a few weeks later, after Franklyn's death, I obtained through
a gardening friend the unlisted number of the nursery he and
Ron own and operate, and gave them a call. It was Ron who
answered and when I told him about the research and writing I
was doing, he said, "Sure, why don't you come out and talk to
us. Rodney and I have some definite ideas about all this." It was
late afternoon when I arrived at Mosswood Perennials, driving
down a narrow lane after leaving the highway about fifteen
minutes outside of Victoria. At the end of their short driveway
is a ranch-style bungalow. The home with its five acres of property sloping down to a small spawning stream is leased from an

aging gentlemen in his mid-eighties whom Ron and Rodney care for. They make all his meals and tend to his personal needs so that he can stay at home until he dies. Ron and Rodney modified the existing forty-five-year-old trees and shrubs and expanded to create the unusual nursery and stunning garden that is Mosswood Perennials. Customers can stroll through the results of their labour (ongoing since 1990), before making their choices from the small nursery at the top of the hill. Free-range chickens cackle in a large pen near the entrance and while you're paying for your plant purchases you can also pick up a dozen of the area's best eggs. Open only three days a week, with no advertising and no listed number, the nursery is known by word of mouth to all serious gardeners in a region renowned for gardeners.

Ron, ten years younger than Rodney, is the inspiration, knowledge, and driving force behind the garden and business — Rodney admits that until he met Ron in the late 1980s he knew next to nothing about plants. Ron is the born gardener. When he was just eight months old, his mother wrote in his baby book "Ron seems to be taking an interest in horticulture," describing how he would constantly crawl into the centre of the garden to seemingly examine the plants and flowers. As a teenager, when others his age were drinking, partying and obsessed with cars, Ron would be hiking in the mountains, collecting wildflowers to press.

They give me a tour of the perennial garden, and enormous vegetable garden, which supplies all their produce for an entire year. In the unfinished basement they show me newly hatched chicks living in an incubator, and next to it a heated propagating case for seedlings newly built from what was the former bed of a recently deceased friend. "We think Sybil would approve," they laugh, "she was always very practical." And then we make ourselves comfortable on the chairs and sofa of their living-room to talk about life and death and dying. Ron tends to be the more serious, earnest one; Rodney is more irreverent and offhand. Together, they have been present at more than fifteen deaths. They tell me stories about the lives and deaths of friends and relatives.

One moment we were laughing as Ron told an hysterically funny story about struggling to fulfil a woman's dying wishes by dressing her corpse in a 1930s velvet wedding dress she had grown five sizes too big to fit into. The next moment I was moved to tears as Rodney described the death of his father. Never had I met two people so in touch and untroubled by their own mortality or that of others. They live in full awareness of death, in acceptance of it, and yet were full of life and laughter and compassion and love. "We treat life and death as celebrations," Ron said. I felt honoured to be with them, as if by simply talking to them I, too, acquired that peace. Rodney admits that he hasn't always been comfortable with death; it has evolved over the last ten years as part of facing his looming mortality from AIDS, and by being around others who are dying. For years he denied his real sexuality by trying to live as a straight man. He was married and is still extremely close to his ex-wife. He fathered and raised a child, Julia, now grown, whom he adores. In the early 1980s he finally acknowledged openly to himself and to others that he was gay. Then, only a short time later, he learned he had been infected with HIV. "Drag, eh?" he says, and laughs. Rodney has remained remarkably healthy and strong for the ten years since the test, in part he believes through attention to eating wholesome food prepared from their garden, and maintaining a positive mental outlook. Only in recent months had he begun to show the first signs of ill health. Shortly after they met, Rodney told Ron he was infected with the virus that causes AIDS. Ron said, "It's okay, it makes no difference to me." Ron is healthy and has never been tested for HIV. In a discussion with his doctor a few years back, they reviewed the last twenty years of his life, and his relationship with Rodney. Since he had always practised safe sex, there was little or no chance he had been exposed. He behaves, however, as if he has been exposed, paying attention to keep himself healthy. His comfort with death, while nurtured by working with dying people, has its origins from the time when he was nineteen and survived a near fatal car accident, in which his back was broken. He realized then that being dead would simply be like going to sleep and not waking up. "From that point, death lost its fear for me."

Both Ron and Rodney have made living wills and talked about what they want for their medical care with each other. "The greatest fear in the AIDS community is that your mind will go from AIDS dementia and you will lose the ability to make decisions. That's why you have to be clear with others what you want and leave instructions," said Rodney. They both support legislative change to allow euthanasia and assisted suicide. They feel rational individuals facing terminal illness should be free to decide when and how they wish to die. They know friends who have kept a bottle of barbiturates on hand, just in case. For themselves, however, controlling the timing of their death is not a huge issue anymore. It is almost as if they have moved beyond it. Because they do not fear death, they feel no pressing need to control it. As we say goodnight under brilliant stars, the sound of the wind rustling through the trees, I feel as if I have had a rare experience; some of their comfort with death has rubbed off on me. I feel free and alive, with a heightened awareness and a sensitivity. "Keep in touch," they tell me, and I do. Over the next half year I visit them every two months or so at the nursery, or keep in touch by phone. Over the summer of 1994 Rodney is hospitalized with pneumonia. He becomes weak and anaemic and begins to lose weight. He rebounds a bit in the fall. We sit out under the trees in the nursery, laughing and talking in late September. Rodney looks thin and tired, but is still full of good humour and wry observations. They tell me about scattering Franklyn's ashes in a beautiful ceremony at China Beach on the west coast of Vancouver Island.

Rodney says how he wants to have his ashes spread in two places, some at China Beach as the waves roll in and some at a little swimming hole on the Cowichan river where he used to spend time when he was growing up. There is a wild onion patch by the water and some rocks, and he would sit there if he was troubled or pensive and listen to the water rush by. "I want to leave a bit of myself there, maybe just an arm and a leg," he says, smiling.

In late December of 1994, I realize it has been more than two months since I have seen or talked to them. I am hesitating to call. I feel anxious, afraid to pick up the phone. Every time I think of calling, a knot of anxiety comes into my stomach, and I put it off for another day. I realize I am afraid to hear that Rodney is sick again, or worse, dying. I am afraid to have Ron tell me that Rodney is about to go. I guess I am not as comfortable with death as I thought I was. When I recognize this, I call Ron the next day and tell him about my fear of calling and asking "How's Rodney doing?" only to hear him reply, "Not well." Ron understands: "That's your anxiety about death, Anne, not ours. Don't worry about asking us what's going on. We are completely accepting of whatever happens. Rodney knows that his time is limited." And then I ask, "So, how's Rodney doing?" and Ron replies, "Not well . . . he's in the hospital right now. Why don't you come out and see us." That evening when I go out to the hospital, Rodney is in a room with four beds on the seventh floor. An intravenous line is running massive doses of antibiotics into his veins. He has been there two days, fighting *pneumocystis carnii pneumonia*, an opportunistic infection common to AIDS. Ron is sitting on Rodney's bed massaging his legs. He has brought a fresh batch of chicken vegetable stew made from all their home-grown ingredients, as he does for all of Rodney's meals, so that he doesn't have to eat hospital food. In the room are three other young men, all with serious illnesses. One fellow in the bed beside Rodney's has just been diagnosed with terminal liver cancer. His bed curtains are drawn and the family members who come and go from behind the curtain have red eyes and drawn faces. They look shell-shocked. "It's been very hard for him and his family," says Rodney sympathetically. "We've talked a bit — I hope we'll talk some more." I tell Rodney how I had felt I was quite comfortable with death and dying until I realized that I was reluctant to phone him. "You know," he says, "I think you should follow my decline and death. Just stick around and see how it goes. I think I'm pretty comfortable, but you never know until it's happening to you. Maybe we'll both learn something."

In the two years of research and writing that has gone into this book, I have learned a great deal about what we might consider to improve the process of dying, including the controlled availability of voluntary euthanasia and assisted suicide. People on both sides of the issue agree that our relationship with death has become warped and distorted. Where the disagreement arises is in the solution for society. Some believe that allowing euthanasia and assisted suicide skirts the real problem and, indeed, is an outgrowth of the same motivation that has been driving modern medicine for the past forty years: a desire to control death and to take away its power. Many, particularly those in the field of palliative care medicine, reject euthanasia or assisted suicide out-of-hand and instead call on the improvement of palliative care, of doctor-patient communication, of the awareness of the option to refuse treatment and reject high technology. While they admit that persuasive arguments can be made on the individual level for euthanasia or assisted suicide, they believe at the societal level it is just too risky to implement. Margaret Sommerville, the director of the McGill Centre for Medicine, Ethics and Law, compares it to a stone thrown into a pond, the ripples of which would then rock the care for the elderly and the vulnerable, the doctor-patient relationship, even the way our children and our grandchildren die in the future. Like four of seven senators on the Special Senate Committee on Euthanasia and Assisted Suicide, Sommerville and others stress that we cannot in any way lessen the centuries-long prohibition against killing another person, even in compassion and even at the person's request, because its impact would be felt across society.

Sommerville even suggests that it is better to keep the practices of assisted death underground, secretive, and unregulated, rather than risk turning them into an accepted, legitimate forms of death. Describing the physician who either knows, suspects, or ought to know that a patient is obtaining a prescription in order to stockpile the medication to commit suicide, Sommerville told the Senate committee: "I do not think we need to be absolutely frenetic about stopping people from doing that. On the other hand, even at the expense of individual decision-making, we can't have that become the accepted situation." To many others, that is the worst route we can take, far more dangerous to society and harmful to individuals than attempting to draft legislation to regulate the practices. Keeping the status quo keeps patients and doctors using deception and outright lies to disguise what they are doing; it creates inequitable access so that some patients may find a sympathetic doctor and others may search desperately in vain for one; it hinders open communication and an honest exploration between patient and doctor about why the patient wants to die in the first place; it prevents the possibility that through open discussion an alternative solution, such as better pain relief or more support at home, can be found to remove the desire to die; and it precludes the ability for scrutiny and accountability of the decisions that are made.

We know from Russel Ogden's research, from professionals who appeared before the Senate committee, from individuals

who talked to me for this book, that assisted suicide and euthanasia is already occurring in a clandestine fashion in this country as did back room abortions thirty years ago. Some of the
cases of assisted suicide are bungled or botched in a terrible
way. The law, which so many people argue must remain in
place to keep our society safe, is simply not being upheld.
In the United States, Jack Kevorkian's assistance with more
than twenty-four suicides is glaring evidence as to how unenforceable laws have become in preventing aid-in-dying. Even
after Michigan legislators specifically wrote a law to curtail his
activities, a jury refused to convict him and Dr. Kevorkian
continues to help people die.

In Canada, six times between 1991 and the spring of 1995, individuals who openly admitted to compassionately helping others
to die have received a conditional discharge, or a suspended
sentence: Andrew Sikorski in Toronto who turned up the morphine drip for his father dying in hospital; nurse Scott Mataya in
Toronto who injected a dying patient with potassium chloride;
Dr. Alberto de la Rocha in Timmins who injected his patient
with potassium chloride; Cheryl Myers and Michael Power in
Halifax who smothered Myers' father; Jean Brush in Hamilton
who stabbed her demented husband and herself; and Robert
Cashin in Edmonton who gave his mother pills.

    Cashin, forty-six years old, cooked, cared for and lived with
his sixty-eight-year-old mother who was dying of metastasized
breast cancer. In the preceding months she had stopped eating
and shrunk to only sixty pounds. She had repeatedly asked her
son not to let her suffer. On October 18, 1994, Cashin sat on
his mother's bed and placed in her hand one Ativan pill after
another, which she then placed in her mouth. She consumed
somewhere between fifty to one hundred pills and rapidly fell
asleep. Cashin confessed what he had done to his girlfriend,
his brother and a homecare worker almost immediately. The

homecare worker called the police. Murielle Cashin was rushed to hospital where doctors tried to resucitate her; she died three days later. Cashin was charged with attempted murder, but pleaded guilty to a reduced charge of administering a noxious substance. He was given a suspended sentence in April of 1995. The judge at the sentencing said: "Given the fact that this was an act of love, however misguided, I feel it would be contrary to the principles of law to incarcerate you." The Cashin case, as well as the others that preceded it aptly illustrate, "the growing gap between ideological support for the law and the realities of current law enforcement," notes John Hofsess, director of the Right to Die Society of Canada.

That gap grew even greater with a seventh case that hit national headlines in the fall of 1995. Mary Jane Fogarty and Brenda Barnes were best friends. Fogarty, thirty-nine, was an insulin-dependent diabetic. Barnes, thirty-six, was a part-time waitress whose life had been filled with poverty, abuse and neglect. She had long battled serious depression and had attempted suicide more than thirty times before. On May 25, 1994, Barnes finally succeeded by injecting insulin into her abdomen with Fogarty's syringes. A month later, largely because a suicide note was found written in Fogarty's hand, Fogarty was charged with aiding and abetting the suicide, the first case under that charge to come to trial since the death of Kolitalik in the Arctic thirty years before. Even after a two-week trial in Halifax, the true details of the case were so unclear that serious questions still remained. Fogarty's lawyer claimed her client had no idea her friend was intent on suicide and she had given her the syringes so she could shoot up street drugs to battle her depression. Fogarty claimed she had no knowledge that Barnes had taken the insulin out of her purse. The prosecution claimed Fogarty supplied both the insulin and the needles because she hoped to benefit from Fogarty's life insurance. It was clear the jury sided with the prosecution's versions of events when it found Fogarty guilty of assisting the suicide and supplying the insulin. But after taking almost two months to consider the sentence, Justice John Davison decided prison was not warranted and gave Fogarty three years probation, three-hundred hours of community work, and a suspended sentence. "The whole case had many troubling elements," notes John Hofsess, "but if even under such murky and provocative evidence, a judge deems that a prison sentence is not warranted, then clearly the existing law is becoming unenforceable."

Many jurisdictions seem to be taking the approach of turning a blind eye. In British Columbia in the fall of 1993, for example, the Ministry of the Attorney General released guidelines that effectively say that charges in any euthanasia or assisted suicide cases will only be laid where there is a substantial likelihood of conviction, and the public interest requires a prosecution. "In essence, the B.C. guidelines say 'we will look the other way'. Hear no evil, see no evil, speak no evil. To me, such an unregulated system is the worst we can have," said Scott Rowand, president of the Toronto Wellesley Hospital. Rev. Ralph Mero, of the Washington State's Compassion in Dying, an organization that helps terminally ill patients die under strict criteria, says the opportunities for exploitation are always greatest where things are done secretly. "Where there are no guidelines, no peer review, no second opinion, no records kept, no reporting, when people are afraid to even talk about it — that is the situation where people will be driven by their own personal conscience or other motivations. They may make a right or wrong decision and no one will know," he says.

It is not difficult to predict what will unfold over the next ten to twenty years if the status quo is maintained: those forces pushing the issues — the aging of the Baby Boom generation, rising individualism, disillusionment with medical technology, declining religion, continued impact of AIDS, cancer and a growing demand for control of death — will continue to exert their pressure. More and more individuals will either challenge or simply ignore the law. Those who are caught breaking the law, when charged, will receive suspended sentences or acquittals until eventually prosecutors won't even bother to bring charges any more. Doctors, emboldened by the lack of penalty for the acts, and following their own personal set of criteria, will begin to write fatal prescriptions for patients, or give them lethal injections. There will be *de facto* widespread acceptance of euthanasia and assisted suicide but with one major problem: we will have no way of controlling it. We will not have a regulatory scheme to ensure the decisions are being made in a consistent, thorough and effective fashion that is open to public scrutiny. We will not have a clearly defined consensus about when it is appropriate to resort to euthanasia. We will not have a way of assessing whether or not the best of palliative care was offered to the patient, whether depression was examined, whether other options had been tried before resorting to taking the life.

We need to view legislation to allow euthanasia or assisted suicide not as a way to liberate the practice, but as a way to restrict it to the situations that we, as a society, deem appropriate. Professor Ruud de Moor, a sociologist at the Catholic University of Brabant, in Tilburg, Netherlands believes that all Western nations, whether they want to or not, will soon be forced to write legislation for euthanasia and assisted suicide to regulate the practice.

"At present, legislation on euthanasia is mainly viewed as an opening to it, but very soon it will become a necessary instrument to prevent unacceptable situations," he said. "If the community itself has no longer the power to maintain a necessary minimum of rules, the state has to impose them as a morally neutral guardian of human rights and society's vital interests." That trend appears to have already begun. In Oregon in November 1994, the first bill in the world to allow assisted suicide was passed by referendum, although it quickly became mired in court challenges. In the spring of 1995, the government of the Northern Territory of Australia became the first jurisdiction in the world to bring a right-to-die bill into force. After months of divisive lobbying by public interest groups, and after a sixteen-hour debate by the elected politicians, the bill passed by fifteen votes to ten. Under its guidelines, a patient suffering from an illness that has been diagnosed as terminal by two doctors (one of whom must have a background in psychiatry) can ask for a fatal prescription or a lethal injection. Alternatives, such as palliative care, must have been found wanting and the patient must wait at least nine days, as a cooling off period, before the request is fulfilled. Three other Australian states are now considering euthanasia bills.

Sharon Carstairs, one of the senators on the Special Senate Committee on Euthanasia and Assisted Suicide, urged Canadian politicians to bring in legislation to set down the rules in law. Commenting on the Fogarty case, she said, "We can't leave it up to the courts to make law."

What might Canadian legislation look like and how should it work? In recent years there have been numerous models proposed. Toronto's Dying With Dignity favours guidelines similar to those of the Netherlands. Russel Ogden has proposed "Aid-in-Dying Boards" composed of a cross-section of professions with designated counsellors who review applications from patients. Others, such as Timothy Quill, the drafters of the Oregon bill, B.C. Chief Justice Allan McEachern and Supreme Court Chief Justice Antonio Lamer, have put forward procedural safeguards limiting the acts only to assisted suicide. B.C. ethicist Eike Kluge has extended the process to include the ability for duly appointed health care proxies to apply to a superior court for euthanasia on behalf of incompetent individuals.

The quality and value of any new law for euthanasia and assisted suicide would depend on its ability to ensure that assistance with death is kept safe, effective and equitable. One would want the law to provide for the scrutiny of decisions both before and after the death takes place, not simply after the fact when it is too late to reverse the decision. If the process of obtaining permission beforehand were too bureaucratic, time consuming, onerous or expensive, the average person, however, would be unable to use it. One would want to ensure that any individual asking for help to die was making a free, voluntary and durable request in full knowledge of the available alternatives. Therefore the procedure for obtaining permission would need to be sensitive enough to detect instances of coercion, incompetency, depression or other mental illness, or hesitancy in patients' requests, and leave ample room for patients to change their minds even after permission is granted. Nor would one want the process to alienate or antagonize the relationship between patients and their doctors, coming like a legalistic wall between them. Any regulation for assistance with death would need to enhance communication between patients and doctors about the dying process, so that, like the Dutch, the benefit of a liberal approach to euthanasia would not come solely from the act itself, but from the ability of the doctor and patient to talk openly about it, using the discussion to pinpoint a patient's particular fears and concerns about dying. Dying patients would need to know that euthanasia or assisted suicide is potentially available if they really need it, without committing to it or making a rush decision. The right to die, however, must not impose on the individual doctor a corresponding duty to furnish a death where the doctor is reluctant to do so. Instead, the doctor would simply be given the discretion to be involved.

Doctors or individuals who perform euthanasia or assisted suicide with disregard for the established procedures would have to be penalized in some manner. There will always be individuals who decide to take matters into their own hands, who don't follow the guidelines or don't apply for permission, and simply perform the act. Authorities must be given the legislative muscle to ensure that individuals comply with the procedural safeguards by being able to bring appropriate charges against them. Finally, accurate data on the number and circumstances of acts of euthanasia or assisted suicide for statistical analysis and regular publication would have to be routinely collected in order to monitor the safety and effectiveness of the legislation.

Among the dozens of legislative drafts that have been proposed, many of which were presented to the Special Senate Committee, the one by University of Toronto law professor Bernard Dickens seems to most closely meet the above criteria. Under Dickens' proposal, the Criminal Code would continue to make it illegal to counsel or coerce an individual to commit suicide, but would be ammended by an exception to allow aiding and abetting suicide, or the consent to have death inflicted by another person, if the individuals involved had obtained permission for the acts under a strict procedure. The law might work something like this for a fictional patient, John Smith, who has metastasized cancer. Soon after his terminal cancer diagnosis, John could tell his doctor that he is in favor of euthanasia and he believes that as his disease progresses he will not want to go through the final stages and will want help to commit suicide. The doctor would be able to reassure him that court permission was possible and that she will be there for him. The discussion about euthanasia could be used as a springboard to a wider discussion about death and dying, about John's particular fears and worries. John would be comforted by knowing he had a way out if he needed it; the doctor would be attuned to what, for John, was a particular anxiety — pain, loss of independence, nausea, whatever. Their communication would be enhanced and John could put the concern aside for the time being. When John decided he was ready, he could inform the doctor that he wanted to go ahead with obtaining court permission for the assisted death. The doctor, if she agreed with John's request at the time, would arrange for a second opinion, ideally with a doctor experienced in palliative care who would ensure that John was competent and informed of all available alternatives. With that documentation John and the doctor would apply to a family court.

Some people, such as Chief Justice Lamer, Chief Justice McEachern and Eike Kluge, have suggested the application should be made to a superior court because of the profound nature of these decisions. Applying to the Supreme Court of Canada or those of the various provinces, however, could prove too costly, time-consuming, and overly precautious in the case of a competent individual like John Smith. We simply need a judge to supervise the process and to ensure it occurs with openness and accountability. The judge's role is not to make the decisions, rather to review and scrutinize the decision of the patient and the doctors to ensure that decisions have been arrived at with due care and with consideration of all the facts. Family court judges in Canada are now, on occasion, called into hospitals to adjudicate in difficult cases, for example, when doctors and parents do not agree on the correct course of treatment for a sick child. Such hearings have been known to convene within thirty minutes. Applications could take place at the patient's bedside in the hospital, in the home, or in a court room, without the need of lawyers to represent all parties. Therefore, the family court has the flexibility, the economy and the existing structure to cope with requests for euthanasia or assisted suicide.

The judge, if not satisfied with any part of the application, would have the power to require further evidence from witnesses such as family, or friends, or John himself, or to order psychiatric evaluations, counselling, or a separate palliative care assessment. If she was satisfied that John's request was voluntary, durable and rational, and his suffering unrelieved by other options, she could issue permission for euthanasia or assisted suicide to proceed. The permission would be registered with the local coroner. The decision as to whether John consumed pills on his own, or if the doctor gave him an injection would be left to John and his doctor to decide, taking into account the safest, most effective method in light of his illness. If John chose assisted suicide, but he vomited the medication during the act, the court permission would extend to allowing the doctor to give him a lethal injection.

Some draft proposals have put an arbitrary expiry date on court permissions for euthanasia or assisted suicide. Justices Lamer and McEachern imposed a thirty-one-day limit. Kluge and Dickens both propose a period of six months. For the legislation to be truly beneficial for people facing a terminal illness, however, a longer window of permission may be most helpful, perhaps even one to two years. The progress of a terminal illness can be so uncertain, with sudden remissions or plateaus in the course of the disease, that a patient like John, who may be temporarily feeling okay might feel compelled to end his life because his permission will soon expire. As well, experience from the Netherlands shows that one of the main benefits of allowing euthanasia is the reassurance the patient receives from knowing he can have it. That reassurance is most helpful early in the course of a terminal disease (so much so that most patients who request euthanasia in Holland don't go on to eventually need it). Knowing that one has the permission in hand early on in one's terminal disease may confer a psychological advantage over being forced to wait to obtain permission during the agony of the final months. At any time, John, or his proxy, may rescind the permission by notifying the court. The doctor may refuse to honour the request if she feels the conditions under which the permission was obtained no longer apply. When and if John decides the time has come to end his life, the doctor in the presence of a witness will ask him a final time if he has any hesitation. After the act has been done, the doctor will notify the coroner, with documentation from the witness, that the court permission was acted upon with the patient's final consent. Each year the regional coroner would tally and report the number of euthanasias or assisted suicides to a federal office, which would compile the Canadian numbers and publicly issue an annual report.

Many commentators restrict the acts of euthanasia or assisted suicide solely to competent individuals, but that discriminates against suffering individuals who have lost competency through disease, particularly elderly people who develop Alzheimer's or senility. What the court needs to know is that, at one point, the individual in question was competent, knew what he or she wanted and executed a witnessed advance directive. For those individuals, the only change to the above procedure would be that the application, this time, would be to a superior court and others, such as advocacy groups, could apply for judicial permission to intervene against the application to present their point of view. Take the case of Cecil Brush, the eighty-two-year-old Hamilton man suffering from Alzheimer's disease who was stabbed and killed by his wife, Jean, who also stabbed herself but did not die. It was the second time the couple had tried to commit suicide. Under this draft legislation, if Cecil Brush had prepared an advance directive while he was still competent, setting out the conditions under which his life would become intolerable to him, Jean Brush could then apply to the court on her husband's behalf to end her husband's life. The superior court judges could review Cecil Brush's prior stated wishes, hear from expert witnesses, from interveners from Alzheimer's or seniors' groups. The judges might refuse to grant permission and instead require evidence about the availability of home care, respite and support for Jean. As Jean Brush's lawyer, Frank Genesee stated, such an application would be a "911 call to the community." The judges, however, might find that ending Cecil's life in this situation was indeed what the elderly man had stated he wanted, that no other options were adequate to alleviate the suffering, and the court was satisfied that euthanasia was justified in this situation. However, if Cecil Brush had left no advance directive and there was no evidence of his prior stated wishes, the court could not rule in favour of death.

Some, like Kluge, would extend the court procedure to allow proxies to apply on behalf of individuals who have never been competent, such as Tracy Latimer and others like her. The reasoning is that it is discriminatory to give competent, or once-competent individuals more rights than never-competent individuals. While on the surface this may seem reasonable, it is dangerous ground. When the decision to allow deliberate death is rooted in informed consent and individual choice, we are on firm footing. There is little or no danger that someone will be killed against their will. Substituted decisions, however, are a moral minefield. British and U.S. courts, in the ruling on Tony Bland which allowed doctors to stop his feeding via a tube, and on that of Joseph Saikewicz, which allowed doctors to forego questionable chemotherapy for the mentally handicapped man's leukemia, have made what are essentially subjective decisions about what is best for another person without the individual's knowledge about what that choice would be. In the cases of Bland and Saikewicz, what was at stake was the withholding or withdrawing of treatment, not a deliberate injection. It may be a fine line, but for now at least, in the case of incompetent individuals, we need to discriminate and not allow others to give fatal injections to non-consenting individuals, if only because it is too close to what happened in Nazi Germany. There are other legal arrangements, not seen as being discriminatory to incompetent individuals, where a level of competency is a prerequisite: to be legally married the individuals involved must be able to say "I do," to drive a car requires a level of skill and competency.

The last essential step in our new law would be to create a realistic penalty for those individuals or doctors who might enact a mercy killing, or perform euthanasia without judicial permission, or outside of the legislative framework. Under the present law in Canada, the charges of first and second degree murder carry a mandatory life sentence on conviction, a requirement that ties the judges' hands and removes from them any flexibility to let the punishment fit the crime. The Criminal Code for murder should be amended to include the charge of third degree murder, for which the punishment could be up to life imprisonment, but left to the court's discretion. Bernard Dickens first proposed the category of third degree murder ten years ago in efforts to deal with the reluctance of prosecutors to charge, and juries to convict, individuals who mercy-kill out of misguided compassion, because of the minimum life term. A category of third degree murder would put in place a mechanism to punish those who act outside the guidelines and thereby give us the protection we seek for inappropriate killings that have no place under euthanasia law.

Whether or not the law is changed, there is much that can be done now to improve the process of dying for many individuals, including ensuring that the general public is kept informed of the steps they can take to help them achieve a peaceful death. Families, when they don't know what a loved one would have wanted, often feel compelled to agree to treatment or life-support for a patient in case they appear callous, indifferent, unloving, or even greedy for an inheritance. We need public education campaigns to encourage individuals to write out living wills. We need to inform ill or dying individuals of their right to obtain information from their doctors about their illnesses, the expected medications or medical treatments, the option of palliative care and the predictable pathway of their decline, so they can think about choices for the end of life in advance of a crisis. If the doctor does not share information or communicate effectively, the patient should seek a new doctor. We need to promote and support dying at home or a hospice rather than dying at the hospital. "If you don't want a high-technology death, stay away from places that provide high-tech medicine," notes Callahan.

Much of the improvements in dying can come about by addressing how hospitals and the medical profession deal with death and terminal disease. A start would be to require hospitals, doctors, and nursing homes to raise, in a sensitive and compassionate fashion, the issue of advance directives, "Do Not Resuscitate" orders, and choices at the end of life with patients for whom there is a predictable pathway of decline — such as patients with AIDS, Alzheimer's, untreatable cancer, chronic lung disease and neuromuscular disorders. Medical education needs to address the pervasive denial of death in the medical culture and the attitude that death is a medical failure. The reality of death should be integrated into the teaching program. For example, textbooks on cancer should include chapters on cancer deaths, detailing ways to keep patients comfortable during the dying process. As Callahan notes, physician training should instil a sense of sharing responsibility for the quality of a patient's death. Doctors' communication skills — primarily the ability to talk to patients in clear, open and appropriate terms — should be stressed in medical school. Role-playing and sensitivity training could help them learn how to talk to dying patients, how to deliver bad news and how to help patients plan ahead for their medical treatment. Palliative care training should be compulsory in medical school and no doctor should graduate without knowing how to give effective pain relief and how to provide symptom management. Practising doctors already in the field should be required to take a certificate in palliative care to upgrade their skills. All regional hospitals and cancer treatment centres in Canada should have access to a medical consultant with expertise in palliative care or develop a comprehensive palliative care program. Community-based palliative care programs, linked with a back-up medical support and hospital services, should be encouraged and funded by local governments. Home care services, enabling dying patients to stay at home with adequate support for their caregivers, should be ensured by local and provincial governments. The cost of home care should be fully covered by provincial health insurance to remove the financial burden from families who look after patients at home. Respite care, which enables families looking after patients to have a break, should be widely established.

The medical fee schedule should be restructured to encourage a move away from its high-tech, intervention focus to give more support and remuneration to doctors who take the time to discuss options, avoid unnecessary intervention, or give palliative care. For example, under the present situation, a doctor will be paid more for putting in a feeding tube than for undertaking a long discussion with the family in which the decision is made not to put in a feeding tube. Perhaps the answer might lie in putting more doctors on salaries (generous ones to adequately reward them for the skill, training and stress demanded by their jobs). As for the witholding and withdrawal of treatment, national standards and guidelines about when such acts are appropriate need to be determined, setting out the decision-making steps that must be taken to ensure consistency in the decisions, and outlining the proper procedure after the life-support has been removed. There needs to be consensus about what the appropriate procedure is for patients who are removed from respirators who do not die quickly, but struggle, convulse and gasp for breath. The majority of money and effort devoted to medical research has been aimed at finding cures and defeating death, with little attention paid to how to improve the quality of dying patients' lives. More research needs to be conducted regarding effective pain and symptom management, with the focus on finding better drugs or techniques to combat pain and address distressing symptoms. Perhaps most importantly, as individuals, we need to begin talking about death and accepting the reality of death, neither courting it, nor ignoring it, but trying to obtain, if not a perfect peace in our war against it, a partial truce. In that, we might all learn a bit from Rodney.

The two weeks in hospital on constant intravenous antibiotics took a lot out of Rodney. When I talked to him on the phone shortly after he was discharged home, he sounded down and tired. "I feel pretty shitty," he says. "The antibiotics are like chemotherapy, it starts out okay but by the last two doses I just didn't want to do it. It made me feel sick. All I'm doing now is lying in bed, recovering from it. I feel really out of it. I haven't been eating — so that makes me really weak." When I see him a few weeks later, he has rebounded somewhat. He is still thin and pale, but his appetite is back. We sit at the kitchen table on a cool February day and eat warming bowls of Ron's lentil soup. "He's a good cook, isn't he?" he says. We talk more about life than death on this day. He tells me, with affection, about his daughter, Julia, who lives off the land with her boyfriend on Lasqueti Island, one of the B.C. Gulf Islands. He talks about his time in the Yukon first working for former federal politician Eric Neilsen on his ranch as a cook, then getting a job as big game guide. From the time his infection with the HIV was found, Rodney always rejected the experimental antiviral drugs and experimental treatments offered by the medical profession. He declined using AZT — in its early years he had seen too many friends become sick with it. In recent years friends of his are now combining low doses of AZT with a new antiviral drug called 3TC, and seem to be doing well with them, but he still prefers the herb and diet route. "At this stage of our understanding about AIDS, I think there is no right way or wrong way to fight it. Each person has to find what is right for them. What feels good. This is the right way for me."

It is mid-May before I see him again. I had been busy with my family, with writing and interviewing, and I had hardly noticed

the time going by — when you are healthy time can fly like
that. But when you are ill, it is a different story. In those ten
weeks, Rodney had taken a dramatic turn for the worse. I
received a call one morning from Rae Westcott, the palliative
care social worker, saying Ron and Rodney had misplaced my
phone number and wanted to see me. Rodney was very sick
and might not last long. I called immediately and arranged to go
out the next day. When I arrive Rodney is lying in a hospital
bed that they have rented and placed in a spare room in the
house. He is impossibly thin, and covered with a rash of itchy
red splotches. He gives me a wan smile and I sit on a stool by the
bed as he tells me the sequence of events that led to this day.

Through March and early April he felt pretty good. He
regained some of his strength and was even able to go out in the
garden to do some light work. He knew he wasn't completely
well, however, because he found that he was unable to read —
he didn't have the stamina or the interest — something unusual
for him because all his life he'd had a stack of books on the bedside table. "It just didn't seem important any more." At the end
of April he started to feel devastatingly tired and his bones began
to hurt. Tests in hospital revealed what doctors believed was
mycobacterial avium complex (MAC), a type of bacterial infection in the tuberculin family, though less virulent than tuberculosis. The organisms, commonly found in the soil and water,
pose little threat to healthy people, but for an individual with a
compromised immune system they can be deadly. The *Merck
Manual*, a doctor's desk reference and the most widely used
medical text in the world, says of MAC in the patient with AIDS:
"combinations of anti-mycobacterial drugs have reduced bac-
teriemia and temporarily improved symptoms, but no regimen
has been truly successful and the disease carries a grave prognosis." Rodney's doctors suggested a heavy course of antibiotics,
but Rodney wasn't sure whether it would be worth it. "I said,
I'll try it, but if I don't like it, I'm going to stop. I stopped after

two days. It made me feel too sick. My GP was upset because he thought I should do it. But I said, what is the point? Why prolong it?"

He asked to be referred to the palliative care program and he returned home to die. For two weeks now he has been on morphine for the pain in his bones. He is comfortable and his mind is fairly clear, but the morphine seems to be causing some side-effects — at least he thinks it is, it is hard to tell what is the MAC and what is the morphine. He is nauseated almost constantly — he thinks that is the morphine because it seems to directly correlate to when he takes the pills. The rash could be caused by either the drug or the infection. He has had a recurring feeling that a hand is resting on his thigh. He will be asleep or lying with his eyes closed and he will feel like someone is touching him. "I open my eyes and there is nothing there."

"Is it scary?" I ask.

"No, it's kind of neat, actually. I don't know who it is, but it is sort of comforting."

What is most disconcerting to him, however, is how weak and unsteady he has become so fast. A few days earlier he had attempted to get out of bed on his own, and, putting on his housecoat, he tried to flip the sleeve right side out. He suddenly crumpled and fell hard on the floor. "It really hurt and I am still badly bruised, my back and tail bone, I can't lie on it, I have to be on my side. But what was worse was that it really shook me. It seemed to knock the last bit of energy out of me and I feel afraid to get out of bed."

Ron comes in briefly from where he has been dealing with customers in the garden. He seems sad and subdued. It's been hard he says, his head is not in the business with Rodney sick. "Right now is the busiest time of year, but it is hard to face the customers when you feel like crying," Ron says. He is leaning against the jam of the bedroom door, and he begins to reminisce about the way they built the business together. "It is hard to

believe we've done it for six years. A chapter is coming to an
end with Rodney dying."

Rodney's concern now is how much time he has left to
live. The palliative care team told him anywhere between
three to six weeks or longer. "I want it to be shorter, because
I'm ready to go," says Rodney. As we talk, Rodney suddenly
seems to become very tired. The words come slowly from his
mouth, as if it takes effort to bring them forward to his lips
from his brain. There are long pauses in between words and
sentences. He closes his eyes now and again as if gathering
strength, takes a deep breath and then speaks a phrase or two
more, then pauses again.

"I'm going to let you get some sleep," I say as I give him a
hug and tell him I'll see him in a few days.

I go out again four mornings later and I am feeling emotional, unsettled. Rodney is lying in his hospital bed with the
blankets tucked right up to his chin and his thin arms and
shoulders poking out at the top. Bony protuberances stick up
like tent poles in the blanket — his hip bones, knees, wrists,
feet. He starts talking about feeling so sleepy. "I could sleep
twenty-three hours a day," he says. "Just close my eyes and it is
there. It's my body making the transition. Shutting down, I
think." I start to cry as he talks. I tell him that today I am having a hard time with his dying. I want to be there with him but
I worry that because I am a journalist and I am writing about
what is happening to him that I may be exploiting his death, his
private time, his personal transition. I feel conflicted about my
role and my writing about it. "Don't worry," he tells me
warmly. "I think our spirit guides brought us together. Maybe
by chronicling my dying you can help other people, bring
them some comfort, let them come to some peace in their own
mind. I want you to be here."

As he talks, it seems as if he has fallen asleep and then with a
big breath, he continues, slowly, deliberately with the words.

Every now and then his body will twitch and jerk — these are called myoclonic jerks. "It just happens — I have no control of it. It can be dangerous if I have a drink in my hand — it's all over me," he says with a smile. With his talk about spirit guides, I ask him to tell me about his religious beliefs — something in our many times together we have never talked about.

"I guess I am most along the Buddhist lines, but I am not a Buddhist. If anything, I am just a joyful being. A joyful being who has a real appreciation of the mysteries of life."

Although he still wants to drink water, Rodney has almost stopped eating, in part, because food would make him nauseated. But he has stopped, too, to help speed his death. "I want to keep it moving along." Ron is making him yogurt smoothies, blending fresh fruit with plain yogurt, which Rodney still finds refreshing. Have they needed the palliative care team to come out to help keep him comfortable? "No, they are really for crises," Rodney says.

"We don't have crises, do we?" Ron says.

They talk about how some people are having a hard time with Rodney's impending death. Friends and family who always knew he had HIV and then AIDS can't quite believe that this time it is really it. Rodney has always radiated good health. It always seemed like he would be the one to beat it. His ex-wife is having a difficult time, but his daughter Julia is calm and accepting. "She is too much like you to act any differently," Ron says. Rodney tells me that on her last visit, his daughter told him that she is pregnant, just a few weeks along, and due in December. He is very excited and happy for her. "That is one of the reasons I want to go quickly," Rodney says. "I want her to have enough time to grieve, to get my death behind her so that it doesn't interfere with her joy of the baby."

Ron tells me that some people who come to see Rodney "flutter around" him in nervous energy, fidgeting and fixing things in their discomfort around death. It is exhausting to

Rodney. Sometimes the medical people — nurses, doctors, homecare workers — are the worst for being uptight around him. "It seems that some of them are more anxious about death than anybody. They want to do something about it. They can't be still." Some visits take too much out of him, says Ron. "I think we will tell some people that they should just come and say their goodbyes. Not keep coming back. It is too hard on you. Okay?" says Ron.

"Okay," says Rodney.

"I think we'll also tell people no more evening visits, it's too exhausting for you. Just the mornings, Okay?"

"Yeah, that's better. Mornings are better."

After I leave him, to my amazement, I feel an extraordinary sense of peace and a heightened sense of awareness. My brain feels free of clutter, of the endless lists of "must do that, got to remember this" that usually preoccupy it. It feels as if my perceptions have all been honed. I am hit with the smell of the trees and flowers. The colours and the air seems more sharp and redolent. I find myself noticing details — like the firm, strong, tanned legs of three young girls walking down Government Street — and having simultaneous recall of an appropriate line of poetry, "A simple child that feels its life in every limb, what should it know of death?" I am amazed that in this heightened state I can recall a line of a Wordsworth poem from my distant past. When next I visit, a few days later, I mention this hyperawareness to Ron as we sit outside in the garden while Rodney is sleeping. Ron is not surprised. "Being with Rodney, with someone who is dying, is like doing meditation. You focus on what is important. Your brain was cleared of all the usual stuff and it left your mind free to absorb new things and make new associations."

Over the next week, I am struck by the difference that suddenly appears in Rodney's face. His teeth and cheeks have become so prominent, angular. His face has lost so much weight that the underlying bone structure of his skull is almost visible.

His eyes seem to have changed. He doesn't look like himself. "Yeah I know," he says when I tell him. "People have told me that. Weird, eh?" He is speaking so softly now that I can hardly hear him. Everything is an effort these days, he tells me. Standing up now makes him nauseated, and he vomits. In the bath he will tremble and shake uncontrollably and he feels afraid that he will fall. "It is sponge baths for me now. I find it too frightening to get up. Too hard." He has been drifting in and out of awareness. "I can't keep track of the days now. I don't know what day it is. I don't like that."

He is in more pain now and the palliative care doctor is going to come and see if his medication can be altered to improve his comfort. He takes 30 mg of M.S. Contin (morphine sulfate) in the morning, 30 mg in the afternoon and 30 mg at night, but yesterday he had to take two breakthrough doses. It seems clear that having a conversation now with Rodney is simply too taxing for him. I offer, instead to rub his feet with calendula oil to help ease a sore spot on his heel where his foot has laid against the sheets. "Oh, I could have you do that for hours," Rodney says as he lies back and closes his eyes. For me, massaging his painful feet fulfils my need to feel useful and be a comfort to him. For the next two weeks when we visit, our conversation is minimal, but I make a habit of giving him a long foot massage each day.

June 2, 1995, is Rodney's forty-seventh birthday. He has been in bed at home for a month. It is almost impossible to talk to him now. His voice is almost a whisper, his teeth and jaw are clenched. He has lost so much weight that his face is like a skeleton. He spends most of the time with his eyes closed. He has been hallucinating more. A week earlier when I visited he told me an elaborate, frightening story about how he had fallen out of bed and been stuck there for twenty minutes calling and nobody had come. His details were so specific that when Ron comes in the room, I mention how scary his fall must have been. "You didn't fall," says Ron. "You were hallucinating. Remember how Jim said that Richard kept feeling that he had fallen and he'd still be right in the bed. I think that is what is happening to you."

Rodney seems perturbed. "Well," he says. "That gives me something to think about."

Today on his birthday he is at one moment clear, the next clouded. Fortunately he has no pain — after her visit a week earlier the doctor added the pain reliever Entrophen to his regimen and it seems to have worked well. But he is hallucinating more frequently. He says in a whisper to me. "Everything is blue with black lines."

"Is that what you are seeing?" I ask.

"No," he says. "That's what it is." With conversation so difficult, I massage his feet. Rodney's eyes roll up into his head and soon he falls asleep. I quietly leave the room and I wonder to myself if he will live through the weekend.

On the following Monday I meet Ron as I am pulling into the driveway and I brace myself to hear of further decline, but Ron surprises me. "He had a good weekend. He's remarkably clear. He wasn't in pain so I decided that if the Entrophen seemed to be working so well, why not try to drop the afternoon dose of morphine and see if he became more lucid. He cleared right up." Since Saturday he has been on only two doses of morphine a day and his appetite has begun to return. When I see Rodney inside, he is ambivalent about the return of his hunger. He has eaten a mango and some cherries. Being hungry would usually be seen as a good sign, but he wonders if it will only slow down the process of dying. "Maybe this means I'll last longer. I don't know what to do. I'll have to think about this." He still is extraordinarily tired and talking is difficult. I massage his feet and he drifts off to sleep.

Over the next week, to everyone's amazement, Rodney seems to be making a recovery. His pain is controlled by the

Entrophen and by mid-week, Ron has stopped giving him any morphine at all. Rodney is clear and his appetite has returned with a vengeance. "He asked me what he should do about it and I said, look, if you feel like eating, eat. I'd love to have you around longer. Do what feels right. Maybe you can get strong enough to sit in the garden." Rodney craved red meat so Ron cooked a tiny piece of steak, just to see of Rodney could stomach it, and cut it up in small cubes. "Before I could even turn around it was gone and he was asking for more."

Into the next week the recovery is still continuing. Rodney has been off all morphine for ten days and has no pain. When I arrive he is sleeping in the bedroom so Ron and I sit in the living-room and talk about the turn around. He tells me that Rodney's voice has returned strong and clear. So has his appetite. "He's eating like a horse — last night he had chicken, this morning scrambled eggs." said Ron. "It's all very confusing, actually. For both of us. Rodney's head is all ready for death, but his body isn't. He asked me whether I thought he should be eating. I said, you do whatever feels right. For me, I don't know what to think. I was sort of mentally preparing myself for him being gone. Trying to imagine what I would do. But now there is this hope that maybe he could get better. I'm all for him sticking around longer. It would be great if he could get back his strength so that he could walk in the garden again, go outside. It's all pretty stressful, actually. The uncertainty. I don't know if we should be feeling optimistic. We just have to see what happens." Ron then tells me that the night before he and Rodney had joked, "Oh no, what's this going to do to Anne's book? Everyone is going to expect Rodney to die." We hear him rousing in the next room and we go in to see him. Already his face is beginning to fill out and lose its death's mask appearance.

"So Rodney, you're eating like a horse."

"Yeah, weird, eh?" he says.

"Ron tells me you're worried about the ending of my book."

"Yeah, sorry about that."

He smiles. We are all smiling.

"Look Rodney," I say, with a grin. "If you feel like eating, you eat. I don't want you to worry about that. Don't die on account of my book. I'd love to give it a surprise ending."

Over the next two months, Rodney does indeed make a comeback. He slowly gains weight. One day Ron helps him out of the house and into the truck, his first time out of the bedroom for more than six weeks. He drives him into town for an appointment with a chiropractor. Rodney stares out of the window in wonder and amazement at the clouds, the trees, and the passing scenes. "I started to cry. It just seemed so overwhelming. I was going 'Wow! Look at that cloud, isn't it beautiful!' I just never thought I would be seeing that sort of thing again."

While he still feels tired and must sleep for many hours every day, he is well enough to sit in the living-room and watch Wimbledon tennis matches, or sit for short periods in the garden. He and Ron begin to take more trips, going up to Duncan to visit Rodney's mother. "It feels so good just to get out of bed, I was getting so tired of those four walls."

In the last week of July, Rodney undergoes a blood transfusion to boost his dangerously low hemoglobin count. As August approaches Ron and Rodney plan an eight-hour trip in the truck to the Interior to visit Ron's family for an annual get-together. Sitting that long for the drive is going to be hard on Rodney — particularly because he still has so little padding on his bones. But he wants to do it. He is feeling optimistic. "Maybe I can make it to December. It is not that far away now. I could hold my grandchild, that would be really great, and then after that, I could die."

Yet, despite his optimism, he is keeping his options open. He and Ron have begun to research botanical poisons that Native Americans used to commit suicide — with their knowledge and ready supply of plants, that option seems like the most logi-cal form of self-deliverance to have on hand if there comes a time that he needs a way out. "We find it very comforting to know that he could simply eat a plant or something and be gone. We may never use it, but it is nice to know it is there," Ron says.

For now, however, Rodney can cope. Who knows, how-ever, what lies in the future? Rodney has also thought ahead to other choices, too. If the pain returns, he'll go back on mor-phine. If his hemoglobin count drops so low again, however, he probably won't have another blood transfusion. "It means my marrow isn't making new blood cells and as my count falls, I would just slip into a coma — and that would be an okay way to die. Not so great for Ron, mind you, who has to wait while I go through it, but okay for me."

As I listen to Ron and Rodney, I realize their balance and perspective about the process of Rodney's dying is what more of us need to have. Of course, Rodney has known for ten years that he would die of AIDS. He has had time to adjust to the real-ity of his own death. Yet, like Rodney, each one of us is mortal, but in our denial of death, our refusal to think or plan for its eventuality, we act as if it's not going to happen to us. Ron and Rodney are informed and realistic about what lies ahead; they are neither fixated on death, nor avoiding it. They are weighing various possibilities, looking at the medical choices they might make that could lead to a more peaceful death for Rodney, such as refusing a blood transfusion, or taking morphine. They are talking openly to each other about what is going on; talking about the pain, the sadness, the loss, the fears; they are talk-ing openly with friends, family and health professionals. In their back pocket, luckily for them and unfortunately missing for many others, is the option of an assisted suicide. They hope, however, that Rodney's dying never gets to a point where they must use it. They are taking each day as it comes, enjoying it for what it is worth. And reassessing it tomorrow. A time will come when the balance changes. For now, Rodney feels okay, so pass the barbequed chicken. Maybe he won't die tomorrow, and maybe it won't be next week, or even next month. He will enjoy what he can, while he can. He knows, for certain, that one day, probably soon, the time for his death will come. Just as it will come for each and every one of us.

Epilogue

S OON AFTER Ron and Rodney returned from the trip into the Interior a stabbing nerve pain began to radiate up Rodney's legs from his feet. It was excruciating and unrelieved by morphine. Its constant presence kept Rodney awake at night. He became restless and started losing interest in food. Ron noticed that Rodney seemed to be quietly fading away. The twinkle in his eye was gone, his hugs to visiting friends seemed uncharacteristicly vacant and unfeeling, as if the real Rodney had left already. I visited again on Monday, August 14. Rodney lay on the couch in the living room, his face drawn in the constant struggle of fighting his foot pain. Ron began to cry, releasing months of pent-up emotions and grief, talking about how difficult it was to see Rodney disappear before his eyes and how he didn't want him to die. "Maybe I've been holding you back," Ron cried. "I haven't been giving you real permission to go." As Ron cried, Rodney lay on the couch nodding his head, saying almost nothing.

Over the next few days, Rodney rapidly declined, as if Ron's emotional unburdening had been the signal he'd been waiting for. By Wednesday he was pale and listless. He refused supper and stayed in bed. On Thursday the palliative care team started

Rodney on an extremely low dose of Dilaudid to keep him comfortable. Ron and Rodney had their last conversation Thursday morning. By Thurdsay evening Rodney's breathing had become so laboured Ron sat by his bed until the early hours of morning in case Rodney died. By Friday morning pneumonia had set in. He lasted through most of the day and at 7:38 p.m. as Ron sat by the bed, Rodney opened his eyes and wordlessly turned his head looking towards Ron. Ron placed his hand on the side of his face. "Close your eyes and sleep," he told him. "You'll be okay and I'll be okay." Rodney took his last breath and died.

Just as Rodney did with his father, Ron kept Rodney's body in the room for twenty-four hours, allowing friends and family to come and say their goodbyes. Five days later, while candles still burned for Rodney in his bedroom, 200 friends gathered in the garden and as evening descended over the trees and flowers, sadness mingled with laughter and rose up to the stars. In mid-September, Ron and Julia took a portion of Rodney's ashes to the banks of the Cowichan River and spread them over the wild onion patch. And on a sunny day in early October, Ron took Rodney's remaining ashes in a bowl to the west coast of Vancouver Island, and climbed down the steep, wooded embankment to the sands of China Beach. He placed the bowl in the sunshine beside him and for more than seven hours he and Rodney's ashes enjoyed the warming rays, as they had so often done in the past. Later, as the sun began to disappear into the clouds along the horizon and the tide came in, Ron walked with the bowl into the gentle surf and scattered Rodney's ashes by handfuls along the wave tops, watching how the particles sparkled against the sand. As the setting sun danced on the water, the receding waves gently carried Rodney's ashes out into the Pacific Ocean.

Further Reading

Hundreds of articles and books on euthanasia, assisted suicide, death and dying, as well as historical texts, were consulted in the research of this book. In many cases those specific sources are stated directly in the text, for example Thomas More's Utopia, and are therefore not mentioned here. For those with interest in the topic, some of the following books and articles may be useful.

Alexander, Leo. "Medical Science Under Dictatorship." *New England Journal of Medicine* 241, no. 2 (July 1949): 39–47.

American Thoracic Society, Board of Directors. "Official Statement on Withholding and Withdrawing Treatment." *American Review of Respiratory Disease* 144 (1991): 726–731.

Anonymous. "It's Over Debbie." *Journal of the American Medical Association* 259, no.1 (Jan.8, 1988): 272.

Battin, Margaret P. *The Least Worst Death: Essays in Bioethics on the End Of Life*. New York: Oxford University Press, 1994.

Brody, Howard. "Assisted Death — Compassionate Response to Medical Failure." *The New England Journal of Medicine* 327 (Nov. 5, 1992): 1384–1386.

————. *The Healer's Power.* New Haven: Yale University Press, 1992.

Burleigh, Michael. *Death and Deliverance: "Euthanasia" in Germany c. 1900–1945.* New York: Cambridge University Press, 1995.

Callahan, Daniel. *The Troubled Dream of Life: Living With Mortality.* New York: Simon & Schuster, 1993.

Canadian Pediatric Society, Bioethics Committee. "Treatment Decisions for Infants and Children." *Canadian Medical Association Journal* 135 (1986): 447–448.

Coughlin, Joe. "Open Season: Children Are Victims of Society, Not Their Disabilities." *Abilities* (Spring 1995): 41–42.

Davies, Nick. "Helping Patients to Die." *The Melbourne Age* (Melbourne) (March 25, 1995): A1.

Derksen, Jim. "Deadly Compassion, Fearsome Kindness." *Abilities* (Spring 1995): 43–45.

Deux, Kay, and L. Wrightman, eds. "Social Influence and Personal Control." *Social Psychology in the 1980s.* 4th ed. Monterey: Brooks/Cole Publishing Company, 1984.

Dworkin, Ronald. *Life's Dominion: An Argument about Abortion, Euthanasia and Individual Freedom.* New York: Alfred A. Knopf, 1993.

Foley, Kathleen. "The Relationship of Pain and Symptom Management to Patient Requests for Euthanasia." *Journal of Pain and Symptom Management* 6 (1991): 289–297.

Frankl, Viktor, E. *Man's Search For Meaning.* 3rd ed. New York: Washington Square Press, 1984.

Gaylin, W. et al. "Doctors Must Not Kill." *Journal of the American Medical Association* 259, no. 14 (April 8, 1988): 2139–2140.

Gomez, C.F. *Regulating Death: Euthanasia and the Case of the Netherlands.* New York: Free Press, 1991.

Gourevitch, Danielle. "Suicide Among the Sick in Classical Antiquity." *Bulletin of the History of Medicine* 43 (1969): 501-518.

Gray, Madeline. *Margaret Sanger: A Biography of the Champion of Birth Control.* New York: Richard Marek Publishers, 1979.

Greenhouse, Linda. "Court Order to Treat Baby Prompts Ethical Debate." *The New York Times* (New York) (Feb. 20, 1994): 12.

Greenway, Norma. "Women 'Victors' in Population Control Plan," *The Vancouver Sun* (Vancouver) (Sept. 9, 1994): A11.

Griffiths, John. "Assisted Suicide in the Netherlands: The Chabot Case." *Modern Law Review* 58, no. 2 (March 1995): 232–248.

———. "Recent Developments in the Netherlands Concerning Euthanasia and Other Medical Behavior that Shortens Life." *Medical Law International* 1 (1995): 347–386.

———. "The Regulation of Euthanasia and Related Medical Procedures that Shorten Life in the Netherlands." *Medical Law International* 1 (1994): 137–158.

Hendin, Herbert. *Suicide in America.* New York: W.W. Norton & Company, 1995.

Hendin, Herbert. "Scared to Death of Dying." *The New York Times* (New York) (Dec. 16, 1994): A27.

Hobbs-Birnie, Lisa. *Uncommon Will: The Death and Life of Sue Rodriguez.* Toronto: Macmillan Canada, 1994.

Humphry, Derek. *Final Exit.* Eugene, Oregon: Hemlock, 1990.

Hutchinson, Brian. "Latimer's Choice." *Saturday Night* (March 1995): 38–43.

Jenish, D'arcy. "What Would You Do?" *Macleans* (Nov. 28, 1994): 16–22.

Kolata, Gina. "Withholding Care From Patients: Boston Case Asks, Who Decides?" *The New York Times* (New York) (April 3, 1995): A1.

Langer, E. and J. Rodin. "The Effects of Choice and Enhanced Personal Responsibility for the Aged: A Field Experiment in an Institutional Setting." *Journal of Personality and Social Psychology* 34, no. 2 (1976): 191–198.

————. "Long-term Effects of a Control-Relevant Intervention With the Institutionalized Aged." *Journal of Personality and Social Psychology* 35, no. 12 (1977): 897–902.

Lifton, Robert J. *The Nazi Doctors: Medical Killing and the Psychology of Genocide.* New York: Basic Books, 1986.

Maxwell, J.H. "The Iron Lung: Halfway Technology or Necessary Step?" *The Millbank Quarterly* 64, no. 1 (1986): 3–25.

McLaren, Angus. *The Bedroom and the State: The Changing Practices and Politics of Contraception in Canada,* 1880–1980. Toronto: McClelland & Stewart, 1986.

Mitchell, Alanna. "Father wanted to end girl's pain, jury told." *The Globe and Mail* (Toronto) (Nov. 9, 1994): A1.

Nagle, Patrick. "Dawson battle 'costly mistake.'" *The Vancouver Sun* (Vancouver) (July 29, 1983): A1.

Neu, Steven and Carl Kjellstrand. "Stopping Long-Term Dialysis." *New England Journal of Medicine* 314 (Jan. 2, 1986): 14-20.

Nuland, Sherwin. *How We Die: Reflections on Life's Final Chapter.* New York: Alfred A. Knopf, 1994.

Ogden, Russel D. *Euthanasia, Assisted Suicide and AIDS.* Pitt Meadows, British Columbia: Perrault Goedman, 1994.

"On Euthanasia." *Canadian Medical Association Journal* 17 (1927): 957–958.

Pless, J.E. "The Story of Baby Doe." *New England Journal of Medicine* 309 (1983): 664.

Quill, Timothy. "Death and Dignity: A Case of Individualized Decision Making." *New England Journal of Medicine* 324 (1991): 691–694.

————. *Death and Dignity: Making Choices and Taking Charge.* New York: W.W. Norton & Company, 1993.

————. "Doctor I want to die. Will you help me?" *Journal of the American Medical Association* 270, no. 7 (Aug. 18, 1993): 870–873.

Quill, Timothy, C.K. Cassell, and D. Meier. "Care of the Hopelessly Ill: Potential Clinical Criteria for Physician Assisted Suicide." *New England Journal of Medicine* 327 (1992): 1380–1384.

Rachels, J. "Active and Passive Euthanasia." *New England Journal of Medicine* 292, no. 2 (1975): 78–80.

Ramsey, P. "The Saikewicz Precedent: The Courts and Incompetent Patients." *Hastings Center* Report 8, no. 6 (1978): 36–42.

Reed, James. *From Private Vice to Public Virtue: The Birth Control Movement and American Society.* New York: Basic Books, 1978.

Rinpoche, Sogyal. *The Tibetan Book of Living and Dying.* San Francisco: HarperSanFrancisco, 1992.

Rhoden, N.K. and John D. Arras. "Withholding Treatment from Baby Doe: From Discrimination to Child Abuse." *Millbank Memorial Fund Health Quarterly* 63, no. 1 (1985): 18–51.

Schöne-Seifert, Bettina and Klaus-Peter Rippe. "Silencing the Singer: Antibioethics in Germany." *Hastings Center Report* 21, no. 6 (1991): 20–27.

Seguin, Marilynne. *A Gentle Death.* Toronto: Key Porter, 1994.

Siegel, Karolynn. "Psychosocial Aspects of Rational Suicide." *American Journal of Psychotherapy* 40, no. 3 (July, 1986): 405–418.

Simmons, Leo. *Role of the Aged in Primitive Societies.* London: Arenon Books, 1945.

Sissons, Jack. *Judge of the Far North.* Toronto: McClelland & Stewart, 1968.

Smeida, N.G. et al. "Withholding and Withdrawal of Life Support From The Critically Ill." *New England Journal of Medicine* 322 (1990): 309–15.

Solomon, Andrew. "A Death Of One's Own." *The New Yorker* (May 22, 1995): 54–69.

The Special Senate Committee on Euthanasia and Assisted Suicide, Report of. "Of Life and Death." Ottawa: Ministry of Supplies and Services, 1995.

Thomas, N. "Pain Control: Patient and Staff Perceptions of PCA." *Nursing Standards* 7, no. 28 (Mar 31–Apr 6, 1993): 37–9.

Van der Berge, C.J. "Mercy Murder and Morality." *Hastings Centre Report* 19 (1989): 47.

Van der Maas, Paul et al. "Euthanasia and Other Medical Decisions Concerning the End of Life." *The Lancet* 338 (Sept. 14, 1991): 669–674.

Van der Wal, Gerrit and R. Dillmann. "Euthanasia in the Netherlands." *British Medical Journal* 308, no. 21 (May 1994): 1346–1349.

Vaux, Kenneth. "Debbie's Dying: Mercy Killing and the Good Death." *Journal of the American Medical Association* 259, no. 14 (April 8, 1988): 2141.

Yu, V.Y.H. "Selective Non-treatment of Newborn Infants." *Medical Journal of Australia* 161, no. 21 (November 1994): 627-629.

Index